The Ups and Downs of Affirmative Action Preferences

Contents

∽

The Ups and Downs of Affirmative Action Preferences

∽

M. Ali Raza,
A. Janell Anderson, and
Harry Glynn Custred, Jr.

PRAEGER

Westport, Connecticut
London

100

#41211275

Library of Congress Cataloging-in-Publication Data

Raza, M. Ali
   The ups and downs of affirmative action preferences / M. Ali Raza,
A. Janell Anderson, Harry Glynn Custred, Jr.
     p.   cm.
   Includes bibliographical references and index.
   ISBN 0-275-96713-1 (alk. paper)
   1. Affirmative action programs—United States. 2. Affirmative
action programs—Law and legislation—United States. I. Anderson,
A. Janell. II. Custred, Harry Glynn, 1939-   . III. Title.
HF5549.5.A34R39   1999
331.13'3'0973—dc 21   99-15395

British Library Cataloguing in Publication Data is available.

Library of Congress Catalog Card Number: 99-15395
ISBN: 0-275-96713-1

First published in 1999

Praeger Publishers, 88 Post Road West, Westport, CT 06881
An imprint of Greenwood Publishing Group, Inc.
www.praeger.com

Printed in the United States of America

The paper used in this book complies with the
Permanent Paper Standard issued by the National
Information Standards Organization (Z39.48-1984).

10 9 8 7 6 5 4 3 2 1

Preface

In November 1996, when California voters amended the state constitution to ban racial preferences in public higher education, they were responding to the blatant use, by university and college administrators, of race as a criterion for student admissions and faculty hiring. Proposition 209 (as the amendment was popularly known) was necessary because these administrators have been protected from outside scrutiny through a long tradition of academic freedom that allowed them to pervert priorities in academia to the point where ethnicity and skin color became major determinants of administrative decision making. Had the universities used this criterion carefully and limited it to being a "plus factor" as barely permitted in the *Bakke* decision (1978) for student admissions, the voters of California would not have found it desirable to totally ban the use of racial preferences in public higher education. When confronted with questions as to the extent of the use of race and ethnicity, the higher education establishment dismissed the queries as unworthy of serious consideration. Later, when the general public raised the issue, the university administrators invoked the mantra that these preferences were essential to maintain "diversity" and touted "multiculturalism" as necessary for excellence. Once academic rationale retreated from the merit principle and the notion of measurable individual ability, there was no logical point at which nonmerit factors could be contained first, in student admissions, and then, in faculty hiring. At this point, the moral high ground was lost by the advocates of preferences in higher education, and the result was the campaign to pass Proposition 209 and to ban racial preferences in California's public sector. These efforts, begun by a few academicians, grew into a movement in California with national implications.

This phenomenon in California, however, was in part a reflection of nationwide rethinking and reevaluation of the concept of affirmative action that was transformed from its original intent of compensatory relief for proven cases of individual discrimination into a policy of reparation to achieve proportional outcomes for racial and ethnic minorities. This transformed policy gave its practitioners both redemptive solace and the chimera of an expanded egalitarianism. Slowly, though, those who were dispreferred put some dents in the new meaning of affirmative action by using the forum of the courts to undermine the practice of unadulterated race-conscious admissions into professional schools and the granting of government contracting. In the 1980s, the U.S. Supreme Court began to restrict the use of race as a criterion for decision making by public agencies. Exception to this policy was permitted only when it met the standard of strict scrutiny and compelling governmental interest in remedying the past wrongs. Even under those circumstances, the Court required that the remedies provided must not unduly trample the rights of innocent third parties. In addition, the use of racial categories requires the institution to demonstrate that it has engaged in past racial discrimination and that the effects of this are still present.

The movement against preferences, particularly in public education, public employment, and public contracting, is not confined to California. The State of Washington Civil Rights Initiative, patterned after that of California, was passed by the voters in November 1998 by a comfortable 16 percent margin (58 percent to 42 percent). Efforts are also being made in a number of other states to replicate the success of these measures despite the refusal in late January 1999 of Florida's Republican governor, Jeb Bush, to support a similar initiative in that state. Ward Connerly, who spearheaded the drive in California, was unfazed by this development and vowed to press on with the campaign to give voters of several other states a chance to express their views in referendums on this pivotal issue. It is interesting to note that the State of Washington voters banned preferences despite the fact that the political campaign to preserve them was actively supported by Vice President Al Gore, the National Education Association, AFL-CIO, and some powerhouses of private enterprise such as Boeing, Microsoft, and Starbucks.

The courts continue to hand down decisions declaring race-based decisions of government entities to be unconstitutional. For instance, in November 1998, the First U.S. Circuit Court of Appeals (which covers Maine, Massachusetts, New Hampshire, Rhode Island, and Puerto Rico) ruled that the race-based admissions policy at three of Boston's prestigious schools was unconstitutional. The case involved 15-year-old Sarah Wessmann, a white student who was denied admission into Boston Latin School despite her superior scores as compared to those of minority students accorded admission. This was a particularly important ruling because it was the first time a U.S. Court of Appeals had ruled that affirmative action preferences were unconstitutional in student admissions at a public school.

In 1996, such preferences at the university level were declared unconstitutional in the case of *Hopwood v. University of Texas*. Similarly, in January 1999, a U.S. District Court judge ruled that the University of Georgia's race-based admission policy, followed between 1990 and 1995, was unconstitutional. The Court rejected the defense argument that the preference policy was necessary to maintain "diversity." There are many other cases of preferential treatment in the pipelines of the nation's courts. Progress is being made in other court proceedings against racial preferences in university student admissions. Reverse discrimination cases filed by the Center for Individual Rights against the University of Washington and the University of Michigan were progressing in early 1999, and their outcomes are likely to have a major impact on the national debate on this issue. Knowledge of the national context of affirmative action is necessary for an understanding of what happened in California. Thus, we discuss here at some length the national picture in order to frame the California scene.

Introduced in Chapter 1 is the theme that the quest for equality before the law and belief in individual rights were distorted by judicial activism in race relations and by the influence of elites on public policy. Also discussed is the Civil Rights Act of 1964, as amended in 1972, and the beginning of affirmative action based on the controversial concept of *underutilization* defined in terms of demography and geographical area.

In Chapter 2, the way in which the concepts of affirmative action, initially enacted to be a means of providing compensation to individuals for intentional discrimination, mutated into an ideology, and an industry, of mostly race-based preferences is described in detail. The role of the Supreme Court in a series of decisions that helped to build a rationale for group-based rights and that eroded the idea of individual rights is also discussed.

Chapter 3 describes how the Supreme Court, in a series of decisions, reevaluated its previous holdings on race- and gender-based government affirmative action policies and sharply reduced the extent of preferences granted under the Civil Rights Act of 1964. Also discussed are controversies concerning student admission policies and important U.S. Courts of Appeals decisions involving public educational institutions.

In Chapter 4, there is a discussion of the Clinton Administration's efforts to protect preferences in government programs in the wake of the Courts' new hostility to those preferences. Also described is *the celebration of diversity* through a regime of hiring quotas, cash awards, and other benefits reserved for underrepresented faculty in the California State University system.

Chapter 5 discusses the controversy aroused by the Western Association of Schools and Colleges when it insisted that over 140 four-year colleges and universities in California, Hawaii, and Guam under its jurisdiction demonstrate their "commitment to diversity" as a condition of accreditation. Also described in this chapter is the account of the first major public disclosure of data on the magnitude of race-based preferences in student admissions at the University of California, San Diego, School of Medicine, and UCLA's law school. The medical school's data in particular convinced Ward Connerly, a regent of the university, of the unfairness of the system, leading him to successfully launch a campaign that abolished preferences in student admissions, employment, and contracting—first in the University of California through a resolution by the Board of Regents and later in the whole of California through Proposition 209.

Chapter 6 discusses how the idea of a law to ban preferences originated with and was developed by Glynn Custred and Thomas Wood. It also discusses their efforts to garner political support and the ultimate success of the constitutional amendment at the polls through the invaluable leadership of Ward Connerly and California's then-governor Pete Wilson.

Chapter 7 details the failed court challenges to Proposition 209, which was passed by the voters in November 1996, the subsequent unsuccessful efforts to repeal California statutes that conflict with the provisions of Proposition 209, and the failure of Congressional leaders to enact legislation to at least partly replicate the California constitutional amendment.

Acknowledgments

We are pleased to express our appreciation to Professor Charles Geshekter and attorneys Robert Corry, and Harvey Zall for providing some of the material used in this book. We are, of course, responsible for the interpretation of that material.

We thank Lyn N. Popovich for keyboarding the manuscript and Gary Krebs for reproducing it. Thanks are also offered to Sharon L. Zettlemoyer, Secretary of the Department of Organizational Behavior and Environment, California State University, Sacramento, for assisting us in the performance of our departmental and school responsibilities, thereby making it possible for us to devote some of our time to the preparation of this manuscript. Thanks also to Judy Cardanha for her conscientious editorial assistance and to Jerry and Ellen Cook for providing data on preferences in the University of California, San Diego, School of Medicine.

1

⌇

The Origins of Affirmative Action

Two principles are so deeply rooted in the American consciousness that they have been called the American Creed. These principles contribute in a basic manner to defining America as a nation and, on the individual level, constitute for the vast majority of the American people the very definition of fairness and justice. These two principles are *individual rights* (the right of individuals to advance as far as their talents, their demonstrated abilities, their experience, and their application permit without undue restrictions imposed on them by the government or by an oppressive majority) and *equality before the law* (one law for everyone, not different laws for different classes of citizens).

There has always been a gap between these ideals and the way they have been practiced, especially with regard to black Americans, a significant segment of the American population that has been systematically excluded from the mainstream throughout most of American history. From the very inception of the nation, however, voices were raised against this discrepancy—first, in opposition to slavery, the most extreme form of exclusion and the greatest affront to the core principles of the nation, and then, against segregation, which evolved after the Civil War and lasted until the middle of the twentieth century.

NATIONAL CONSCIENCE AND THE QUEST FOR EQUALITY

It was not until the 1940s that social, economic, and political forces began to change the context in which racial exclusion thrived. Then in the 1960s a new consensus of inclusion materialized, based on the morality of the nation's guiding principles and unified in an effort to close this gap once and for all. Nathan Glazer described this as a trend "to ever widen the circle of those eligible for inclusion in the American polity with full access to political rights." By 1975, when Glazer wrote those words, the circle embraced "all humanity, without tests of race, color, national origin, religion or language" as indeed "premature hyperbolic statements made as long as 200 years ago suggested it would."[1] The process of full economic inclusion, however, was another thing, a process that is still underway.

While a new national consensus was developing in the mid-1960s, forces were working in the opposite direction partially in response to the slowness in eradicating economic disparities between minority and majority populations despite political and legal guarantees. Over the past 30 years, these forces have crystallized into a new regime of racial, ethnic, and sexual preferences that reasserts and expands America's obsession with race confirming the historic pattern of racial categorization and preference in the United States, albeit with different beneficiaries and different victims. The gap between principle and practice, thus, remains open with potentially baleful consequences for the future. In this chapter we will briefly examine the rise of this new regime and the statutory and regulatory provisions that ban discrimination in employment.

The seeds of the new regime were planted in official acts that propelled civil rights forward in the 1950s and the 1960s, first in *Brown v. Board of Education* (1954) and then in the Civil Rights Act of 1964. The National Association for the Advancement of Colored People (NAACP) chose to challenge the separate-but-equal doctrine in the public schools by appealing to the Fourteenth Amendment's "equal protection" clause, which applies to state government. The problem for the Warren Court, no supporter of segregation, was that there was nothing in the words, the Court interpretations, or the history of the Fourteenth Amendment to unequivocally declare segregation unconstitutional. In fact, eminent historian Henry Steele Commager explained to the NAACP that the framers of the amendment did not "intend that it should be used to end segregation in the schools." He urged them not to base their case on the Fourteenth Amendment.[2] Given the nature of the law, the only way the court could overturn separate-but-equal doctrine standing in the way of full inclusion was by overturning judicial precedent, which most judges at the time were unwilling to do.

A new era in the judiciary, however, was dawning, and *Brown v. Board of Education* was its debut, what Max Boot in his recent critique of the courts has called the "Magna Carta of judicial activism."[3] Justices Felix Frankfurter and Earl Warren were the advocates of this new activism, persuading the other justices to a unanimous decision based not on the words of the constitution but on their own moral sentiments, shared by a growing consensus, and justified by what turned out to be faulty sociology. Capturing the gist of the opinion, headlines in the May 8, 1954, issue of the *New York Times,* read "A Sociological Decision: Court Founded Its Segregation

Ruling On Hearts And Minds Rather Than Laws," and James Reston wrote that "the Court's opinion reads more like an expert paper on sociology."[4] Historical forces ultimately broke the back of Jim Crow, which for a fleeting moment led to the triumph of color-blind law and the principles on which it is based. Social forces also created the context in which those principles were betrayed and that created the system of racial and ethnic preferences we have today.

From the 1940s until the middle of the 1960s, mainline civil rights organizations were firmly committed to the principles of individual rights and equality before the law. These principles, however, were quickly abandoned as these organizations came nearer their goals. Whitney Young of the Urban League was one of the early backers of a new regime of preferences, calling for "a decade of discrimination in favor of black youth" and urging the board of directors of the National Urban League to endorse "a compensatory, a preferential Marshall Plan for black America."[5] This view was also enunciated at the highest level of government when President Lyndon Johnson, giving the commencement speech at Howard University in 1965, said that freedom was not enough; that "you do not take a person who for years has been hobbled by chains and liberate him, bring him up to the starting line of a race and then say, you're free to compete with all the others, and justly believe that you have been completely fair. . . . It is not enough just to open the gates of opportunity. All our citizens must have the ability to walk through those gates."[6]

This was the first official announcement of a federal endorsement of the principle of equality of results, a principle that would be put in place by bureaucrats as they bypassed the law and exceeded their authority in the name of racial justice. The result is the system we have today, which operates to distribute benefits to and to impose handicaps on individuals because of their race, ethnicity, and sex—a betrayal of the ideals of individual rights and equality before the law on which old patterns of exclusion had foundered.

As soon as it became clear that a new regime was forming, political entrepreneurs hastened to exploit the situation and to climb on board. Anyone who could make a case of victimhood did so. Thus the racially and culturally diverse category "Hispanic" was created. And soon American Indians (later to be called Native Americans) and Pacific Islanders were included in the lengthening list of preferred groups. What began as a means of redressing old wrongs against blacks, a people who had helped build the country from its very beginnings, soon mutated into a system in which immigrants just off the boat, or just across the border, who had never suffered discrimination in the United States (and whose ancestors had never suffered such discrimination) were immediately eligible for preferred status. This included wives and daughters of middle- and upper-class families who were in a position to trump black males in employment and contracting.

To prefer one group over another because of race means discrimination against members of another group in order to accommodate the quota. The reality of this fact is not acknowledged by advocates of preferences. When advocates are forced to admit this, they usually point to past discrimination as justification for the new regime. White males had the advantage in the past, they say, and now it's our turn. This pleading for special treatment brings up such questions as: Why should a young white man be held liable today for what his father or grandfather might have done? Why should a young black man receive special privileges because someone of another generation may have suffered? And what about second- or third-generation sons and daughters of working class "white ethnics" who had a hard enough time assimilating in a new nation under new economic conditions? They were not even present here during slavery, nor were they benefiting from segregation when it was still in place. Why should a new generation pay for a past in which they had no part? Are the sins of the fathers being visited on the sons?

The present system of preferences in the United States is nothing more than a variation on a very old and apparently tenacious system of discrimination.[7] The difference is that Jim Crow excluded blacks from a viable and just system of rights. The present system aims to replace those rights with a regime in which all individuals, not just those of a designated class, are subject to classification and restriction by a more powerful managerial bureaucracy. This represents a new vision of the nation and a more authoritarian way of doing business.

This new regime has also spawned a new industry that feeds off the spoils generated by government. This industry consists of bureaucratic preference enforcers, grievance lawyers, "diversity consultants" and "diversity managers," ethnic and racial interest groups, ideological groups, practitioners of ethnic politics (especially in higher education), and race agitators. The members of this industry maintain their influence and make their comfortable living by exploiting the tensions inherent in a diverse society. To keep the bounty coming, they stir up resentment, further dividing people in our society.

Such a massive betrayal of core principles would not have been possible without the acquiescence of the American elites. In this regard, John D. Skrentny observed that the present regime of racial and ethnic preferences was ironically "largely the construct of white male elites who have traditionally dominated government and business."[8] *Elites* are those in society who, through their political or economic position and their control of symbols and communication, coordinate action and focus attention in a way that helps keep the society working, that gives it direction, and that allows it to overcome collective crises. Corporate and governmental bureaucratic managers, along with the judiciary and those who manage information in universities and the media, all comprise what sociologists call *strategic elites* in the United States.

A number of observers have noted that since the 1960s these elites have drifted away from the rest of society ideologically, thus creating a gulf between themselves and the rank and file. Racial and ethnic policies are one of the most mischievous results of this gulf. On the one hand, elites have given up on the American Creed and on the hope that racial harmony will prevail if left to people of goodwill to sort things out under just laws and without pernicious government meddling. Instead, there reigns among elites a pessimism that such problems are insoluble. This is one reason, said Christopher Lasch, why American politics does not deal with substantive issues.[9]

The moral consensus, which by then dominated popular opinion, also contributed to this process by discouraging people of good will from criticizing what some even then perceived as dangerous trends. Optimism that we could bend the rules a bit to bring excluded minorities into the mainstream as quickly as possible greased the wheels for the preference regime and made possible intimidation through political correctness. It is ironic that optimism was soon dampened by the belief that once legal barriers were removed, blacks would be immediately integrated into society and become almost indistinguishable from whites. This was a utopian ideal on the part of those whites who had little or no contact with blacks, except perhaps middle-class blacks who were poised to take advantage of the new opportunities available. The long history of exclusion and diverse perceptions within the black community made quite unrealistic policies that were predicated on the kind of immediate integration imagined by white liberals.

At first, the failure of immediate integration was interpreted as white intransigence. But as white resistance to black progress diminished and the numbers still did not come out right, racism could no longer explain the delay. Questions as to what might be wrong inside the black community could not be broached without the questioner being accused of "blaming the victim." It was thus impossible to pursue rational inquiry into problems of integration, which left only one explanation—*racism* (a term that mutated into the notion of "institutional racism")—and one remedy—a government command system. Given the fashionability of governmental intervention, this was not considered so unattractive by many observers. This, in turn, was related to still another factor in the mindset of elites, namely a growing conviction that maybe blacks really needed the paternalistic big government. This, too, is a concept that easily found a home in elitist mentality and that was reinforced by some leaders of the black community who demanded special dispensation for their victimized constituencies.

Another factor in elite mentality is white guilt. Shelby Steele believes that white liberals feel guilty for the advantage they have enjoyed in the past and, thus, have sought preferences for blacks as a way of achieving self-redemption. The effect is that "guilt that preoccupies people with their own innocence blinds them to those who make them feel guilty," says Steele, "and yet it has the same effect as racism since it makes blacks something of a separate species for whom normal standards and values do not automatically apply."[10] This is a resource that the grievance industry readily exploits. White guilt and its manipulation by political entrepreneurs thus creates a symbiosis between them and elites seeking absolution.

A PERIOD OF DECISION

What started as a gathering of forces and a growing moral consensus to close the gap between society's principles and practices has been transformed into a system of racial and ethnic preferences that increasingly strains at the seams of society. Some people claim that without preferences, there would not have been the progress toward equality that has been made over the past 30 years. This opinion ignores the trends building in the 1940s and 1950s and the growing consensus of inclusion that was essential in breaking segregation and in creating a new climate in race relations in America. It also ignores the fact that, generally, preferences benefit those minorities already in the middle class who are capable of advancing on their own. In fact, preferences have been called a fast track for the minority's middle class, leaving completely unaddressed the plight of a large segment of the minority population—those who are at the bottom.

This false solution creates a host of problems of its own. It creates a conflict of principles between the general public and the elites, thus preventing the consensus necessary to move toward greater racial harmony. In fact, preferential policies do just the opposite, namely pit one group against another. Preferences, therefore, are a formula for increased balkanization, in which intergroup tensions are increased and unity impaired or destroyed, all for the benefit of an expanding bureaucracy and an exploitative preference industry based on victimization and grievance. Finally, there is the damage done to the supposed beneficiaries of preferences by reinforcing negative stereotypes of minorities and stigmatizing them in the workplace even when they may be the best qualified for the jobs they hold. This, in fact, may account for the "black middle-class rage" that is supposed to haunt many successful blacks.

At the beginning of the 1990s, intimidation, political correctness, and guilt squelched honest debate on the important issues. All the while, the corruption and corrosiveness of this system continued unabated. It seemed that nothing could be done about it. Yet other changes were slowly growing, as was seen in sporadic protests and in a zigzag trend in the federal courts. The only way to force the issue, it seemed, and to bring it into the realm of public debate and even to move toward the beginning of a solution, was to let the people have a say on policies that were literally transforming their country into a balkanized state. And the only vehicle by which this could be brought to the people was by means of a popular initiative. Thus was born the California Civil Rights Initiative, later known as Proposition 209, which, as it turns out, not only rent the veil of political correctness and opened the issue to rational debate, but also succeeded in reasserting in the Constitution of the State of California the core principles of individual rights and equality before the law for all Californians, regardless of their race, ethnicity, or sex.

In order to provide national historical context to the issues involved, a note on constitutional amendments is followed by a brief discussion of Title VII (the Civil Rights Act of 1964) and the Presidential Executive Orders that ultimately led to preferences and quotas.

EARLY ATTEMPTS TO END RACE DISCRIMINATION

The first efforts by the federal government to forge equal opportunity and civil rights policies began shortly after the Civil War had ended. But these attempts fell short of the mark.[11] On the other hand, the Civil Rights Act of 1964 seemed destined for success. However, its meaning was greatly altered, transforming it from a policy that prohibited use of color or race in employment, education, and government contracting to a policy of race and gender preferences. How this occurred is the subject at hand.

President Abraham Lincoln's famous Emancipation Proclamation of 1863 was followed by the Civil Rights Act of 1866 that gave "full and legal benefit of all laws" to American citizens. This law, now popularly known as Section 1981, is still in force and is used to combat discrimination, especially in employment. Then in 1868 the Fourteenth Amendment to the Constitution was adopted, guaranteeing due process and equal protection to all citizens against action by state governments. Similar protections against the federal government were earlier provided under the Fifth Amendment, adopted in 1791. The Fifteenth Amendment, adopted in 1870, guarantees all U.S. citizens the right to vote without regard to the individual's "race, color, or previous condition of servitude." Taken together, the Thirteenth (adopted in 1865, abolishing slavery), Fourteenth, and Fifteenth Amendments were enacted to provide equal civil rights to blacks. Despite the Constitutional guarantees, the United States Supreme Court in a series of decisions dating back to 1873 generally denied equality of treatment to blacks.[12] However, in the first half of the nineteenth century, the Supreme Court also gave several decisions that upheld the principle of nondiscrimination.[13]

Starting in 1941, several Presidential Executive Orders were issued, with varying degrees of success, to expand employment opportunities for blacks, particularly in business organizations having contracts with the federal government.[14] Especially significant in this regard was Executive Order 10925, issued by President John F. Kennedy in 1961, which called on federal government contractors to "take affirmative action to ensure that applicants are employed, and that employees are treated during employment, without regard to their race, creed, color, or national origin."[15] This was the first use of the term *affirmative action* in the context of racial discrimination in employment. But the term had previously been used in the National Labor Relations Act (1935) in which the National Labor Relations Board (NLRB) had been authorized to provide affirmative action remedies, such as reinstatement of employees, in cases of management's unfair labor practices concerning employees' labor union activities. [16] From the very beginning in 1940, the NLRB has been asked by the Supreme Court to interpret the term *affirmative action* strictly as remedial for those specific situations in which unfair labor practices have been proved based on "preponderance of the testimony taken."[17] Unlike the National Labor Relations Act, affirmative action as practiced under the Executive Orders and the Civil Rights Act of 1964, particularly in employment, government contracting, and public education, has evolved into quotas and preferences.

THE CIVIL RIGHTS ACT OF 1964 AND ITS AMENDMENTS: EQUALITY OF OPPORTUNITY

The social context of the Civil Rights Act of 1964 included dozens of protest demonstrations against segregated public facilities in the South; the march on Washington on August 28, 1963, in which over 200,000 people participated; the tragic assassination of President John F. Kennedy on November 22, 1963; and the swearing in of Lyndon B. Johnson as president. Developments in desegregation included the famous Supreme Court decisions in *Brown v. Board of Education* (1954 and 1955) in which it was held that the public school district must desegregate with "all deliberate speed"[18] because "separate but equal"[19] schools deny citizens equal protection of the law. The Supreme Court also entered the hitherto purely political arena of determining electoral districts. In *Baker v. Carr* (1962), it held that courts are empowered to determine the legitimacy of legislative apportionment.[20] By expounding on this issue in *Wesberry v. Sanders*[21] and *Reynolds v. Sims*[22] (1964), the "one man, one vote" doctrine was developed that continues to involve the courts in the politics of reapportionment of legislative districts. The Supreme Court ruled that state legislatures must be apportioned on the basis of population.

The Civil Rights Act of 1964,[23] as amended, is an omnibus law that prohibits employers, unions, and employment agencies in interstate commerce from discriminating in employment; prohibits discrimination in places of public accommodation; eliminates segregation in public facilities, such as hospitals, libraries, parks, and museums owned by state or local governments; prohibits discrimination in programs and activities receiving federal financial assistance; provides technical and financial assistance to public schools in carrying out desegregation plans; and provides safeguards for the exercise of the right to vote. There are also several provisions concerning procedural matters, such as the compiling of statistics on voter registration, removal of civil rights cases from state to federal courts, and so forth. The following discussion will focus on employment and public education, including some discussion of public contracting.

Title VII of the Civil Rights Act was originally designed to prohibit discrimination by private sector employers, labor organizations, and employment agencies because of an individual's race, color, religion, sex, or national origin. It is interesting to note that prohibition of sex discrimination was introduced as an amendment during the debate in the House of Representatives. The amendment's real purpose was to kill the bill. There is practically no legislative history for determining the Congressional intent with respect to sex discrimination. Effective July 2, 1965, the law covered every employer in interstate commerce having 100 or more employees and every union having 100 or more members. The law prohibited discrimination in job referrals, hiring, training, apprenticeship programs, and compensation and in other terms and conditions of employment. Excluded from jurisdiction of the Act were the United States government, corporations owned by the United States government, and state and local governments. The Act also established the Equal Employment Opportunity Commission (EEOC), which consisted of five members, not more than three of whom were to be members of the same political party. The members, to be appointed by the President by and with the advice and consent of the Senate, were to serve five-year terms. The President designates one member to serve as chairman of the Commission and one member as vice chairman. The chairman is responsible for the administration of the Commission. The President also appoints, with the advice and consent of the Senate, a General Counsel of the Commission who is responsible for litigation under the Act. The Commission was authorized to receive complaints of discrimination. In case it found the complaint meritorious but was unable to reach a settlement through informal methods of conciliation and persuasion, the complainant was allowed to bring a civil action in a court of law. The Commission on its own was not authorized to lodge a civil action; but the U.S. Attorney General could intervene in civil actions in cases of general public importance. The Act specifically provided that if the respondent (employer, union, or employment agency) "has intentionally engaged in or is intentionally engaging in an unlawful employment practice charged in the complaint, the court may enjoin the respondent from engaging in such unlawful employment practice, and order such affirmative action as may be appropriate, which may include reinstatement or hiring of employees, with or without back pay (payable by the employer, employment agency, or labor organization, as the case may be, responsible for the unlawful employment practice)."[24]

The Attorney General was given the independent authority to bring civil action in a federal court against a person or a group of persons engaged in a pattern or practice of discrimination. Such action may seek a restraining order, injunction, or other such relief. The EEOC was empowered to issue rules and regulations to carry out the provisions of Title VII. Because over half the states already had laws prohibiting discrimination, Title VII barred action by the EEOC until a state agency authorized to provide relief had 60 days to dispose of the case. In other words, a complainant had to resort to the state agency to seek remedy under the state law. In some cases, the relief provided by the state law was superior to that of the federal law.

President Nixon's administration greatly strengthened the equal employment opportunity provisions of the Civil Rights Act of 1964. The amendments passed in 1972 provided the following:[25]

1. While maintaining the right of individuals to seek redress and the right of the Attorney General to intervene, the EEOC was given the authority to bring suits in federal district courts against private sector employers and their agents for their discriminatory practices. The Attorney General of the United States was now given the authority to sue state and local governments. Private parties may file suits against federal agencies.

2. State and local governments and government agencies, including educational institutions, were brought under the jurisdiction of the EEOC. Elected state and local government officials and their staff were excluded from the coverage of this law.

3. Coverage was extended to all employers in interstate commerce employing 15 or more workers. Now unions having 15 or more members were also covered.

4. An Equal Employment Opportunity Coordinating Council was created. It consisted of the Secretary of Labor, the chairman of the EEOC, the Attorney General, and the chairman of the U.S. Civil Rights Commission. They, or their respective delegates, were to coordinate and promote equal employment opportunity in the federal government and recommend changes.

5. A federal government contractor's business, for which an affirmative action plan has been approved by the Office of Federal Contract Compliance within the previous 12 months, cannot be denied a government contract without an administrative hearing for the employer.

The Civil Rights Act of 1964 was the result of many compromises. Its supporters and detractors waged passionate debates in both houses of Congress. Senate debate on House Resolution (H.R.) 7152 lasted nearly three months, totaling over 530 hours. Finally, on June 19, 1964, the Senate cut off debate by a vote of 73 to 27. On July 2, President Johnson signed the historic bill. During these debates, fears were expressed by many legislators regarding the greatly expanded role of government in economic life and the intrusion of government bureaucrats in the employment process of private enterprise. The supporters of proposed legislation assured its critics that the law was simply designed to ensure that all future employment decisions shall be neutral as to an individual's race, color, religion, sex, or national origin and shall not otherwise infringe on an employer's right to hire and deploy his or her labor force.

Concerns and suspicions expressed by the critics were allayed by a number of provisions finally incorporated in the bill that dealt with bona fide seniority imbalances relative to demography. These common concepts, which seemed to have been adequately taken care of in the legislation, have become highly controversial because of their "innovative" applications by government administrators and fractured court decisions over the past several years.

A bipartisan amendment by Senators Everett Dirksen (Republican from Illinois) and Mike Mansfield (Democrat from Montana and Senate Majority Leader) was designed to answer the critics who alleged that Title VII would result in racial balancing and preferential treatment. It states:

Nothing contained in this title shall be interpreted to require any employer, employment agency, labor organization, or joint labor-management committee subject to this title to grant preferential treatment to any individual or to any group because of the race, color, religion, sex, or national origin of such individual or group on account of an imbalance which may exist with respect to the total number or percentage of persons of any race, color, religion, sex, or national origin employed by any employer . . . in comparison with the total number or percentage of persons of such race, color, religion, sex, or national origin in any community, State, section, or other area, or in the available work force in any community, State, section, or other area.[26] (703[j])

In substance, Section 703 provides that barring race- or gender-based discrimination, an employer may pay different wages and fringe benefits to different employees based on seniority, merit, quality or quantity of production, and geographic location of jobs. An employer may also use the results of professionally developed job-related ability tests for employment decisions. The senators supporting H.R. 7152 expressed the belief that these amendments simply recounted what was already obvious in the language and the intent of the main operative provisions (Section 703[a][1]): that an employer or a labor organization shall not discriminate against any individual because of such individual's race, color, religion, sex, or national origin. This was also the view of Michael I. Sovern, Professor of Law at Columbia University (later Dean), and a consultant to the NAACP. Writing in early 1966, Sovern expressed the belief that amendments that added provisions concerning bona fide seniority, merit system, ability tests, preferential treatment, and labor for imbalances were "redundant" and unnecessary and "seem to have been designed solely to reassure the doubters."[27] And indeed doubters there were, including Senators Robert Byrd, Sam Ervin, and Russell Long, who expressed fears that Title VII would result in federal government bureaucrats and agencies exerting pressure on businesses to give employment preference to minorities.

The EEOC's first compliance chief was Rutgers law professor Alfred W. Blumrosen, who had already stated that he declined the narrow construction of race discrimination set out in Title VII and preferred instead a definition that would reduce the disparity between black and white unemployment.[28] Intending to alter the EEOC's authority de facto rather than having to ask Congress for the added authority, Blumrosen arbitrarily decided to require employers to provide his agency with reports concerning the racial composition of the workforce despite the statute's prohibition of such a requirement. Thus armed with the facts of statistical "underutilization" of minorities, Blumrosen provided the basis for ordering preferential hiring of blacks.

In addition, the EEOC allied itself with NAACP attorneys to wage a battle on the "cult of credentialism," in the words of its chief psychologist, William H. Ennis. The effort entailed a litigation attack on employee testing and other employment practices that had a disparate impact on whites and blacks. This unintentional type of discrimination, based on merit and objective test results, also fell due to the misguidance of Blumrosen and the misinterpretation of the Civil Rights Act's clear prohibition of only intentional discrimination in employment. Written by Chief Justice Warren Burger, the *Griggs v. Duke Power Company*[29] decision (discussed fully in Chapter 2) declared the employer to have discriminated against blacks because of its requirement that employees who were promoted must have a high school diploma or a passing grade on intelligence and mechanical-comprehension tests. Thus, the statutory meaning of race discrimination as one of intent in the mind of the employer was radically altered and replaced with a theory of disparate impact.

EXECUTIVE ORDER 11246 OF SEPTEMBER 24, 1965

President Kennedy's Executive Order 10925 was superseded by President Lyndon B. Johnson's Executive Order 11246, issued in 1965.[30] Order 11246, with some amendments, remains in effect and is the epicenter of national debate as to the appropriateness of government's pressuring businesses and public entities in instituting programs of preferences that obviously result in reverse discrimination. President Johnson's Executive Order mostly reenacted the Kennedy Order and expanded its coverage, put more teeth in its enforcement machinery and process, and required more reporting from unions and employers. This new Order covered not only federal procurement contracts but also federally assisted programs. Overall, administration of the Order and the duty of establishing appropriate regulations for compliance were now turned over to the Secretary of Labor.

The Order prohibited discrimination because of race, creed, color, or sex. Subsequent changes call for affirmative action programs for the handicapped and for disabled and Vietnam veterans. However, the discussion here will be limited to programs for racial minorities and women. The main provision of the Order is as follows: "The contractors will not discriminate against any employee or applicant for employment because of race, color, religion, sex, or national origin. The contractor will take affirmative action to ensure that applicants are employed, and that employees are treated during employment, without regard to their race, color, religion, sex, or national origin."

Federally funded or assisted construction contracts are also covered. Noncompliance with the Order or its applicable rules and regulations may result in the cancellation, termination, or suspension of the contract. The contractor may also be declared ineligible for further government contracts. In such cases the Secretary of Labor has provided for show-cause notices and avenues of administrative appeals. All contractors and subcontractors with 50 or more employees and contracts of $50,000 or more are required to file, on standard forms, programs of equal employment opportunity and affirmative action. Government contractors are required to submit affirmative action programs that are "specific and result-oriented." Each "contractor commits itself to apply every good faith effort" to achieve these results (41 Code of Federal Regulations [CFR] Section 60-2.10). An affirmative action program must include a utilization analysis of minorities and women in the contractor's workforce, including goals and timetables to correct the deficiencies "to achieve prompt and full utilization of minorities and women, at all levels and in all segments of its workforce where deficiencies exist."

A government contractor must furnish the total number of male and female incumbents of each job title belonging to each of the following groups: blacks, Spanish-surnamed Americans, American Indians, and Asian Americans. The term *underutilization* is purported to mean that a contractor has fewer minorities or women in a particular job group "than would reasonably be expected by their availability." The Secretary of Labor has delegated the responsibility for enforcement of the Executive Order to the Office of Federal Contract Compliance Program (OFCCP). It, in turn, monitors the activities of various contracting agencies.

Labor organizations are indirectly affected because government contractors who employ union members are bound by the covenants of nondiscrimination and affirmative action signed by them. Labor unions, however, are directly covered by the special regulations issued by the Secretary of Labor to govern apprenticeship programs. They require unions to follow policies and programs of nondiscrimination and affirmative action. The affirmative action obligations of contractors and subcontractors both in construction and nonconstruction contracts depend on whether the OFCCP thinks that there is "underutilization" (also referred to as "disparity") of minorities and whether a contractor is "putting forth every good faith effort to make its overall affirmative action program work."

At least in theory, Executive Order 11246 of 1964, as well as the Executive Orders preceding it, called for equal employment opportunity. The idea of "underrepresentation" based on statistical disparities was an implant of the compliance branch of the EEOC, which shifted the focus of law from the prerequisite of intentional discrimination for remedy to a theory of "underrepresentation" and "disparate impact." This shift was, in turn, embraced by a majority of Supreme Court justices, as described in Chapter 2.

Mindful of the fact that under Executive Order 11246 and its applicable regulations contractors and subcontractors of federal and federally assisted projects and institutions required bidders to submit plans for equal employment opportunity and affirmative action, the Philadelphia Federal Executive Board, on November 30, 1967, put into effect an affirmative action plan. It required each bidder to submit an acceptable written affirmative action plan for minority employment in specified skilled trades as a prerequisite for receiving a construction contract in a project funded or assisted by the federal government. However, Elmer B. Staats, Comptroller General of the United States, in an opinion letter issued in 1968, stated that the affirmative action plan of the Philadelphia Federal Executive Board violated the principle of competitive bidding in government contracts.[31] Enter Attorney General John N. Mitchell and Assistant Secretary of Labor Arthur Fletcher. On June 27, 1969, Assistant Secretary Fletcher issued an order under which bidders on federal or federally assisted construction projects in the five-county Philadelphia area were required to submit "acceptable affirmative action plans" that included specific goals of black employment. The order by Fletcher stated that, because of the exclusionary policies of craft unions, traditionally only a small number of blacks have been employed in skilled trades in construction. After holding public hearings in August 1969, Fletcher issued another order on September 23, 1969, in which he required construction contractors in the five-county Philadelphia area to meet the standards of black employment for each of the following four years in the six skilled trades specified in the order. Starting with 1970, the employment of blacks was required to be between 4 and 9 percent, increasing to 9 to 15 percent in 1971, 14 to 20 percent in 1972, and 19 to 26 percent in 1973. Attorney General Mitchell, in an opinion letter dated September 22, 1969, and addressed to the Secretary of Labor, dismissed the argument that the affirmative action program imposed by federal government would inevitably result in reverse discrimination.[32]

Several contractors challenged the Philadelphia Plan, arguing that, among other things, it contradicts the Civil Rights Act of 1964, which states that the statute does not require an employer or a labor organization to grant preferential treatment to any individual or group; that there has been no judicial finding of past discrimination by employers; that it violates due process rights of contractors; and that "underrepresentation" of blacks in the six specified skilled trades is attributable to the hiring-hall referral policies of unions rather than to the alleged "exclusionary" policies of employers. Assistant Secretary Fletcher had stated that because of discrimination in the five-county Philadelphia area, blacks comprised only approximately 1 percent of the specified skilled trades, even though they constituted about 30 percent of the total workforce in the construction industry.

The Court of Appeals confirmed the judgment of the district court and rejected all the arguments of contractors.[33] The Court of Appeals held that the limitations of the Civil Rights Act did not prevent the Executive Branch from granting preferential treatment and that courts must give great deference to an administrative agency's interpretation of Executive Orders and regulations. The Court also rejected the argument that the affirmative action program violates due process rights of employers. It said: "the specific [affirmative action] goals may be met, considering normal employee attrition, and anticipated growth of the industry, without adverse effects on the existing labor force." Earlier, on October 27, 1969, Comptroller General Staats had advised the Secretary of Labor that his (Staat's) office considered the Philadelphia Plan to be in contravention of the Civil Rights Act of 1964 and that the "distinction between quotas and goals was largely a matter of semantics." The Supreme Court denied the contractors' petition to hear the case[34] and set the locomotive of race- and gender-based quotas toward the destination of equal results.

NOTES

1. Nathan Glazer, *Affirmative Discrimination: Ethnic Inequality and Public Policy* (New York: Basic Books, 1975), p. 22.

2. Paul Craig Roberts and Lawrence M. Stratton, *The New Color Line: How Quotas and Privilege Destroy Democracy* (Washington, D.C.: Regnery Press, 1995), p. 39.

3. Max Boot, *Out of Order: Arrogance, Corruption, and Incompetence on the Bench* (New York: Basic Books, 1998), p. 104.

4. Roberts and Stratton, *The New Color Line*, p. 44.

5. Terry Eastland, *Ending Affirmative Action: A Case for Color Blind Justice* (New York: Basic Books, 1996), p. 43.

6. Ibid., pp. 39-40.

7. Thomas Sowell, *Preferential Policies: An International Perspective* (New York: William Morrow and Company, Inc., 1990).

8. John David Skrentny, *Ironies of Affirmative Action: Politics, Culture and Justice in America* (Chicago: University of Chicago Press, 1996), p. 5.

9. Christopher Lasch, *The Revolt of the Elites and the Betrayal of Democracy* (New York: W. W. Norton and Company, 1995).

10. Shelby Steele, *The Content of Our Character* (New York: St. Martin's Press, 1990), p. 87.

11. James MacGregor Burns, *The Workshop of Democracy: From the Emancipation Proclamation to the Era of the New Deal* (New York: Vintage Books, 1985),

p. 47; John Hope Franklin, *From Slavery to Freedom: A History of Negro Americans*, 3rd ed. (New York: Vintage Books, 1969), pp. 187-190.

12. See for example: *Slaughter House* cases, 83 U.S. 36 (1873); and The Five Civil Rights Cases, 109 U.S. 3 (1883); also see: "Civil Rights Cases," Kermit L. Hall (ed.), *The Oxford Companion to the Supreme Court of the United States* (New York: Oxford University Press, 1992), p. 149; *Plessy v. Ferguson*, 163 U.S. 537 (1896).

13. *Buchanan v. Warley*, 245 U.S. 60 (1917); *Shelley v. Kramer*, 334 U.S. 1 (1948); also see: Francis A. Allen, "Remembering *Shelley v. Kramer*," *Washington University Quarterly* 67 (1989): 709-735; Missouri ex rel. *Gaines v. Canada*, 305 U.S. 337 (1938); *McLaurin v. Oklahoma State Regents*, 339 U.S. 637 (1950); *Sweatt v. Painter*, 339 U.S. 629 (1950).

14. Executive Orders: No. 8802 in 6 *Federal Register* (1941): 3109; No. 9346 in 8 *Federal Register* (1943): 7183; No. 10308 in 16 *Federal Register* (1951): 12303; No. 10479 in 18 *Federal Register* (1953): 4899.

15. 26 *Federal Register* (1961): 1977.

16. Section 10(c) of the Public Law No. 101, 80th Congress (as amended).

17. *Republic Steel Corporation v. NLRB*, 311 U.S. 7 (1940).

18. 349 U.S. 294, 300-301 (1955).

19. 347 U.S. 483 (1954). Segregation in school system of the District of Columbia was also held to be in violation of the due process clause of the Fifth Amendment of the United States Constitution in *Bolling v. Sharpe*, 347 U.S. 497 (1954).

20. 369 U.S. 186 (1962).

21. 376 U.S. 1 (1964).

22. 377 U.S. 533 (1964).

23. 42 U.S. Code (1964) as amended.

24. 42 U.S. Code, Section 706(g) 78 Stat. 253 (1964).

25. For the 1972 amendments, see: Arthur B. Smith Jr., *Employment Discrimination Law: Cases and Materials* (Indianapolis: Bobbs-Merrill Company, 1978), pp. 1210-1223.

26. Section 703(j).

27. Michael I. Sovern, *Legal Restraint on Racial Discrimination in Employment* (New York: Twentieth Century Fund, 1966), p. 70.

28. For a detailed review of Blumrosen's initiatives in developing a theory of workforce "underutilization," see: Paul Craig Roberts and Lawrence M. Stratton, *The New Color Line: How Quotas and Privilege Destroy Democracy* (Washington, D.C.: Regnery Publishing, 1995), pp. 88-93; and see pp. 94-95 for William H. Enneis' ideas about "credentialism."

29. 401 U.S. 424 (1971).

30. 30 *Federal Register,* 12319 (1965). For a brief retrospective of the Executive Orders from 1941 to 1967, see: *Legal Aid Society of Alameda County v. Brennan*, 381 F. Supp. 125 (N.D. California 1974), Note 1. For more details of these Orders, see: *Farmer v. Philadelphia Electric Company*, 329 F. 2d 3 (3rd Cir.

1964), 5-7; and *Contractors Association of Eastern Pennsylvania v. Secretary of Labor*, 442 F. 2d 159 (3rd Cir. 1971), 168-171.

31. See Comptroller General Elmer B. Staats's objections to the Philadelphia affirmative action preference plan in his letter to the U.S. Secretary of Labor, August 5, 1969, 115 *Congressional Record* (December 18, 1969): 17204-17206, and his statement before the Subcommittee on Separation of Powers, Senate Committee on the Judiciary, on the Philadelphia Plan, 115 *Congressional Record* (December 18, 1969): 40026-40029.

32. 115 *Congressional Record* (December 18, 1969): 17204-17206.

33. *Contractors Association of Eastern Pennsylvania v. Secretary of Labor*, 442 F. 2d 159 (3rd Cir. 1971).

34. 404 U.S. 854 (1971).

2

∽

From Individual Rights to Group Preferences: Supreme Court Decisions (Griggs to Metro Broadcasting)

The history of civil rights in the United States would have been radically different if, on May 18, 1896, the Supreme Court had followed the wisdom and thinking of Justice John Harlan who in his dissenting opinion in *Plessy v. Ferguson* said: "Our Constitution is color-blind, and neither knows nor tolerates classes among citizens. In respect of civil rights, all citizens are equal before the law."[1] But a majority of Justices upheld the Louisiana statute that required the railway companies to provide separate but equal accommodations for whites and nonwhites. Justice Harlan had warned in his dissenting opinion that the doctrine of separate but equal would prove to be pernicious in its consequences. Eighty-three years after *Plessy*, a similar prophetic warning was given by Justice William Rehnquist, who, in his dissent in *United Steelworkers of America v. Weber* (1979), decried the race-based preferences given in a training program for skilled craft jobs. This time the dispreferred person was white. Justice Rehnquist predicted that by upholding race-based preferences in that case, the Court had opened a Pandora's box for later courts that will face the impossible task of rationalizing this anomaly.[2]

In this chapter we discuss how the Supreme Court in the past three decades has tried to deal with the issues of equality versus preferences and of color blindness versus color consciousness under the Civil Rights Act of 1964. The perennial issue of race has once again come to dominate education and employment policies. Challenges to these preferences are currently major themes in politics, public policy, and American jurisprudence.

FROM DISPARATE TREATMENT TO DISPARATE IMPACT

Even before the Civil Rights Act of 1964, the Supreme Court had dealt with the issue of unequal treatment in employment. It struck a blow against race discrimination when, in *Steele v. Louisville and Nashville Railroad Company* (1944) and *Wallace Corporation v. National Labor Relations Board* (1944), it declared that a labor union having the right of being the exclusive bargaining agent of employees has the corresponding duty of "fair representation" of all members of the bargaining unit, the majority as well as the minority. The union in this instance had discriminated against a black employee.[3]

The first case concerning Title VII of the Civil Rights Act to reach the Supreme Court was *Griggs v. Duke Power Company* (1971).[4] The employer, a North Carolina company, required a high school diploma or the passing of a standardized intelligence test and a mechanical comprehension test for transfer from its Labor Department to higher paying departments of Coal Handling, Operations, Maintenance, and Laboratory Testing. (The passing scores approximated the national median for high school graduates.)

Prior to the passage of the Civil Rights Act, blacks were restricted to the Labor Department. Since 1955, the company had followed a policy of requiring a high school education for appointment to any department except Labor and for transfer from the Coal Handling to Operations, Maintenance, or Laboratory. In 1965, the policy of restricting blacks to the Labor Department was abandoned. The company instituted a new policy under which an employee had to meet the aforementioned requirements for assignment to a department other than Coal.

A class action suit by the NAACP on behalf of black workers challenged the company's qualification requirements as discriminatory. The Supreme Court rejected the company arguments that Title VII clearly permits an employer "to give and to act upon the results of any professionally developed ability test," as long as it is not intended or used to discriminate because of race. Ironically, the Court also found it immaterial that there was no finding of discriminatory intention in the adoption of the high school diploma and test requirements. To the contrary, the company had a policy of helping the undereducated employees by underwriting two-thirds of the cost of tuition for high school education. There was also no evidence, nor had the plaintiffs alleged, that the company had in fact discriminated against any individual black worker as the Civil Rights Act required. The Supreme Court ruled: "Under the [Civil Rights] Act, practices, procedures, or tests neutral on their face, and even neutral in terms of intent, cannot be maintained if they operate to 'freeze' the status quo of prior discriminatory employment practices."[5]

In its opinion, statistics spoke louder than intent. So the fact was that in North Carolina, according to the 1960 census, because 34 percent of white males had completed high school and only 12 percent of black males had done so, whites did better on the company's requirements than blacks. "This consequence would appear to be directly traceable to race." The Court, relying on the Guidelines on Employment Testing Procedures developed and promulgated by the EEOC in August 1966 and August 1970, said, "[t]he Act proscribes not only overt discrimination but also practices that are fair in form, but discriminatory in operation. The touchstone is business necessity."[6] The Court also wanted the educational and testing requirements to "have a manifest relationship to the employment in question." The EEOC Guidelines were uncritically accepted by the Court as "entitled to great deference," even though they do not have the same legal authority as regulations.

The *Griggs* decision, in effect, gave birth to the doctrine *of disparate impact,* in which an employment practice or requirement is violative of the Act if it disqualifies substantially more members of a protected class than it does whites and if it cannot be shown to significantly correlate with job performance. The decision also voided the conditions incorporated into the Civil Rights Act that an employer could legally administer professionally developed ability tests and that only intentional treatment was considered a violation of Title VII. Furthermore, in *Griggs,* the Supreme Court immensely expanded the operative provision of the law, Section 703(a)(1), by changing it from individual rights to group rights. Thus, individuals who themselves may have suffered no harm could claim remedy simply because of their membership in a particular race or ethnic group. The decision, coupled with the EEOC Guidelines on Employment Testing and Selection procedures, has led to lowered standards and "race norming." In desperate efforts to meet quotas and thereby to avoid lawsuits, employers have practiced reverse discrimination against better qualified candidates. This is a particularly contentious issue in public employment.

In 1978 the EEOC issued Uniform Guidelines on Employment Selection Procedures, which provided the four-fifths, or 80 percent, rule as evidence of disparate impact:

Adverse impact and the "four-fifths" rule. A selection rate for any race, sex, or ethnic group which is less than four-fifths (4/5) [of the rate for the group with the highest rate] will generally be regarded by the Federal enforcement agencies as evidence of adverse impact, while a greater than four-fifths rate will generally not be regarded by Federal enforcement agencies as evidence of adverse impact. Smaller differences in selection rate may nevertheless constitute adverse impact, where they are significant in both statistical and practical terms or where a user's actions have discouraged applicants disproportionately on grounds of race, sex, or ethnic group.[7]

The four-fifths concept was termed by the EEOC as merely a "rule of thumb." The testing and measuring precepts proposed by the EEOC were severely criticized by businesses, unions, academicians, and many individual citizens.[8] However, they were promulgated anyway. The Guidelines and its accompanying statistical validation requirements are given great deference by the courts despite the fact that they are not regulations and courts are not obliged to follow them. The Supreme Court in *Albemarle Paper Company v. Moody* (1975)[9] and *Washington v. Davis* (1976)[10] relied heavily on the EEOC's employee selection guidelines.

The Supreme Court averted a potential disaster by ruling in *Washington v. Davis* (1976) that the Police Department of the District of Columbia did not violate the equal protection rights of black applicants who had failed a test that was "designed to test verbal ability, vocabulary, reading, and comprehension." The plaintiffs had alleged that because four times as many blacks as whites had failed the test, it was invidiously discriminatory. They claimed to be the victims of adverse impact and, consequently, were deprived of the Fifth Amendment's equal protection guarantee. By the time *Washington v. Davis* reached the Supreme Court, a number of U.S. Circuit Courts had held that even without intentional discrimination, adverse impact of a personnel test would be sufficient to prove racial discrimination violating the equal protection clause. The Supreme Court disagreed with "the view that proof of discriminatory racial purpose is unnecessary in making out an equal protection violation."[11] The Court said that adverse impact theory, though sufficient for the Title VII violation involved in *Griggs*, is not an adequate basis to prove violation of the equal protection clause of the Constitution.

To prove violation of the equal protection clause, a party must demonstrate discriminatory intent or purpose. Disproportional impact of a personnel test in this case by itself was deemed an insufficient basis for relief. The test itself was developed by the U.S. Civil Service Commission and used generally throughout the federal service. The Supreme Court said that the government is not prevented "from seeking modestly to upgrade the communicative abilities of its employees rather than to be satisfied with some lower level of competence, particularly where the job requires special ability to communicate orally and in writing."[12] The Court said that the Constitution allows the government to administer a test that is neutral on its face and serves a rational purpose. A contrary decision would have jeopardized the use of this verbal skills test throughout the U.S. Civil Service System and equated the requirements of proofs of discrimination under Title VII of the Civil Rights Act of 1964 with the equal protection clause of the Fifth Amendment.

The color blindness of Title VII of the Civil Rights Act of 1964 and alleged violations of the Civil Rights Act of 1866 (42 U.S.C., Section 1981) were the subjects of *McDonald v. Santa Fe Trail Transportation Company* (1976).[13] Two whites sued the company and Local 988 of International Brotherhood of Teamsters (union) alleging discrimination because of their race. In 1970, while employed by the company, they and a black employee were jointly and severally charged with stealing 60 one-gallon cans of antifreeze being carried by Santa Fe. The company fired the two whites but retained the black employee. The whites pursued their claim of discrimination through the grievance procedure of their collective bargaining agreement, but they did not receive satisfaction. In the suit, they alleged that the company and the union had discriminated against them because of their race. Both the U.S. District Court and the Court of Appeals held against the petitioners.

The Supreme Court, in its opinion delivered by Justice Thurgood Marshall, said that Title VII of the Civil Rights Act of 1964 prohibits employment discrimination against "any individual" because of "such individual's race" and prohibits discriminatory preferences for any racial group, minority, or majority. The opinion also quoted from the Congressional Record and cited several decisions of EEOC "to the effect that Title VII was intended to 'cover white men and white women and all Americans'." The Court said that the company may decide that dismissing an employee for stealing is an appropriate penalty but that this criterion must be applied alike to members of all races. The union was also criticized by the Court for shirking its duty and acquiescing in racial discrimination against the petitioners.

The first case challenging racial preference in university admissions to reach the Supreme Court involved Marco DeFunis Jr., who was denied admission by the University of Washington Law School despite academic credentials that were far superior to those of minority students accorded admission (including blacks, Chicanos, American Indians, and Filipinos).[14] But by the time the Supreme Court heard oral arguments in 1974, it was informed that DeFunis had already almost completed his education and was registered for his final academic quarter. Therefore, the Supreme Court considered the case moot. However, several of the Justices believed that the Court should have resolved the constitutional issue of equal protection of the law that, if left unanswered, will "inevitably return to the federal courts."

The constitutional issue postponed by the Court in *DeFunis* in 1974 confronted the Supreme Court again four years later in the now famous *Regents of the University of California v. Bakke*.[15] The Medical School of the University of California at Davis had a special admissions program operating with a separate committee, a majority of whom were members of minority groups, defined as blacks, Chicanos, Asians, and American Indians. Allan Bakke, a white man, applied to the Davis Medical School in 1973 and 1974 but was rejected both times. In both years, minority applicants were admitted under the special program with grade point averages and Medical College Admissions Test (MCAT) scores substantially lower than Bakke's. Thus, it was a classic case of race- and ethnicity-based preferential treatment resulting in reverse discrimination against a better qualified candidate. Bakke filed a suit alleging violation of his rights under the equal protection clause of the U.S. Constitution, the California Constitution, and the Civil Rights Act of 1964.

The U.S. Supreme Court ordered Bakke's admission and invalidated the Medical School's special admissions program. However, by a five-to-four vote, the Justices ruled that the university may take race into account as *one* plus factor in its admissions policy. Justice Lewis Powell provided the swing vote in a three-way fractured opinion. The university had argued that its minority admissions programs established "goals" of minority representation. *Bakke* labeled them a racial quota. The Court said that it was simply a "semantic distinction." It further stated that a state university may have a genuine compelling interest in having a diverse student body. However, ethnicity and race must be considered "a single though important element." The University, on the other hand, was focusing its admissions policy solely on ethnic and racial diversity. Thus, its special admissions program "would hinder rather than further attainment of genuine diversity."

Four Justices (William Brennan, Byron White, Thurgood Marshall, and Harry Blackmun) agreed that racial classifications by a state agency call for strict judicial scrutiny. But in their view, overcoming chronic minority underrepresentation in the medical profession justifies use of race in university admissions policies. The decision in *Bakke* was essentially a straddle by a divided court. It prohibited racial quotas but allowed the use of race as a "plus factor" in student admissions to achieve diversity in state universities. Even then, it would have worked had the leaders of educational institutions accepted and implemented the rule within the strict parameters outlined by the Court. But quotas have been used with impunity not only in public educational institutions but also in other public transactions. (Bakke graduated from Davis in 1982 and now is a physician in Minnesota.)

The equivocation of the court in *Bakke* was described variously as a "Solomonic compromise," "act of statecraft," and "sound compromise."[16] The experience of the more than two decades since that decision indicates that the prognosis of others was closer to the truth succinctly phrased by the *Wall Street Journal* which feared that the ambiguity of the decision left room for "discretionary mischief." Robert Bork, then a professor at Yale Law School, called the decision "unstable" because it did not say how much weight a university may give to race in its admissions policies. Some feared that the decision would lead to evasion and hypocracy in the universities. Justice Blackmun in his *Bakke* opinion had said that "in order to treat some persons equally, we must treat them differently."[17] This Orwellian statement in fact became the ideological basis of the majority opinion a year later in *Weber* (1979).[18]

In 1958, Kaiser Aluminum and Chemical Corporation (Kaiser) opened a plant in Gramercy, Louisiana. It had no in-plant apprenticeship training program for skilled craftspeople such as carpenter, electrician, general repairman, insulator, machinist, and painter. Therefore, the company hired its craft workers from the Gramercy area. Because there were few skilled black craftspeople available there prior to 1974, only 5 of the 273 skilled craftspeople at the Gramercy plant were blacks. The company was unable to attract more black craft workers despite the advertisements targeting black skilled workers. In the Gramercy area, blacks constituted 39 percent of the total labor force. In 1974, Kaiser (which had a total of 15 plants) entered into a master collective bargaining agreement with the United Steelworkers of America. It provided that, instead of hiring craft workers from outside the Gramercy plant, craft training would be conducted in the plant itself. Under the agreement, at least 50 percent of the openings in the training program were to be reserved for blacks until the percentage of black craft workers in the plant approximated the percentage of blacks in the local labor force. Selection into the craft training program was to be based on seniority.

In 1974, in accordance with the collectively bargained plan, 13 craft trainees were selected. Two of the blacks selected had seniority less than several white applicants who were rejected. Brian Weber was one of the whites rejected. He sued, claiming reverse discrimination prohibited by the Civil Rights Act of 1964. His claim was upheld at the District Court level as well as at the Circuit Court level. The United Steelworkers of America, AFL-CIO, appealed the case to the U.S. Supreme Court. Justice Brennan delivered the opinion of the Court and reversed the decision of the Court of Appeals. In doing so, he opined that Title VII does not forbid race-conscious affirmative action plans "voluntarily adopted by private parties to eliminate traditional patterns of racial segregation." Weber argued that Title VII intended to prohibit all race-conscious preferences, but the Court dismissed this as "literal interpretation" of the Civil Rights Act.

Chief Justice Warren Burger in a dissenting opinion said that Title VII, "a statute of extraordinary clarity," directly prohibited discrimination against all individuals and its legislative history makes clear its intent. Justice Rehnquist in an exhaustive dissent (joined by Burger) quoted Congressional leaders of both political parties who, in their debates on the bill containing Title VII, clearly stated that the purpose of the legislation was equality and not preferential treatment. Quoting the District Court's finding, Rehnquist said that Kaiser had agreed to the training plan in order to retain federal government contracts. The Office of Federal Contract Compliance (OFCC) had pressured Kaiser to increase minority workers in craft positions. Said Rehnquist, "The OFCC employs the 'power of the purse' to coerce acceptance of its affirmative action plans."[19] Both the District Court and the Court of Appeals said that the Kaiser plant at Gramercy had not been guilty of past discrimination against minorities. In concluding his dissenting opinion, Justice Rehnquist said: "By going not merely *beyond* but directly *against* Title VII's language and legislative history, the Court has sown the wind. Later courts will face the impossible task of reaping the whirlwind."[20] For over two decades, the Courts have been vainly trying to reconcile the simple and clear language of Title VII with the Orwellian interpretation by the five Justices. Weber, an individual who had done no wrong, was thus made to bear the burden of past societal wrongs against blacks.

The most contentious blueprint of race-, gender-, and ethnicity-based preferences in the federal government is the "Minority Small Business and Capital Ownership Development," or Section 8(a) program. It authorizes the Small Business Administration (SBA) to enter into construction, supply, and service contracts with other federal departments and agencies. The SBA presumes that small businesses owned and operated by blacks, Hispanics, American Indians, and Asian Pacific Americans are "socially disadvantaged." The SBA's Section 8(a) program started in 1969. In 1994 and 1995, it disbursed $4.4 billion and $5.2 billion, respectively, in federal contracts.[21] The program is widely criticized for the fact that most of the contracts are concentrated in the hands of a relatively few companies. For example, in 1994, of the 5,400 minority- and women-owned, SBA-certified "disadvantaged" firms, 1 percent of them got 25 percent of the contracts' dollars, while 56 percent got none. The program allows a firm to remain in the program for a maximum of nine years before standing on its own feet and facing the competition. However, between 1990 and 1993, of the companies that had graduated, 42 percent folded.[22]

The SBA Section 8(a) program was the prototype of the Minority Business Enterprise (MBE) provision of the Public Works Employment Act of 1977, challenged in *Fullilove et al. v. Klutznick, Secretary of Commerce* (1980).[23] The Act set aside 10 percent of federal funds granted for local public works projects to procure supplies and services from minority-owned businesses. The term *minority* was to include blacks, Hispanics, Orientals, American Indians, Eskimos, and Aleuts. The *term minority business enterprise* (MBE) meant that at least 50 percent of its ownership rested with minority-group members. The statute required that the MBE contracts were to be competitively priced, "or might have been competitively priced but for the present effects of prior discrimination." The program was challenged by a group of several associations of construction contractors and subcontractors. They argued that it denied them equal protection of the law, guaranteed under the Fourteenth Amendment to the Constitution.

The Supreme Court also ruled against them. In its decision, it said that a similar program has been in existence under Section 8(a) of the Small Business Act for many years.[24] The Court also quoted from the Congressional debate leading up to the passage of this Act in which it was mentioned that, although minorities constituted 15 to 18 percent of the U.S. population, they received only 1 percent of the federal procurement dollars. In the Court's view, even though this program may work to the disadvantage of some nonminority firms, relying on earlier decisions, it stated that "such 'a sharing of the burden' by innocent parties is not impermissible."[25] In a separate concurring opinion, Justices Marshall, Blackmun, and Brennan applauded the majority opinion. A strong dissenting opinion was written by Justice Potter Stewart and joined by Justice Rehnquist who quoted Justice Harlan's famous dissenting opinion in *Plessy v. Ferguson* (1896), "Our Constitution is color-blind, and neither knows nor tolerates classes among citizens." Therefore, they believed that the contract set-asides were unconstitutional. They said that no race has a monopoly on social or economic "disadvantage."

The decisions in *Griggs v. Duke Power Company* (1971) and *Washington v. Davis* (1976) dealt with a class of individuals who complained that the employers' qualification tests were discriminatory against them (*the disparate impact theory*). The cases of *DeFunis* (1974), *Bakke* (1978), and *Fullilove* (1980) fall into the category *of disparate treatment*, in which an individual claims that he or she was treated less favorably than others because of race, color, religion, sex, or national origin and must give specific proof of discriminatory motive, which sometimes may be inferred logically rather than empirically.

A class action was involved in *International Brotherhood of Teamsters v. United States* (1977) in which the government alleged that a nationwide common carrier was engaged in a pattern or practice of discrimination against its black and Spanish-surnamed employees.[26] All the company employees were represented by the same union. One collective bargaining contract covered Line Drivers (also known as over-the-road drivers) who hauled merchandise over long distances between company terminals. Other bargaining units included Servicemen (equipment maintenance persons) and City Operators—laborers on shipping docks, hostlers, and city drivers who picked up and delivered cargo within a city. The Line Drivers generally earned between $1,000 and $5,000 a year more than the Servicemen and the City Operators. But the Line Drivers worked long and irregular hours away from home and family. The company had a history of filling Line Drivers' jobs with whites. Blacks and Spanish-surnamed employees were hired as Servicemen and City Operators. These two categories also had some white workers. Until 1969, the company had hired only one black as a Line Driver.

The collective bargaining agreement provided that each worker enjoyed competitive seniority only in his or her own bargaining unit. All fringe benefits, layoffs, and recall rights were determined on the basis of bargaining unit seniority. A Serviceman or a City Operator bidding for a job as a Line Driver had to forfeit all competitive seniority and start at the bottom of the Line Drivers' category. Because layoffs, recalls, and fringe benefits were based on bargaining-unit seniority, for a large number of employees, such transfers were not attractive. Consequently, it "locked in" the Servicemen and City Operators in lower-paying and generally less desirable jobs. There was also evidence that over the years, in over 40 specific instances, the company had either ignored the requests for transfer to Line Drivers' jobs or had given false and misleading information to job applicants.

The Supreme Court ruled that the company in violation of Title VII had engaged in a systemwide pattern or practice of discrimination against blacks and Spanish-surnamed people. Even though the thrust of Title VII is on disparate treatment, the Supreme Court in this case, relying on the theory of *Griggs* (1971), said that "Proof of discriminatory motive, we have held, is not required under a disparate-impact theory." Discussing the role of statistics in disparate impact, the Court said: "Statistics showing racial or ethnic imbalance are probative in a case such as this one only because such imbalance is often a telltale sign of purposeful discrimination; absent explanation, it is ordinarily to be expected that nondiscriminatory hiring practices will in time result in a workforce more or less representative of the racial and ethnic composition of the population in the community from which employees are hired."[27] This thinking has contributed to the theory of parity, whose proponents demand equality of results in occupations, professions, student admissions, and sometimes even in college graduation rates. It ignores a whole host of cultural and labor market factors, other than discrimination, that influence individual choices and, consequently, the outcomes. The Supreme Court did say that depending on the facts and circumstances of a case, the "figures for the general population might not accurately reflect the pool of qualified job applicants." For a nonapplicant to get relief, he or she must give evidence that he or she: (1) would have applied but for the discriminatory policy of the company and (2) would have been discriminatorily rejected. He or she must prove both of these assertions as a potential victim of discrimination. The Supreme Court ruled that any minority applicant applying for a Line Driver's job after the passage of Title VII is presumptively entitled to a remedy subject to a showing by the company that its refusal to award that job was not based on discrimination.

Only four weeks after the high court's ruling in *Teamsters*, it handed down its decision in *Hazelwood School District v. United States* (1977).[28] The U.S. District Court had ruled that the Hazelwood School District in St. Louis County, Missouri, had engaged in a pattern or practice of employment discrimination against black applicants for teaching jobs. In determining this discrimination the District Court compared Hazelwood's teacher workforce with the racial composition of its student body. The Supreme Court said that such a comparison was "misconceived." It agreed with the Court of Appeals, which had held that a proper comparison must be made between the racial composition of the teaching staff and "the racial composition of the qualified public school teacher population in the relevant labor market." A relevant labor market area is the geographical area from which the employer draws its workforce. Thus, for instance, for unskilled or semiskilled labor, the relevant area may be the average commuting distance, while for postgraduate engineers, it might be a whole state or a multistate area. In other words, the geographical area used varies from occupation to occupation.

In *Franks v. Bowman Transportation Company* (1976), in the opinion written by Justice Brennan, the Supreme Court said that all those nonemployee black applicants who applied for and were denied over-the-road truck driving positions because of the company's discriminatory policies must be "made whole."[29] This included the right to priority consideration for such jobs, including the seniority each individual applicant would have enjoyed under the existing system but for the discriminatory refusal to hire. The Supreme Court said that the remedial Section 706(g) of Title VII was modeled on the remedial Section 10(c) of the National Labor Relations Act (NLRA). Under the latter statute, as was stated earlier, the National Labor Relations Board (NLRB) is authorized to take affirmative action, including reinstatement of employees with or without back pay, to remedy the effects of unfair labor practices.

Justices Powell and Rehnquist and Chief Justice Burger dissented from that part of the Court's majority opinion that awarded competitive seniority to nonemployee discriminatees. ("Competitive seniority" determines transfers, layoffs, recalls, desirable shift assignments, and promotions. "Benefit seniority," on the other hand, is used for fringe benefits, such as vacations, pensions, and other entitlements.) In their view, award of competitive seniority would hurt innocent employees who had earned their respective seniority credit through conscientious service through the years. In Chief Justice Burger's words, awarding of competitive seniority is tantamount to "robbing Peter to pay Paul."

SUMMARY OF SUPREME COURT'S DECISIONS IN THE 1970s

By the end of the 1970s, the Supreme Court had ruled in a number of cases involving race discrimination in employment and in one case (*Bakke*) involving student admissions into a public university. In broad terms, the majority or plurality opinions had declared the following:

1. An employer must not require a high school diploma or the passing of a standardized intelligence test if such requirements have a disparate impact on a protected class. The tests and educational qualifications must have a manifest relationship to the employment in question. Class action suits may be brought under Title VII. (*Griggs*)

2. A public university must not establish quotas or set-asides that give preference to protected minority students in admissions that result in reverse discrimination. However, public higher educational institutions may give race a "plus factor" to increase diversity. (*Bakke*)

3. A public agency may require its job applicants to pass a personnel test even if it has a disparate impact so long as it is reasonably related to successful job performance and to "modestly" upgrade the abilities of employees. (*Washington v. Davis*)

4. For Title VII violations, it is sufficient to show that a particular employment practice has an adverse impact. But to prove violation of the equal protection clause, a party must show discriminatory intent or purpose. (*Washington v. Davis*)

5. A collectively bargained affirmative action plan in a private sector corporation that gives preferences to protected minorities in employment and apprentice-training programs is permissible even if:

   a. The corporation does not have a history of discrimination against the protected minorities.

   b. It diminishes the benefit of competitive-seniority rights of innocent incumbent nonminority employees.

   c. The "voluntary" collective bargaining agreement incorporating affirmative action preferences for minorities is the result of government pressure threatening cancellation of federal contracts. (*Weber*)

6. The federal government has the power to set aside a portion of federal funds to be allocated to minority-owned contractors supplying goods and services to government departments and agencies. The set-aside contracts must be competitively priced, or "might have been competitively priced but for the present effects of prior discrimination." Even though in passing the statute Congress did not specifically cite discrimination in government contracting in the Supreme Court's view, it is sufficient that there is disparity between the contracts received by minority and nonminority contractors. (*Fullilove*)

7. Collectively bargained provisions are illegal if they discriminate against protected minorities in applying for and appointment to specific jobs in a company for which the applicants have the necessary skills. A competitive seniority system that deters minorities from applying for certain jobs is illegal because it locks them into generally less desirable jobs. Proof of discriminatory motive is not required where there is a pattern or a practice of discrimination creating a disparate impact. In such cases, class action suits are appropriate. Nondiscriminatory hiring practices are expected to result in a workforce representative of the racial and ethnic composition of the labor market. This is the theory of "representativeness/parity." (*Teamsters*)

8. In determining discrimination, comparison of an employer's skilled and college-educated workforce must be in proportion to the racial composition of the qualified labor pool in the relevant labor market. (*Hazelwood School District*)

9. Nonemployee qualified applicants who are denied specific jobs because of the discriminatory policy of the company have a right not only to be appointed to those jobs on a priority basis but also to receive competitive seniority even if it abridges the seniority-based benefits of incumbent innocent nonminority employees. (*Franks v. Bowman*)

As you will see in what follows, the Supreme Court will veer away from these principles in an often zigzag pattern.

BURDEN OF PROOF, SENIORITY RIGHTS, AND RACE-CONSCIOUS REMEDIES

In *McDonnell Douglas Corporation v. Green* (1973), a black applicant alleged that in violation of Title VII he was denied employment because of race discrimination.[30] The Supreme Court by a unanimous decision ruled that for an individual complaint (as compared to a class action) the following guidelines must be used. First, the complainant has the initial responsibility of establishing a prima facie case of race discrimination, which means that the complainant must offer strong enough evidence of violation of his rights that it will necessitate an answer from his opponent. A *prima facie case* is established when the complainant can show that he or she: (1) belongs to a racial minority, (2) was qualified for the job vacancy, and (3) was rejected, and that (4) after his or her rejection, the job remained open and the employer continued to seek applicants having qualifications equivalent to complainant's.

If the complainant fulfills these requirements, then the burden of proof shifts to the employer who must in rebuttal give specific, relevant evidence of some legitimate nondiscriminatory reason for the applicant's rejection. The complainant is given another full and fair opportunity to give evidence to prove that the reasons offered by the employer are a pretext for a racially discriminatory decision. In other words, the burden of proof ultimately remains on the complainant to prove discrimination.

At first blush, the Supreme Court's decision in *Firefighters Local Union No. 1784 v. Stotts* (1984) dealt a major blow to reverse discrimination.[31] It held that courts must respect bona fide competitive seniority rights in layoffs specified in collective bargaining agreements even if they result in undoing a prior Title VII consent decree. The Supreme Court held that the consent decree was silent as to seniority rights, layoffs, and "bump downs" and that there was no indication in the decree that the City modified its bargaining agreement with the union. Because Title VII protects the rights acquired under bona fide seniority systems, "it is inappropriate to deny an innocent employee the benefits of his seniority in order to provide a remedy in a pattern-or-practice suit as this."[32] If, however, individual black employees (rather than as a group) could prove that the Fire Department had discriminated against them, then they would have been awarded a make-whole remedy in the form of competitive seniority. But in this case, there was no evidence that any of the blacks subject to competitive seniority-based layoffs had been victims of discrimination. The Supreme Court said that "a court was not authorized to give preferential treatment to nonvictims." Subsequent lower courts decisions interpreted *Stotts* narrowly, and the Supreme Court itself reduced the potential impact of *Stotts* by upholding affirmative action preferences in two important cases in 1986.

In *Local 28 of the Sheet Metal Workers' International Union v. EEOC et al.* (1986), the Supreme Court ruled that preferences benefiting individuals who are not actual victims of discrimination may be awarded under Title VII.[33] Such preferences are appropriate where there is finding of a pattern or a practice of egregious discrimination or where it is necessary to dissipate lingering effects of pervasive discrimination. In such circumstances, benefits of affirmative action preferences go incidentally to individuals who were not the actual victims of discrimination.

During the trial in 1975, the District Court found that only 3.19 percent of the local Union's membership was nonwhite and that the Union had systematically excluded nonwhites. Consequently, the District Court ordered the Union to establish a 29 percent nonwhite membership goal to be achieved by July 1, 1981. This percentage was equal to the representation of nonwhites in the relevant labor pool in New York City. The Court of Appeals also found that the Union had "consistently and egregiously violated Title VII." Subsequently, in 1982 and 1983 the Union was found in contempt for not following the Court's order. The Union and U.S. Solicitor General Charles Fried (under the Reagan Administration) argued that affirmative action preferences in the form of union membership quotas established by the lower court are specifically prohibited by Section 706(g). In their view, under Section 706(g), preferential relief can only be granted to the actual victims of illegal discrimination. The Supreme Court rejected this interpretation of the statute. The quota plan for union membership, notwithstanding 706(g), was approved by the Supreme Court in a five-to-four vote, while six members of the Court agreed that a lower court may in certain cases impose affirmative action preferences that benefit individuals who are not the actual victims of discrimination.

The principle of restricting affirmative action preferences to actual victims of discrimination was lost when on July 2, 1986, the day *Local 28* was decided, the Supreme Court handed down another ruling involving somewhat similar issues. In *Local No. 93 International Association of Firefighters AFL-CIO v. City of Cleveland et al.*, the Court by a six-to-three vote ruled that a consent decree may provide race-conscious affirmative action preferences, such as promotions, to those who are not the actual victims of race discrimination.[34] This case, while severely limiting the scope of *Stotts*, followed the principle of *Weber* in interpreting Title VII. Under the consent decree, the Fire Department was given a specific quota of positions to be filled by minorities in all categories/ranks of the Fire Department. The life of the decree was four years accompanied by "goals" for promotions for each rank. Assistant Attorney General Reynolds and Solicitor General Fried argued that Section 706(g) of Title VII does not allow the Court to enter a consent decree that provides for race-conscious relief to individuals other than those who have been discriminated against. The Union also argued that even in a consent decree, only a victim-specific remedy can be provided under Title VII. The Supreme Court cited its decision given that day in the case of *Local 28* in which it had held that relief under Title VII may also be provided by a court to individuals "who were not the actual victims of a defendant's discriminatory practices." It said that the EEOC holds a similar view.

Justices White and Rehnquist and Chief Justice Burger dissented. In their view, a consent decree is like any other court decree and should be directed to provide relief only to identifiable victims of racial and ethnic discrimination. In the view of Justice White: "This kind of leapfrogging minorities over senior and better qualified whites is an impermissible remedy under Title VII. . . ."[35] The *Local 28* decision and the one in *Local 93* greatly expanded the authority of courts in decreeing affirmative action preferences and thus marginalizing the principle of *Stotts*.

Although the Supreme Court in July 1986 allowed the courts to give affirmative action preferences to nonvictims in the cases discussed previously, it did so in organizations where there were historical patterns and practices of egregious racial and ethnic discrimination. A few months earlier, in May 1986, it handed down *Wygant v. Jackson School Board of Education et al.*, which articulated important legal principles in affirmative action jurisprudence.[36] Suffering from racial tension, the Jackson (Michigan) School Board of Education in 1972 signed a collective bargaining agreement with its teachers' union that included a clause on affirmative action. It stated that in the event of layoffs, teachers with the most seniority shall be retained, "except that at no time will there be a greater percentage of minority personnel laid off than the current percentage of minority personnel employed at the time of the layoff."[37]

During the 1976–1977 and 1981–1982 academic years, nonminority teachers were laid off while minority teachers with less seniority were retained. Consequently, nonminority teachers sued the school board in Federal District Court for alleged violation of their rights under the equal protection clause of the Fourteenth Amendment. The Federal District Court dismissed the suit and held that racial preferences granted under the collective bargaining agreement need not be predicated on a finding of prior discrimination. In the Court's view, racial preferences designed to provide "role models" for minority children and to remedy "societal discrimination" are permissible under the equal protection clause. The U.S. Court of Appeals upheld the decision and the reasoning of the District Court. The nonminority teachers appealed to the Supreme Court.

The High Court struck down the "role model" theory used by the lower court in justifying racial preferences. In its view, this theory has "no logical stopping point," and it results in discriminatory hiring and layoff practices by the school board beyond legitimate remedial purposes. Any race- or ethnicity-based criteria used by government entities must be subjected to the most rigorous scrutiny (also known as *strict scrutiny*) to ensure that they do not violate equal protection guarantees of the Constitution. There are two prongs of strict scrutiny: (1) there must be a compelling governmental interest, and (2) the means chosen to fulfill that interest must be narrowly tailored. The Court made the following additional points:

- In order to determine underutilization of minority teachers in a public school, the proper comparison must be between the racial composition of the school's teaching staff and that of the qualified teacher population in the labor market from which teachers are recruited.

- There are many reasons for the disparity between the percentage of minority students and the percentage of minority faculty. Many of these reasons are unrelated to racial discrimination. Therefore, disparity between the two groups is *not* a basis for permissible preferential treatment. "The Constitution does not allocate constitutional rights to be distributed like bloc grants within discrete racial groups; and until it does, petitioners' more senior union colleagues cannot vote away petitioners' rights."[38]

Wygant did not produce a majority opinion. The five Justices who reversed the Court of Appeals decision on layoffs included Justice White, who only concurred in the judgment and provided the swing vote. The others were Powell (who announced the judgment and delivered the opinion), Rehnquist, Chief Justice Burger, and Sandra Day O'Connor. Justices Marshall, Brennan, Blackmun, and John Stevens dissented. A friend-of-the-Court brief urging reversal of the Court of Appeals' decision was filed by Acting Solicitor General Charles Fried, among others.

In *United States v. Paradise* (1987), the Supreme Court upheld the lower court's decision that ordered the Alabama Department of Public Safety (Department) as an interim measure to promote one black trooper to corporal for every white promoted to similar rank. This one-for-one promotion quota was to be implemented in the other upper ranks provided that there were qualified black candidates and that a particular rank was less than 25 percent black. This interim measure was to remain in effect until the Department developed and adopted a new promotion plan that did not have an adverse impact on blacks. Justice Brennan announced the judgment and delivered the opinion joined by Justices Marshall, Blackmun, and Powell. Justice Stevens concurred in the judgment and wrote an opinion while Justices O'Connor and Antonin Scalia and Chief Justice Rehnquist dissented. The United States, through Solicitor General Charles Fried, argued that one-for-one promotions were rigid preferential quotas and were not victim specific. Fried did not deny that the Department had a long history of egregious racial discrimination and defiance of previous court orders. A plurality of the Supreme Court rejected the argument and upheld the quota.

The case history went back to 1972 when the United States District Court held that the Department had systematically excluded blacks in violation of their Fourteenth Amendment rights. Consequently, in 1972 the District Judge ordered the Department to hire one black trooper for each white trooper until blacks constituted approximately 25 percent of the state trooper force. The Court of Appeals upheld the order. The United States, through its Solicitor General, argued against the quota calling it neither victim specific nor narrowly tailored, but overly rigid. The Supreme Court's plurality disagreed with the U.S. government's assertion and held that the Fourteenth Amendment permits a race-conscious remedy in a situation where there is long-term systematic and pervasive racial discrimination. A one-for-one promotion requirement does not impose an unacceptable burden on innocent whites, particularly in view of the fact that it does not require layoffs of whites. Justice O'Connor, in her dissent, joined by Chief Justice Burger and Justice Scalia, said that the standard of strict scrutiny requires that the means chosen to remedy discrimination must be narrowly tailored. In her view, the one-for-one promotion plan ordered by the Court far exceeded the percentage of qualified blacks among the troopers.[39]

PREFERENCES IN THE NAME OF STABILITY AND ORDERLY DEVELOPMENT OF THE LAW

In 1978, the Santa Clara County (California) Transit District Board of Supervisors adopted an affirmative action plan for the County Transportation Agency.[40] Women working for the Agency were largely concentrated in office, clerical, and service jobs. A relatively small percentage of women held professional, technical, or administrative positions. Of the 238 skilled craft workers' positions, none was held by a woman. The Agency adopted an affirmative action plan that had a long-term goal "to attain a workforce whose composition reflected the proportion of minorities and women in the area labor force."

A dispute arose when in December 1979 a vacancy for the position of "road dispatcher" became available. It was considered a skilled craft position in which hitherto there were no women employees. Of the 12 county employees who applied for the promotion, 9 were deemed qualified (that included Diane Joyce and Paul Johnson). All 9 were interviewed by a two-person board. Seven of the 9 applicants scored between 70 and 80 and were certified as eligible for selection. Johnson was tied for second with a score of 75 while Joyce was next with a score of 73. After a second interview by a panel of three supervisors, they recommended that Johnson be promoted. However, at the recommendation of the Agency's Affirmative Action Coordinator, the Director of the Agency promoted Joyce. Johnson sued alleging reverse discrimination and violation of his rights under Title VII. The complaint did not raise the constitutional issue of equal protection of the law. The U.S. District Court gave a decision in favor of Johnson while the Court of Appeals reversed that decision, even though there had been no finding of gender discrimination by the Agency. The Supreme Court in 1987 affirmed the holding that such an affirmative action preference was permissible under Title VII. It supported its decision by holding that:

1. The sex of a qualified applicant was considered simply as one factor in promotion.

2. The agency had not set aside any specific number of positions for minorities or women.

3. The affirmative action plan was temporary until the agency's workforce would mirror "in its major job classifications the percentage of women in the area labor market." The plan was to attain a balanced workforce, not to maintain it.

As previously discussed in *Bakke* (1978) and again in *Weber* (1979), the Supreme Court permitted voluntary affirmative action preferences. Thus, Justice Stevens said that even though these preferences are at odds with his understanding of the actual intent of the Civil Rights Act, he is compelled to permit them following the precedents of *Bakke* and *Weber* and thus providing "stability and orderly development of the law."[41] Justice Scalia, in his dissenting opinion, wrote that by permitting affirmative action preference in this case, "we effectively replace the goal of a discrimination-free society with the quite incompatible goal of proportionate representation by race and sex in the workplace."[42] He called the proportional-representation goal "the Agency's Platonic ideal of a workforce."

STRICT SCRUTINY FOR GOVERNMENTAL AFFIRMATIVE ACTION

In 1983, the Richmond (Virginia) City Council adopted an affirmative action plan to help minority construction contractors.[43] Under the Minority Business Utilization Plan, those receiving prime construction contracts from the city were required to subcontract at least 30 percent of the dollar amount of their contracts to minority business enterprises (MBEs). City contracts awarded to minority-owned prime contractors did not have this provision.

The Plan defined an MBE as a business of which at least 51 percent is owned and controlled by a minority. The term *minorities* was defined to include any American citizen who is black, Spanish-speaking, Oriental, American Indian, Eskimo, or Aleut. These minorities did not have to be residents of Richmond or even citizens of the State of Virginia.

The set-aside was justified by the Richmond City Council on the following grounds:

1. The set-aside will promote wide participation by minorities in the construction industry. The City Council simply declared it to be "remedial" in nature.
2. The general population of Richmond was 50 percent black, but during the preceding five years, only 0.67 percent of the City's prime construction contracts had been awarded to minority businesses.
3. There is general discrimination in the construction industry in the City of Richmond and the State of Virginia and around the nation. There are very few minority contractors in local and state contractors' associations.

At the end of 1983, the Croson Company, a mechanical plumbing and heating contractor, was refused a waiver from the set-aside rule. The firm brought an action alleging violation of its equal protection rights under the U.S. Constitution. The Court of Appeals held that the set-aside Plan was unconstitutional because it violated the equal protection rights of Croson. The City of Richmond appealed to the Supreme Court asking for reversal. The Supreme Court affirmed the judgment of the Court of Appeals. In its decision, it gave the following reasons.

1. Richmond's City Council had not shown any record of prior discrimination by the City in awarding construction contracts.

2. "The mere recitation of a benign or compensatory purpose for the use of a racial classification" is an inadequate basis for preferential treatment. A city, unlike the federal government, must make a finding of discrimination before it can justify race-conscious remedies.

3. "[A]n amorphous claim that there has been past discrimination in a particular industry cannot justify the use of an unyielding racial quota." There must be a "strong basis in evidence" for the conclusion that remedial action is necessary. Simply stating that a racial classification is "benign" or legitimate is "entitled to little or no weight."

4. There are many explanations of a dearth of minority contractors, including past discrimination as well as entrepreneurial choice made both by blacks and whites.

5. There is absolutely no evidence of past discrimination against Spanish-speaking people, Orientals, Indians, Eskimos, or Aleuts in the Richmond construction industry. Therefore, there was no legitimate reason for their inclusion in the set-aside program. "The gross overinclusiveness of Richmond's racial preference strongly impugns the city's claim of remedial motivation."

6. The City's program is not narrowly tailored, and, therefore, it does not meet one of the tests of strict scrutiny. In order to determine whether a race-conscious remedy is appropriate, the Court will look at whether race-neutral remedies were tried to cope with racial discrimination.

Various Justices concurred with different parts of the Court's opinion. Justices Marshall, Brennan, and Blackmun dissented. The strict scrutiny standard used by the Supreme Court to determine the permissibility of race- and ethnicity-based preferences in state and local programs has now been extended to federal programs. This development is the result of the Supreme Court's decision in the *Adarand Constructors* case (1995), which will be discussed later.[44] However, there is a case in which the Supreme Court, in deference to Congressional policy, allowed race-based preferences in awarding broadcasting licenses by the Federal Communications Commission (FCC).

Two cases, *Metro Broadcasting Incorporated v. Federal Communications Commission, et al.*, and *Astroline Communications Company v. Shurberg Broadcasting of Hartford Incorporated et al.*, were consolidated and decided by the Supreme Court on June 27, 1990.[45] They both involved challenges to racial preferences given by the FCC. Metro Broadcasting challenged the FCC's policy under which a competitor firm was awarded a broadcasting license on the grounds that the competitor was 90 percent Hispanic owned as compared to Metro Broadcasting, which was only 19.8 percent minority owned. In the other case, a television station in Hartford, Connecticut, suffering from financial difficulties, was allowed by the Commission to be sold to another minority firm under the same policy of giving race based preferences. In this case, the competitor bidder, Shurberg Broadcasting Company, sued on the grounds of violation of its equal protection rights.

It needs to be mentioned that the policy to give race-based preferences was developed and implemented by the FCC under its regulatory powers and was not a statutory mandate from Congress. The FCC has the exclusive authority to grant broadcasting licenses based on "public convenience, interest, or necessity." Under this broad authority in 1978, the FCC began a policy of giving a "plus" to minority status in the allocation of broadcasting licenses. (This "plus" factor has its origin in Justice Powell's opinion in *Bakke*—the case handed down on June 28, 1978.) The FCC's policy on racial preference was inaugurated at the same time. Until that time, the FCC had followed a race-neutral policy in awarding licenses.) The FCC defined the term *minority* to include blacks, Hispanics, Eskimos, Aleuts, American Indians, and Asian Americans.

Justice Brennan delivered the opinion of the Court, joined by Justices White, Marshall, Blackmun, and Stevens. The majority opinion upheld racial preferences on the grounds that minorities were underrepresented in broadcasting and that giving them preferences in licenses will create diversity in the use of airwaves belonging to the public. The Court also said that such "benign" preferences "serve important governmental objectives . . . and are substantially related to achievement of those objectives." Justice O'Connor wrote the dissenting opinion, in which Chief Justice Rehnquist and Justices Scalia and Anthony Kennedy joined. In their view, the Constitution treats citizens as individuals and not as groups. The majority opinion has reduced the equal protection standard from strict scrutiny of compelling governmental objectives to a lower standard of "important governmental objectives." There is no precedent in Supreme Court cases for this lowered standard, nor is there any support for it in the Constitution.

In March 1995, the Congress repealed a 17-year-old tax break (signed into law by the President on April 11) that was originally designed to increase minority ownership of broadcasting companies.[46] It was widely believed that big companies had used the tax breaks to save millions of dollars in federal taxes by using minority business partners simply as a means of meeting the diversity criterion. The catalyst for change in the law was a proposed deal by Viacom of $2.3 billion in which a minority businessman had planned to invest only $2 million. If approved, Viacom would have saved approximately $400 million by deferring indefinitely capital gains taxes. During the Senate debate on this preference, one senator remarked that there was no discrimination in the sale of broadcast licenses justifying the tax break. "If you have blue skin . . . and have the money to buy, you can," said Senator Bob Packwood (Republican, Oregon).[47] As discussed later by us, on June 12, 1995, the Supreme Court in *Adarand Constructors* overruled *Metro Broadcasting* and reasserted the test of strict scrutiny for governmental racial classifications.

On February 19, 1992, in *Lamprecht v. FCC*, the U.S. Court of Appeals for the District Court of Columbia Circuit in a two-to-one ruling held that a policy of the FCC to give women preference over men in awarding broadcast licenses is unconstitutional because it denies equal protection of the law to men.[48] Clarence Thomas, now a Supreme Court Justice, wrote the opinion joined by Judge James Buckley, who also wrote a concurring opinion. (It is permissible for a Supreme Court Justice to return temporarily to the lower court to finish the work on decisions after appointment to the High Court. Consequently, Justice Thomas, who was promoted in November 1991, received permission from the Supreme Court to issue the ruling as an Appeals Court Judge.)

The Court's majority said that "the government has failed to show that its sex preference policy is substantially related to achieving diversity on the airwaves. We, therefore, hold that the policy violates the Constitution."[49] The minority opinion in *Metro Broadcasting* (1990), majority opinions in *Lamprecht* (1992) and *Croson* (1989), and plurality opinion in *Wygant* (1986) presaged the severe restrictions on the use of race and sex in public employment and public contracting permitted by the Supreme Court. The next chapter deals with developments in employment law and public policy in the post–*Metro Broadcasting* era.

NOTES

1. *Plessy v. Ferguson*, 163 U.S. 537, 559 (1896); also see: Nell Irvin Painter, "Legal Brief: A Great Divide," *New Yorker*, May 6, 1996, 126; and Charles A. Lofgren, *The Plessy Case* (New York: Oxford University Press, 1987).

2. *United Steelworkers of America v. Weber*, 443 U.S. 193, 255 (1979).

3. *Steele v. Louisville and Nashville Railroad Company*, 323 U.S. 192 (1944); *Wallace Corporation v. National Labor Relations Board*, 232 U.S. 248 (1944).

4. *Griggs v. Duke Power Company*, 401 U.S. 424 (1971).

5. Ibid., 430.

6. Ibid., 431.

7. 29 Code of Federal Regulations (CFR) Section 1607.4(d).

8. *Daily Labor Report*, A-4, Bureau of National Affairs (April 6, 1978); and 71 *Daily Labor Report*, A-3, Bureau of National Affairs (April 12, 1978). For a thorough discussion of this issue, see: Barbara Lindemann Schlei and Paul Grossman, *Employment Discrimination Law*, 2nd ed. (Washington D.C.: The Bureau of National Affairs, 1983), pp. 92-97.

9. *Albemarle Paper Company v. Moody*, 422 U.S. 405 (1975).

10. *Washington v. Davis*, 426 U.S. 229 (1976).

11. Ibid., 245.

12. Ibid., 246.

13. *McDonald v. Santa Fe Trail Transportation Company*, 427 U.S. 273 (1976).

14. *DeFunis v. Odegaard*, 416 U.S. 312, 350 (1974).

15. *Regents of the University of California v. Bakke*, 438 U.S. 265 (1978).

16. Terry Eastland and William J. Bennett, *Counting by Race* (New York: Basic Books, 1979), pp. 175-178.

17. *Bakke*, 407.

18. *United Steelworkers of America, AFL-CIO v. Weber*, 443 U.S. 193 (1979).

19. Ibid., 223.

20. Ibid., 255.

21. Figure for 1994 from: *Business Week*, March 27, 1995, 70; figure for 1995 from: *Wall Street Journal*, 18 April, 1996, B2.

22. Data in this paragraph from: Catherine Yang and Mike McNamee, *"Affirmative Action: 'A Hands Up, But Not a Handout,'" Business Week*, March 27, 1995, 70, 72.

23. *Fullilove, et al., v. Klutznick, Secretary of Commerce*, 448 U.S. 448 (1980).

24. Section 8(a) of the Small Business Act of 1953, Pub. L. 85-536, Section 2, 72 Stat. 389.

25. *Albemarle Paper Company v. Moody*, 422 U.S. 405 (1975); and *Franks v. Bowman Transportation Company*, 424 U.S. 747 (1976).

26. *International Brotherhood of Teamsters v. United States*, 431 U.S. 324 (1977).

27. Ibid., 340, Note 20.

28. *Hazelwood School District v. United States*, 443 U.S. 299 (1977).

29. *Franks v. Bowman Transportation Company*, 424 U.S. 747 (1976).

30. *McDonnell Douglas Corporation v. Green*, 411 U.S. 792 (1973).

31. *Firefighters Local Union No. 1784 v. Stotts et al.*, 467 U.S. 561 (1984).

32. Ibid., 575.

33. *Local 28 of the Sheet Metal Workers' International Union v. Equal Employment Opportunity Commission, et al.*, 106 S. Ct. 3019 (1986).

34. *Local Number 93, International Association of Firefighters AFL-CIO v. City of Cleveland, et al.*, 478 U.S. 501 (1986).

35. Ibid., 534.

36. *Wygant v. Jackson Board of Education, et al.*, 476 U.S. 267 (1986).

37. Ibid., 270.

38. Ibid., 281, Note 8.

39. *United States v. Paradise, et al.*, 480 U.S. 149, 199 (1987).

40. *Johnson v. Transportation Agency, Santa Clara County, California, et al.*, 480 U.S. 616 (1987). For study of the interaction of human relations, law, and justice, see: Melvin I. Urofsky, *A Conflict of Rights: The Supreme Court and Affirmative Action* (New York: Charles Scribner's Sons, 1991).

41. *Johnson*, 644.

42. Ibid., 658.

43. *City of Richmond v. J. A. Croson Company*, 109 S. Ct. 706 (1989).

44. *Adarand Constructors Incorporated v. Federico Pena, Secretary of Transportation, et al.*, 115 S. Ct. 2097 (1995).

45. *Metro Broadcasting Incorporated v. Federal Communications Commission, et al.*, and *Astroline Communications Company v. Shurberg Broadcasting of Hartford Incorporated, et al.*, 110 S. Ct. 2997 (1990).

46. Pam Slater, "Death of a Deal," *The Sacramento Bee*, April 7, 1996, E1, E3. Concerns minority tax incentive (known as Section 1071).

47. "Senate OKs Repealing of Broadcast Tax Break," *The Sacramento Bee*, March 25, 1995, F1. For further information on this issue, see: Mark Lewyn, "The Wrong Way to Open the Media to Minorities," *Business Week*, January 16, 1995, 33; Grey Forster, "Tax Breaks for Being Black," *Wall Street Journal*, November 8, 1995, A18; Gautam Naik and Daniel Pearl, "Pulling the Plug? Sale of Wireless Slots Is Turning into a Flap on Affirmative Action," *Wall Street Journal*, March 17, 1995, A1; and Jackie Calmes, "Senate Committee Votes for Repealing Tax Break Crucial to Viacom Cable Sale," *Wall Street Journal*, March 16, 1996, A3.

48. *James Thomas Lamprecht v. Federal Communications Commission*, 958 F. 2d 382 (D.C. Cir. 1992).

49. Ibid., 398.

3

❧

One Step Backward and Two Forward

CIVIL RIGHTS ACT OF 1991 AND RELATED CASES: REPAIRING THE DAMAGE

The Civil Rights Act of 1991 was the outcome of prolonged negotiations among the Senate liberal Democrats, their counterpart Republicans, and the Bush Administration. The negotiations, lasting for almost two years, led to a compromise bill signed by President George Bush on November 21, 1991.[1] It became effective the same day. The Act was largely designed to repair what its proponents felt was the "damage" done to the law of employment discrimination by the Supreme Court in a series of decisions handed down in 1989 and one in 1991. Following are brief descriptions of the main points of law involved in each case and the "repair work" done by the Civil Rights Act of 1991.

Wards Cove Packing Company v. Atonio[2]

As discussed in the preceding chapter, in *Griggs v. Duke Power Company* (1971), the Supreme Court had ruled that an employment practice (e.g., requiring a high school diploma or a passing score on an aptitude test) that has a disparate impact on a protected class is illegal unless it can be shown that it was "business necessity" and has a "demonstrable relationship to successful performance of the jobs." The term *manifest relationship* was also used in the case. Other employment measures or tests without discriminatory impact could also serve the employer's legitimate interest in efficient productivity.

In *Wards Cove* (1989), the Supreme Court said that "business necessity" simply means that the challenged employment practice or test significantly serves the employer's legitimate goals: "there is no requirement that the challenged practice be 'essential' or 'indispensable' to the employer's business for it to pass muster."[3] The decision also required that the plaintiff isolate and identify the specific employment practices that are allegedly responsible for disparities/adverse impact on the protected group as measured statistically. This requirement of *particularity* now has been incorporated into the 1991 statute. An exception is provided where a complainant can show that the employer's decision-making process is such that its various elements cannot be separated. The new law requires the employer to demonstrate that the challenged practice that creates disparate impact on a protected group "is job related for the position in question and consistent with business necessity." (The statute, however, failed to define the term *business necessity*.)

Price Waterhouse v. Hopkins[4]

The Court ruled in *Price Waterhouse* (1989) that an employer is not liable under Title VII if he can prove by a preponderance of evidence that he would have made the same decision in the absence of discriminatory reason. Known as *mixed motive decisions*, they involve both lawful and discriminatory reasons. In a mixed motive case, the 1991 statute allows the Court to award a complainant attorney's fees and costs as well as declaratory and injunctive relief. But in such a case, the employer cannot be ordered to hire, promote, or reinstate the complainant or to award back pay or damages. Section 703 of Title VII has been amended by the 1991 statute by the addition of the following subsection: "(m) Except as otherwise provided in this title an unlawful employment practice is established when the complaining party demonstrates that race, color, religion, sex, or national origin was a motivating factor for any employment practice, even though other factors also motivated the practice." Reviewing this particular provision of the 1991 statute, David Cathcart and Mark Snyderman stated, "*Weber* and *Johnson* may no longer be good law."[5] Later in this chapter and in Chapter 7, we will discuss developments in the form of Supreme Court cases decided since 1991 that strengthen the belief/prognosis of Cathcart and Snyderman.

Patterson v. McLean Credit Union[6]

This case involves Section 1981 of the Civil Rights Act of 1866, which states interalia that all persons shall have the same right "to make and enforce contracts." Violation of one's right under this Section gave the complainant the right to sue for unlimited compensatory and punitive damages plus equitable relief. The complainant could also ask for a jury trial. Under this

Section, private employers regardless of size could be sued, and the plaintiff could go directly to Court rather than through the Equal Employment Opportunity Commission (EEOC). Compared to Section 1981, only those employers who had 15 or more workers were under the jurisdiction of Title VII. Furthermore, jury trials or damages were not available under Title VII.

In *Patterson* (1989), the Supreme Court held that Section 1981 of the Civil Rights Act of 1866 was applicable only to intentional discrimination in the initial making and enforcement of employment contracts, not to postformation conduct. The Court said that Section 1981 was not applicable to racial harassment. The Civil Rights Act of 1991 amended Section 1981 to include postformation conduct encompassing the total contractual relationship.

Martin v. Wilks[7]

Many employment discrimination disputes are settled through consent decrees in which the parties make an agreement under the sanction of the Court. Such an agreement is enforceable through a Court Order. Often these decrees involve affirmative action plans that have potential adverse impact on current employees and future applicants. In *Martin v. Wilks* (1989), the Supreme Court held that persons who were not parties to the original suit that led to a consent decree have the right to institute a lawsuit challenging hiring and promotion decisions made pursuant to that decree. This right to challenge exists even though the challengers had knowledge of the proposed consent decree and had the opportunity to object to its terms but failed to do so.

The Civil Rights Act of 1991 reversed the Supreme Court's decision in *Martin v. Wilks*, and bars its challenges to programs implemented under consent decrees in two situations: (1) where the challengers prior to the judgment or order had notice of the proposed judgment or order and reasonable opportunity to object; and (2) where the challengers' interests were adequately represented by someone who had previously challenged the judgment or order on the same legal grounds and in a similar factual situation.

Lorance v. AT&T Technologies, Incorporated[8]

In *Lorance v. AT&T Technologies* (1989), the Supreme Court ruled that in the case of a seniority system the statute of limitations begins to run at the time the system is adopted. The Civil Rights Act of 1991 overturned this decision, and it provides that where a seniority system is adopted by an employer for intentionally discriminatory purposes, the time for filing a complaint with EEOC starts (1) when the employee becomes subject to the seniority system or (2) when the employee experiences the injury by the application of the seniority system.

Equal Employment Opportunity Commission v. Arabian American Oil Company[9]

The Civil Rights Act of 1991 also reversed the decision of the Supreme Court in *EEOC v. Arabian American Oil Company* (1991), in which it had held that the protection of Title VII does not extend to U.S. citizens employed by U.S. employers abroad. However, U.S. employers have been exempted from liability if compliance with this law would cause the employer to violate the law of the foreign country in which a workplace is located. U.S. citizens working for U.S. employers abroad were also given protection under the Americans with Disabilities Act of 1990.

Until the Civil Rights Act of 1991 was passed, Title VII did not provide for jury trials. Now plaintiffs have the right of jury trials and compensatory and punitive damages. Monetary awards prior to this Act were restricted to reimbursement for back pay or other equitable relief such as reinstatement. The act places caps on total damages that can be awarded to each complaining party meeting certain specified conditions.

The Act prohibits race norming in recruitment or referral of applicants or candidates for promotion. The practice of "race norming" refers to adjusting the scores or using different cutoff scores for employment-related tests on the basis of race, color, or gender. This practice had been around for years in the United States Employment Service where the General Aptitude Test Battery was widely used for vocational counseling and job referrals. Before the practice of race norming was banned in 1991, an estimated 3,000,000 people had been hired by employers based on racially normed scores. As discussed later in this chapter, many of the elite universities in America in effect use race norming in student admissions policies. The Civil Rights Act of 1991 also provided for a Glass Ceiling Commission to study the obstacles facing women and minorities in upward economic mobility in organizations and to prepare recommendations for the advancement of women and minorities. Rules for the burden of proof in employment discrimination cases have also been provided.

STRICT SCRUTINY TAKES TOLL ON PREFERENCES

Even before the Supreme Court gave its precedent-setting decisions in *Adarand v. Pena* (1995)[10] and *Missouri v. Jenkins* (June 1995)[11] on racial classification by government agencies, U.S. lower courts had been handing down a number of decisions severely critical of expansive affirmative action preferences. Following is a discussion of some of these cases.

Podberesky v. Kirwan

On October 27, 1994, a three-judge panel of the U.S. Court of Appeals for the Fourth Circuit in *Podberesky v. Kirwan* unanimously struck down a scholarship program of the University of Maryland established exclusively for African-American students.[12] The estimated value of each scholarship was approximately $33,500. Daniel J. Podberesky, a Hispanic freshman at the university, met academic requirements of the scholarship but was denied consideration. He sued the university, but in May 1991 the U.S. District Court ruled against him. The District Court upheld the scholarship program on four grounds: (1) poor reputation of the university within the African-American community, (2) underrepresentation of African-Americans in the student population, (3) low retention and graduation rates of African-American students, and (4) a campus atmosphere perceived by African-American students as hostile.

The Court of Appeals, on October 27, 1994, reversing the District Court's decision, said that the race-based scholarship program was not "narrowly tailored to serve its stated objectives" and, therefore, did not meet the strict scrutiny criterion as laid down by the Supreme Court in its decisions, particularly in *Wygant* (1986), *Bakke* (1978), and *Croson* (1989). The Court of Appeals said: "While the inequities and indignities visited by past discrimination are undeniable, the use of race as a reparational device risks perpetuating the very race-consciousness such a remedy purports to overcome. . . . It thus remains our constitutional premise that race is an impermissible arbiter of human fortunes."[13]

The Appeals Court rejected the reasons given by the lower court for its decision because:

- The state's history of past segregation "is not the kind of present effect that can justify a race-exclusive remedy."

- The claimed hostility does not stem from the university's discriminatory acts of the past. Several northern universities suffer from comparable racial problems.

- Lower graduation rates and higher attrition are the result of economic and other factors, not of past discrimination.

- The University should have considered race-neutral alternatives to achieve its objectives.

- The scholarship program is not narrowly tailored because it is open to non-Maryland residents. In fact, 17 of the 31 scholarships went to out-of-state blacks.

In light of the above, the Appeals Court said, "The program more resembles outright racial balancing than a tailored remedy program. As such, it is not narrowly tailored to remedy past discrimination. In fact, it is not tailored at all."[14]

The decision was viewed as a serious setback for race-exclusive scholarships. Of the estimated $30 billion scholarship and loan programs in the nation as a whole, only about 3 percent of them are reserved for one race only.[15] The ruling caused consternation among university officials who support and administer such scholarships. It was a defeat for the Clinton Administration, particularly because it had supported the university's position. The Justice Department under President Bush had not taken a position in this case. In May 1995, the U.S. Supreme Court, without comment, let stand the Court of Appeals decision.[16] Richard A. Samp of the Washington Legal Foundation, which represented Podberesky, predicted lawsuits seeking punitive damages if the institutions do not act in good faith in implementing the decision. The University of Maryland's President called the Supreme Court's action "deeply saddening." The Fourth Circuit Court of Appeals covers Maryland, North Carolina, South Carolina, Virginia, and West Virginia; for these states, the Court of Appeals' decision is binding. This Court of Appeals' decision is the highest level ruling so far on minority scholarships. Finally, at the end of 1995 after five years of litigation, a check for $32,863, equal to the cost of four years of education at the University, was paid to Daniel J. Podberesky. Additionally, his lawyers received a total of $436,000 from the university and the State of Maryland as representation costs.[17]

Some proponents of racial preferences, such as Deval L. Patrick, Chief of the Justice Department's Civil Rights Division in President Clinton's first term, and Robert H. Atwell, President of the American Council on Education, at once bemoaned and belittled the potential consequences of the *Podberesky* decision. In reality, that decision has enormous potential consequences as indicated by the wide press coverage given to the case as it progressed through the various courts.[18] Despite the February 1994 guidelines of the U.S. Department of Education that allow race-based preferences "to promote diversity," a number of institutions will have to take steps to eliminate any racial exclusivity from their scholarship programs. Otherwise, they are likely to be targets for litigation and claims for damages.

UC Berkeley's Boalt Hall

While the Courts have been ruling against blatant racial preferences, in 1992 the U.S. Department of Education's Office for Civil Rights, after a two-year investigation, determined that the University of California at Berkeley School of Law (Boalt Hall) had been practicing reverse discrimination in student admissions.[19] It is appropriate here to describe in some detail the preference program at this school. Boalt Hall has had an affirmative action program in student admissions since 1968. In 1978, it established a program of giving "special consideration" to minorities with the "goal" of achieving a student body composition of 8 to 10 percent of blacks, 8 to 10 percent of Hispanics, 5 to 7 percent of Asians, and 1 percent of Native Americans. The school has achieved that goal every year since 1978. It is noteworthy that these preferences were not designed to remedy any prior discrimination.

The program instead was meant to bring about "educational diversity" and to remedy the underrepresentation of ethnic minorities in the legal profession. Of the 4,000 to 6,000 applications received every year, Boalt Hall admitted about 270 in its first-year class. In its admissions criteria, it used an index score made up of each applicant's LSAT score and undergraduate grade point average (GPA) adjusted for quality of undergraduate school and age of degree. Each applicant's race or ethnicity was noted on the file. An applicant was placed in one of the four admission ranges (A, B, C, or D) depending on his or her index score. Separate Admissions Committees considered the applications of each racial or ethnic group. The candidates within each racial or ethnic group were compared with the members of that group. The U.S. Department of Education, Office of Civil Rights, found that "if the Director [of Admissions] determines that Boalt Hall will fall short of its goal for admission of persons from a particular special consideration group, he will generally bypass applicants on the wait list until he reaches a person who is lower in rank order on the list, but who is a member of the desired special consideration group."[20] The U.S. Department of Education concluded: "In practice, Boalt Hall administered its program of special consideration in a manner designed to ensure that the affirmative action percentage goals would be met."[21]

Simply stated, the Law School first set up a quota for each minority group and then systematically went about filling it. In the process, it insulated each minority group from competition with the other ethnic groups to chieve its "goals." Given these findings and to avoid being sued, in September 1992, the Law School entered into a "Conciliation and Settlement Agreement" with the Office of Civil Rights, U.S. Department of Education, under which it agreed that: (1) it will not set aside seats for admission into the Law School based on race, color, or national origin of applicants; (2) it will not consider applications from minorities separately from others; and (3) admissions will not be based solely on the color, race, or national origin of applicants.

After signing the agreement, Herma Hill Kay, Dean of Boalt Hall, denied that the School used racial quotas in its admission policies.[22] The *Sacramento Bee*, however, in its editorial, called it "a quota under whatever name" and "a matter or affirmative discrimination."[23] Michael L. Williams, Assistant Secretary of the U.S. Department of Education and in charge of the Department's Office for Civil Rights, said that Boalt Hall's "goal, in effect, ended up being a quota."[24] Robert Atwell, President of the American Council on Education, the largest group representing institutions of higher education, called the Conciliation Agreement ending quotas "a real blow to the efforts to achieve racial diversity."[25] The findings of race quotas at Berkeley's Law School elicited considerable media coverage.[26] Michael S. Greve, Executive Director for the Center of Individual Rights, in an op-ed piece said that quota systems are being practiced by "virtually all competitive law schools."[27] Similarly, Richard Samp, Chief Counsel for the Washington Legal Foundation, a public interest law firm, commented that reverse discrimination, like that of Boalt Hall, "goes on everywhere."[28]

Piscataway Board of Education v. Taxman

In May 1975, the New Jersey State Board of Education adopted an affirmative action policy under which the most qualified candidates were to be hired.[29] If candidates were equally qualified, then a candidate meeting the affirmative action criterion was to be hired. The program was not designed as a remedy for any prior discrimination. As a matter of fact, both the plaintiff and the defendant agreed that the affirmative action program was not remedial, and no charge of alleged racial discrimination had been previously filed with the appropriate state or federal government agencies. There was no underutilization of blacks in the relevant qualified labor pool.

On September 1, 1980, the Piscataway Board of Education hired two teachers of business education: Sharon Taxman (a white) and Debra Williams (a black). In 1989, the school district needed to reduce the size of its business education department. In the past, seniority ties were broken by drawing lots. But this time, in an effort to implement its affirmative action policy, the school district terminated Sharon Taxman in May 1989 and abolished one teaching position. The U.S. Department of Justice, in support of Taxman's claim of reverse discrimination, instituted the suit under Title VII of the Civil Rights Act against the Board of Education in Piscataway.

The Board sought to justify its affirmative action plan and its decision to terminate Sharon Taxman in order to promote "racial diversity for education's sake." The Board conceded that the program of affirmative action was not remedial in purpose. The District Court's ruling in favor of Taxman said, "Faculty diversity 'for education's sake' is not a permissible purpose under controlling Title VII case law." The Court also held that the Board had failed to demonstrate a compelling interest in apportioning jobs on the basis of race. The "role model" theory has been rejected by the Supreme Court. The Board then appealed the District Court's decision.

The U.S. Department of Justice initially supported Sharon Taxman in the Third Circuit Court of Appeals. However, a few months after the appointment of Deval L. Patrick, Assistant Attorney General for Civil Rights, the Clinton Administration in August 1994 switched sides. It sought leave from the Court of Appeals to file a friend-of-the-court brief seeking to reverse the judgment of the District Court stating: "Upon further review, the United States believes that the District Court announced an unduly narrow interpretation of the permissible bases for affirmative action under Title VII." [30] The *New York Times* reporting this story stated that Deval "Patrick did not cite a precedent for such a switch."[31] In his defense, Patrick stated that "the [Court's] position was wrong," while Taxman's attorney called the switch "unethical and reprehensible."[32] In an unambiguous eight-to-four ruling of major importance, the U.S. Court of Appeals for the Third Circuit, on August 8, 1996, held that the Board of Education's policy of affirmative action preference based on race was unlawful. "It is clear that the language of Title

VII is violated when an employer makes an employment decision based upon an employee's race."[33]

The *New York Times,* in an editorial entitled "A Blow to Affirmative Action in Schools," commented that restrictions on affirmative action have become "the judicial order of the day."[34] Sharon Taxman, after seven years of court fights, finally had won the right of equal treatment. However, the Piscataway Board of Education appealed the case to the U.S. Supreme Court. On January 21, 1997, Associated Press reported that the Supreme Court asked the Clinton Administration whether it thought the Board had violated the white teacher's rights when it laid her off instead of an equally qualified black colleague. The Supreme Court wanted the Clinton Administration to state its position before deciding whether to hear the appeal.[35]

In response to the Supreme Court's instructions to file a brief as to the Administration's position in the case of *Piscataway Board of Education v. Taxman* (decided by the U.S. Court of Appeals in August 1996), the Justice Department, on June 5, 1997, formally requested the Court *not* to hear the case. The Clinton Administration in its brief argued that the Supreme Court should not hear the case because in its view it was unrepresentative of "real life experience."[36] At the same time, the Administration contended that "narrowly tailored" affirmative action in "the real world" designed to promote diversity "can be constitutional." However, in its friend-of-the-court brief, the Clinton Administration did not give a satisfactory explanation as to why it had supported the race preference in this "unrepresentative" case in the Court of Appeals. Rejecting the Justice Department's entreaty, on June 27, 1997, the last day of the Court's term, the Supreme Court agreed to hear the *Piscataway Board of Education* case.[37] The Justice Department was worried that the Supreme Court would further limit the parameters of affirmative action preferences. This was of particular concern to hundreds of institutions of higher education that use race and ethnic preferences in student admissions and faculty appointments.[38] The proponents of affirmative action called the prospect of limitations on the diversity policy "scary." They realized that the Clinton Administration, in this case, did not have "enough ammunition to win."[39]

As if two previous switches by the Clinton Administration in this case were not enough, on August 22,1997, the Justice Department, after three years of internal philosophical and political debate, changed its position again. This time, in its 29-page brief submitted to the Supreme Court, it conceded that the Piscataway school district's decision to lay off the white teacher in order to retain an equally qualified black teacher to maintain racial diversity was not legally permissible. It urged the Supreme Court to nullify in this case only that part of the Court of Appeals ruling that had barred all affirmative action preferences in hiring and promotion decisions. Thus, in the Administration's view, providing a diverse faculty may justify "a tailored use of race in employment decision."[40] However, the National Association for the Advancement of Colored People (NAACP) was satisfied with the brief's overall support of affirmative action.

The foes of racial preferences were understandably disappointed when, on November 21, 1997, the news broke that in this case, which had been litigated for nine years, the Board of Education had in fact capitulated and decided not to pursue it any further before the Supreme Court. In the settlement, the Board of Education agreed to pay $433,500 to Sharon Taxman and her lawyers. Interestingly enough, 70 percent of this money was contributed by a coalition of civil rights groups that included among others the NAACP, the Reverend Jesse Jackson, and the Black Leadership Forum. This stunning development was viewed by the pro-affirmative action groups as an effort to buy time for a better test case, while the opponents of affirmative action preferences variously labeled it as "playing a shell game" or "dodging a bullet."[41] The *New York Times* in its editorial viewed avoiding a high court ruling under the circumstances "a smart move."[42] Despite the settlement of this case, all sides believe that sooner or later the Supreme Court will issue a definitive ruling on affirmative action preferences in employment.[43]

University and Community College System of Nevada v. Yvette Farmer

Occasionally, advocates of race-based employment preferences have scored some court victories. One such example comes from the Supreme Court of Nevada in a case involving a clear preference given to a candidate because of his race. In this case, Yvette Farmer, a white female sociologist, was initially denied faculty employment while the job was given to Johnson Makoba, an equally qualified black immigrant from Uganda. The curriculum vitae of these two candidates indicated them to be equally qualified. A year later, in 1991, the Sociology Department hired Farmer but at a salary that was $7,000 less than was initially paid to Makoba. Furthermore, Makoba received an additional raise after a year of employment that brought the annual pay gap between him and Farmer to $10,838. The university explained the initial pay difference to be the result of a bidding war between two prestigious universities that had scheduled job interviews with Makoba. However, the University of Nevada openly admitted that in hiring Makoba and giving him premium pay, racial preference was used in order to increase minority faculty representation. The Supreme Court of Nevada in a three-to-two decision held that the university had used race as only one of the factors in making the faculty appointment. The Court further stated: "We also view the desirability of a racially diverse faculty as sufficiently analogous to the constitutionally permissible attainment of a racially diverse student body countenanced by the *Bakke* Court."[44] On March 9, 1998, the U.S. Supreme Court without comment declined to review the case.[45]

Cheryl J. Hopwood, et al., v. State of Texas: Bakke II

No case since *Bakke* (1978) involving institutions of higher education has had such an impact as the one involving Cheryl Hopwood and the University of Texas.

The case involved the University of Texas Law School, which had denied admission to Cheryl Hopwood, who is white, raising a severely handicapped daughter, had paid her way through college working at least 20 hours a week, and maintained a 3.8 GPA.[46] In the Law School Admissions Test (LSAT), she was ranked at the 83rd percentile. The Law School receives approximately 4,000 applications annually and accepts only 500 for its first-year classes. (The Law School had practiced racial segregation until 1950, when the U.S. Supreme Court in *Sweatt v. Painter* held that the Law School established for blacks was inadequate and unequal.)[47] The Law School assigned a "Texas Index" to each applicant. It is a composite of each applicant's LSAT score and a GPA multiple. The School for many years had maintained a "goal" of achieving a student body composed of 5 percent blacks and 10 percent Mexican-Americans. Applications from minorities were considered by a minority admissions subcommittee and were not compared to those of nonminority applicants. In 1992, four white applicants, including Hopwood, were denied admission even though Hopwood had a Texas Index of 199 and the other three had a Texas Index of 197. Only one black applicant from Texas had a score equal to Hopwood's. All of the other 23 black admittees had a score of 197 or below. The Center for Individual Rights, a major public interest law firm in Washington, D.C., took up the cause and provided intellectual and other support for a reverse discrimination suit filed by Cheryl Hopwood and three co-plaintiffs in the U.S. District Court in Austin, Texas. On August 19, 1994, U.S. District Judge Sam Sparks ruled that "affirmative action programs are still needed in our society," and therefore universities may legitimately consider race and ethnicity as one factor in their admission policies.[48] However, a university must not use separate committees to evaluate applications, nor should it use different minimum test scores and GPAs for minority applicants and white applicants. The Judge felt that despite the evidence of the university's race-based preferences, the plaintiffs could not conclusively prove that they would have been admitted but for the discriminatory policies of the university. Therefore, he held that the plaintiffs could reapply for admission without paying the application fee. Additionally, the Court awarded $1 to each plaintiff as nominal damages. The Court denied the plaintiffs' request for compensatory and punitive damages because in its view any harm done was unintentional on the part of the university. The university justified its policy of racial preferences on the grounds that Texas still suffers from the effects of the State's past discrimination. However, over two-thirds of the black admittees were from outside the state. This case was widely reported as *Bakke II!*[49]

On March 18, 1996, the Fifth Circuit Court of Appeals in a three-to-zero ruling held that racial diversity is not a compelling governmental interest that would justify race-based preferences.[50] The U.S. Justice Department's Associate Attorney General John Schmidt called the ruling "startling and wrong."[51] The *Chronicle of Higher Education*, the premier weekly in this field, in its cover story called the decision "A Stunning Blow to Affirmative Action,"[52] while the Executive Director of the Center for Individual Rights, who along with his colleagues represented Hopwood, hailed the ban as a bold step toward color blindness.[53] The supporters of affirmative action charged that the Court of Appeals had misread the case law.[54] The Clinton Administration's Justice Department, nine states, and the District of Columbia, in separate briefs, asked the Supreme Court to strike down the Court of Appeal's *Hopwood* ruling. They were particularly concerned about that part of the decision that declared that: "Justice Powell's view in *Bakke* is not binding precedent on this issue."[55]

Because in our public institutions of higher education throughout the United States race and ethnic preferences in student admissions are defended on the basis of Justice Powell's opinion in *Bakke*, this direct challenge to the very validity of that opinion is unsettling to the advocates of preferences. On April 8, 1996, Georgia's Attorney General Michael J. Bowers, in a two-page letter to the Chancellor of the Board of Regents of the University System of Georgia (which comprises 34 public institutions of higher education), recommended that the Regents should review and revise their student admissions policies of affirmative action if they do not meet the strict scrutiny standards laid down by the Supreme Court in its recent rulings and the Fifth Circuit Court of Appeals' decision in *Hopwood*.[56] Bowers's letter was particularly significant because the *Hopwood* decision covers only the jurisdiction of the Fifth Circuit Court of Appeals comprised of Texas, Louisiana, and Mississippi. On July 1, 1996, the U.S. Supreme Court refused to review the *Hopwood* case, thus leaving intact the Court of Appeals' ruling that the Law School might not use race as a factor in student admissions and that race can be used only to remedy the present effects of a public institution's own discriminatory practices.[57]

Aftermath of *Hopwood*

Some universities are already feeling the reverberations of *Hopwood* and are suddenly facing challenges to their student admissions policies. One such challenge faces the University of Washington, which is being sued by Katuria E. Smith, a white applicant who was denied admission to the University's School of Law in 1994.[58] Her case is being represented by the Center for Individual Rights, which successfully fought the case of Cheryl Hopwood in Texas. Katuria Smith graduated *cum laude* from the University of

Washington's Business School and scored in the 95th percentile on the LSAT. Smith's lawyers from the Center for Individual Rights believe that their client is a victim of reverse discrimination and want appropriate remedy. The case was broadened when Angela Rock and Michael Pyle, who were declined admission into the University of Washington Law School in 1995 and 1996, joined the lead plaintiff Katuria Smith to press their claim against discrimination. The Center for Individual Rights has filed a motion for a class action suit on behalf of "all unsuccessful nonminority applicants to the 1994, 1995, and 1996 incoming classes."[59]

In another case filed by the Center for Individual Rights on behalf of a 16-year-old Corpus Christi girl in the U.S. District Court in Texas, the National Institutes of Health (NIH) and Texas A&M University are being sued for practicing race/ethnicity-based apprenticeship programs in biomedical and behavioral research. The plaintiff in this case alleges reverse discrimination.[60]

Another challenge has been mounted by 11 residents of Georgia against the State University.[61] Seven of the plaintiffs are white and four are black. They charge that affirmative action policies pursued by the University System in effect perpetuate segregation whereby its black colleges have substantially lower admissions and academic standards than their counterpart white colleges. Two of the white plaintiffs complain that the University of Georgia, while rejecting their applications for admission, admitted minority students with lower test scores than theirs. This litigation is of particular importance because it involves a large system that has 19 universities.

The *Hopwood* decision provides an opportunity to reassess university policies of race-based preferences that have become unconscionable and impermissible. Many of the people who initially supported these policies no longer do so.[62] It is ironic that law schools knowing full well the permissible parameters of the law and that separate cannot be equal have been openly defying it and then lying about it. Perhaps no single policy of a university or a corporation is as much denied by their administrators as racial quotas, and yet it is also common knowledge that they in fact encourage them, implement them, and brag about "diversity."

In October 1997, a lawsuit was filed against the University of Michigan on behalf of Jennifer Gratz and Patrick Hamacher. As in the *Hopwood* case, once again the Center for Individual Rights provided the legal counsels.[63] Plaintiff Gratz, now 20, daughter of a policeman, attained a 3.76 GPA and stood thirteenth in her graduating class of 298 in a Detroit blue-collar suburban public high school. She scored 25 out of 36 on the ACT entrance exam. While in high school, she was a math tutor, active in student government, and served as homecoming queen. Despite these qualifications, when she applied in 1994 for the 1995 incoming class, she was denied admission. Similarly, Hamacher, an applicant to the 1997 incoming class, was also denied admission even though he had a 3.32 GPA, scored 28 (84th percentile) on the ACT, had taken a number of advanced placement courses, and had a good record of community service.

The University of Michigan denied them admission because they did not fit into the GRID that was designed to give preference to racial minorities under the "Michigan Mandate," a system designed by the university in 1987. It, in effect, created dual standards for minority and nonminority applicants. Under that system, for example, a white student with a GPA below 3.3 (out of 4.0) and a combined Scholastic Assessment Test (SAT) score of 1,000 (out of 1,600) was automatically rejected after a clerk's review. However, black or Hispanic students with grades above 3.0 and combined SAT scores of above 850 were accepted. The GRIDs, secret charts, and the process became known when Carl Cohen, a Professor of Philosophy at the University of Michigan, requested and received the documents under the Freedom of Information Act. Making this information public brought forth dozens of potential litigants from which the Center for Individual Rights selected Gratz and Hamacher to lead the fight as plaintiffs. The filing of the lawsuit against the University of Michigan resulted in a torrent of stories in the press and commentaries not only about the case[64] but also about the Center for Individual Rights, which took the case pro bono.[65]

Despite data to the contrary, the university insisted that race was considered only as a "plus" factor. This reliance on Justice Powell's opinion in the *Bakke* case and on that solitary Justice's obiter dictum about the university's desire for "diversity" is the single most egregious abuse by elite American universities in their student admissions policies. By using preferences in a dual system during the past decade, the University of Michigan has been able to double the enrollment of minorities to 25 percent. The Admissions Counselors were specifically instructed by the university to use different cutoff points in evaluating the applications of whites and non-whites. The university officials insist that without these preferences the institution will be "resegregated." While awaiting the judicial outcome, Gratz has enrolled as a math major at the University of Michigan's satellite campus at Dearborn where she has made the Dean's List several times; Hamacher is now a pre-med student at Michigan State University. The final outcome of the case is likely to take years. The clarity of its issues and its evidence will make it a prime case for appeal to the U.S. Supreme Court. Finally, the Supreme Court would have the opportunity to revisit the "diversity" and "race-as-a-plus-factor" issues in their empirical form vis-à-vis the Fourteenth Amendment and the equal opportunity provisions of the Civil Rights Act of 1964 (as amended). While this case challenges the undergraduate admissions policies of the University of Michigan, the Center for Individual Rights has instituted another case against the university for denying admission into its Law School for Barbara Cutter. She has a GPA of 3.81 and a score of 161 in the LSAT.

PROGENY OF *CROSON*: HAS THE SUPREME COURT STOPPED ZIGZAGGING?

Despite efforts of proponents of preferences to restrict the scope and impact of the decision in *City of Richmond v. J. A. Croson Company* (1989), its principles have been adopted by lower courts in a number of cases. For the first time, the Supreme Court's majority has said that race-based preferences by state and local government agencies are permissible under the equal protection clause of the Constitution only if they meet the strict scrutiny test. Lower courts immediately started following the precedent.[66]

Where there is "gross statistical disparity" between the proportion of minorities employed and the qualified labor pool in the relevant labor market, then it would be appropriate for public employers to give race-based preferences that are narrowly tailored and flexible and that do not unnecessarily trammel the interests of innocent third parties. Thus, in *Howard v. McLucas* (1989)[67] and *Cone Corporation v. Hillsborough County* (1990),[68] the Courts permitted the use of race-based preferences for minority contractors because of the adequate statistical evidence of discrimination. A public employer implementing an affirmative action plan is required to show that it has a "strong basis in evidence for its conclusion that remedial action was necessary" (*Croson* and *Wygant*). But a plan to end discrimination in employment is not to be equated with achieving racial or gender "parity," particularly in professions and highly skilled occupations.

Since 1989, when the *Croson* decision was given, the Supreme Court has charted a course in which it has been less tolerant of the liberties that public agencies have been taking against citizens' rights to enjoy equal protection of the law. The sole exception was the *Metro Broadcasting* ruling in 1990 when the Court deferred to Congress and upheld a gender-based preference in awarding a broadcasting license. Even that ruling has been overturned, as discussed later, by its 1995 *Adarand* decision. The Supreme Court's fractured decisions in most affirmative action cases prior to *Croson* are not exactly models of either consistency or plain statutory construction of the Civil Rights Act. But since 1989, its decisions give relatively clearer meaning to the term *equality under the law* as it concerns race-conscious public policies. The authors believe that the decisions since 1989 indicate that perhaps the High Court has stopped zigzagging on this important issue. The readers will, of course, make their own judgment after reading the summaries of relevant cases decided between 1992 and 1996.

Freeman v. Pitts

Freeman v. Pitts (1992)[69] involved a school desegregation plan in DeKalb County, Georgia. In 1969, under a consent decree, *de jure* segregation (segregation created specifically by state action for that purpose) was ended.

The District Court issuing the consent decree retained jurisdiction to over-see its implementation. The overall goal of the consent decree was to create a unitary school system. In 1986 the DeKalb County School System (DCSS) petitioned the District Court for dismissal of the consent decree and a dec-laration that a unitary school system had been achieved. The District Court ruled that DCSS had achieved maximum practical desegregation but ordered the school system to allocate resources to remedy the remaining deficiency.

The Court of Appeals held that the District Court must retain full reme-dial authority over the school system for several years "to correct the racial imbalance" even though it may have been caused by demographic shifts. Justice Anthony Kennedy delivered the opinion of the Supreme Court stat-ing that a court may relinquish its supervision of a school desegregation plan in stages. The racial imbalance in the school district was caused by the demographic shift in which the northern half of the county had become predominantly white and the southern half predominantly black. The racial imbalance is not the result of previous *de jure* segregation. Thus, students at various individual schools are a result of demographic shifts and not a vestige of the previous dual system. Once the injury and stigma of the *de jure* segregated system has been ended by creating a unitary system, the school district is not entitled to rearrange attendance zones to achieve balance. "Racial balance is not to be achieved for its own sake. It is to be pursued when racial imbalance has been caused by a constitutional violation."[70] Where resegregation is not a result of law or government action but is due to "private choices," it has no constitutional implication and, hence, is outside the remedial power of a court.

United States v. Fordice

In *United States v. Kirk Fordice, Governor of Mississippi, et al.*, (1992) the Supreme Court held that a state has affirmative duty to ensure that its system of public education is race-neutral and is free from the segregative effects of its previous *de jure* dual system.[71] Mississippi has eight public uni-versities of which five are almost completely white and three almost com-pletely black.

The lower courts had ruled that in these universities the affirmative duty of desegregation was fulfilled when a racially dual structure was formally abandoned. The Supreme Court disagreed with the limited meaning and the interpretation of the concept of desegregation adopted by the lower courts. Justice Byron White, writing for a near unanimous court (with Justice Antonin Scalia concurring in part and dissenting in part), said that the state's affir-mative duty to reform continues "if policies traceable to the *de jure* system are still in force and have discriminatory effects."[72] If such policies influ-ence student enrollment or foster segregation in other aspects of the univer-sity operations and if such policies are not educationally sound and can be practically eliminated, then the state has a constitutional and statutory affirmative duty to dismantle the dual system.

The High Court reviewed four policies of the Mississippi university system: student admission standards, program duplication, institutional mission assignments, and continued operations of eight public universities. The Supreme Court found "unnecessary duplication" particularly of graduate- and post-graduate-level academic programs offered by two or more of the universities. It criticized as "wasteful and irrational" maintaining more universities in the state than necessary. For instance, Delta State and Mississippi Valley are only 35 miles apart, and Mississippi State and Mississippi University for Women are only 20 miles from each other. Disparity in funding between the predominantly white institution and the predominantly black institution was also noted. In light of the preceding, the High Court concluded that, in effect, the state had perpetuated a segregated university system and had not met its affirmative duty to dismantle its dual system. The case was remanded to the district court, and the state was ordered to: (1) end its dual student admissions standards; (2) take into account not only students' ACT scores but also GPAs; (3) eliminate unnecessary duplication in courses, especially graduate and post-graduate academic programs; (4) carefully explore the possibility of closing or merging some of the universities and investigate "whether retention of all eight institutions itself affects student choice and perpetuates the segregated higher education system";[73] and (5) review the mission of the university system and its funding priorities. It is forecast that there will be years of litigation before it is resolved. Nineteen states operate predominantly black colleges and universities. The *Harvard Law Review* considered the *Fordice* decision as a "serious threat to the continued viability of state supported, predominantly black universities in the formerly segregated states."[74]

Shaw v. Reno

A race-conscious state decision was also the topic of *Ruth O. Shaw, et al., v. Janet Reno, Attorney General, et al.,* (1993). According to the 1990 census, the composition of North Carolina's voting-age population included 78 percent white, 20 percent black, and 1 percent each of Native Americans and predominantly Asian. In order to satisfy the reapportionment provisions of the Voting Rights Act of 1965, the state needed to create a second majority-black voting district. North Carolina's General Assembly adopted a redistricting plan that redrew the existing majority-black voting district and created a second one to give blacks greater voting strength. However, both of these districts were geographically bizarre and were described as follows by the Supreme Court:

District 1 is somewhat hook shaped. Centered in the northeast portion of the State, it moves southward until it tapers to a narrow band; then, with finger-like extensions, it reaches far into the Southern-most part of the State near the South Carolina border. District 1 has been compared to a "Rorschach ink-blot test" . . . and a "bug splattered on a windshield."

The second majority-black district . . . is even more unusually shaped. It is approximately 160 miles long and, for much of its length, no wider than the I-85 corridor. It winds in snake-like fashion through tobacco country, financial centers, and manufacturing areas "until it gobbles in enough enclaves of black neighborhoods."[75]

. . .

"One state legislator has remarked that if you drove down the interstate with both car doors open, you'd kill most of the people in the district."

The General Assembly's rationale for the weird redistricting plan was that blacks constituted a majority of the population in only 5 of the state's 100 counties, and that the Attorney General of the United States had approved the configuration. Five voters of North Carolina brought an action against the State of North Carolina and the Attorney General alleging violation of their Fourteenth Amendment rights because of the racially gerrymandered voting redistricting. The Supreme Court struck down the plan, calling it political apartheid. "It reinforces the perception that members of the same racial group—regardless of their age, education, economic status, or the community in which they live—think alike, share the same political interests, and will prefer the same candidates at the polls. We have rejected such perceptions elsewhere as impermissible racial stereotypes."[76]

Missouri v. Jenkins and Miller v. Johnson

In June 1995 the Supreme Court delivered two opinions having a common theme—impermissible race-conscious actions by the state and the misuse of affirmative action. The first case concerned school desegregation, the second Congressional redistricting, and the third federal contract set-asides. *Missouri, et al., v. Jenkins, et al.,* (1995) culminated 18-year-old school desegregation litigation in which the U.S. District Court had ordered the Kansas City, Missouri, School District to pay salary increases to almost all instructional and noninstructional employees in the school district and to continue to fund expensive educational projects.[77] The District Court deemed these measures necessary and appropriate in order to improve the "desegregative attractiveness" of the school district and to reverse the "white flight" to the suburbs. These remedial measures, in the Court's view, were required because student achievement levels of many grades were at or below national norms and because "the school district was far from achieving its maximum potential."

The same District Court Judge who ordered these measures had originally heard and decided the case in 1977. At that time he stated that until

1954, Missouri's law mandated segregated schools for black children and for white children and since that time, the state had maintained a dual school system. So in 1977, the District Court ordered a number of improvements, including full-day kindergarten, expanded summer school, early childhood programs, and early childhood development programs. These "effective school" programs cost the state over $220 million. Then in 1986, the District Court ordered other improvements, including the magnet school program costing the state an additional $448 million. By the time the case reached the Supreme Court, the cost of capital improvements alone had skyrocketed to over $540 million, and the annual desegregation costs approached $200 million. Among the improvements for "quality education" ordered by the District Court were:

> [H]igh schools in which every classroom will have air-conditioning, an alarm system, and 15 microcomputers; a 2,000-square-foot planetarium; green houses and vivariums; a 25-acre farm with an air-conditioned meeting room for 104 people; a Model United Nations wired for language translation; broadcast-capable radio and television studios with an editing and animation lab; a temperature-controlled art gallery; movie editing and screening rooms; a 3,500-square-foot dust-free diesel mechanics room; 1,875-square-foot elementary school animal rooms for use in a zoo project; swimming pools; and numerous other facilities.[78]

The state, having spent over $800,000,000 and seeing no end to the escalating cost, asked the Court to withdraw its mandated salary increases to the school district's 5,000 instructional and noninstructional employees. The state contended that the order for salary increases was outside the scope of the Court's remedial authority. Both the District Court and the Court of Appeals rejected the state's arguments. The Supreme Court said that a desegregation remedy must be no more than "to restore the victims of discriminatory conduct to the position they would have occupied in the absence of such conduct."[79] The simple fact that a majority of students in a school are black does not necessarily mean that it is segregated. This issue must be determined in view of the racial makeup of the school district's population and of whether district boundaries have been drawn neutrally. In the case at hand, the District Court did not find any constitutional violation by the school district that justified the "remedies" imposed on the state. The Supreme Court said that without other evidence of discrimination the Constitution is not violated by racial imbalance in the schools.[80] Black students comprising 68.3 percent of the school district's enrollment reflects demographic shifts and is not a result of a state policy. The Supreme Court said: "The District Court's pursuit of 'desegregated attractiveness' is beyond the scope of its broad remedial authority."[81] The District Court exceeded its authority in endeavoring to eliminate "a condition that does not violate the Constitution or does not flow from such violation."[82] Demographic changes independent of *de jure* segregation plus numerous external factors beyond the control of the school district affect minority enroll-ment and students' achievements.

A separate concurring opinion by Justice Clarence Thomas opened with this poignant statement about the attitude of the District Court: "It never ceases to amaze me that the courts are so willing to assume that anything that is predominantly black must be inferior."[83] He said that "racial imbal-ance" by itself is not necessarily a proof of constitutional violation. The District Court in mandating "magnet" schools is focusing on reversing the "white flight" rather than on remedying the harm done to the black chil-dren by prior segregation. "The mere fact that a school is black does not mean that it is the product of a constitutional violation."[84]

Once again, in *Miller v. Johnson* (1995), the Supreme Court considered the permissible limits of race-conscious decision making by the state.[85] The 1990 census found that blacks constituted 27 percent of Georgia's total population of 6.5 million. Up to that time, the state had only one majority-black Congressional district. The increase in the state's total population entitled it to add one to its ten Congressional seats. Section 5 of the Voting Rights Act of 1965 requires that a Congressional redistricting plan in an area declared as a "covered jurisdiction" by the Attorney General be sub-mitted for approval to the U.S. District Court or to the Attorney General for administrative "preclearance." The provision is designed to ensure full and fair opportunity for the exercise of voting rights by racial minorities.

In 1991, Georgia's General Assembly devised a redistricting plan in which the number of majority-black districts was increased by one to two. There was no evidence that in such redistricting there was any intent to discrimi-nate against black voters. Despite these measures, the U.S. Department of Justice, on January 21, 1992, refused preclearance. In its letter of refusal, it strongly suggested that the redistricting plan should make provisions for three, instead of two, majority-black districts. Georgia's General Assembly redrew the Congressional districts, but the Justice Department once again refused preclearance. Contemporaneously, the American Civil Liberties Union (ACLU) drew up the so-called "Max-black" plan that contained three majority-black districts. The Justice Department relied on that map for its policy response. Having been rebuffed twice by the Justice Department, the General Assembly finally drew up a redistricting plan with the active assis-tance of the Justice Department using the "Max-black" blueprint as its guide. It was precleared by the Justice Department on April 2, 1992. It created a third majority-black district by connecting the black neighborhoods of At-lanta with Savannah on the coast—"260 miles apart in distance and worlds apart in culture."[86] The Supreme Court quoted the Almanac of American Politics, which called the newly created Congressional district a "geographic monstrosity" that defies the generally accepted criteria of voting districts. "In short, the social, political, and economic makeup of the Eleventh Dis-trict tells a tale of disparity, not community."[87]

In the 1992 elections, the newly created three majority-black districts elected three black Representatives. The Supreme Court agreed with the District Court that race was the "overriding and predominant force"[88] in redistricting. This was a clear violation of the right of equal protection of the law. Then quoting from some of its previous decisions, the Supreme Court said: "The idea is a simple one: 'At the heart of the Constitution's guarantee of equal protection lies the simple command that the government must treat citizens as individuals, not as simply components of a racial, religious, sexual, or national class.'"[89]

The Supreme Court recognized that in redistricting, along with such traditional principles as compactness, contiguity, and respect for political subdivisions, race may be a part of "political calculus." However, the Constitution forbids making race a predominant factor, even in the political process of redistricting. The Supreme Court said that it must guarantee equal protection of the law, and in this duty "blind judicial deference to legislative or executive pronouncements of necessity has no place."[90] In this case, the only compelling interest the State Assembly had in its redistricting plan was satisfying the Justice Department's preclearance condition. The redistricting plan met the preclearance condition but violated the Constitution. The judgment of the District Court was affirmed. President Clinton said that the decision was a "setback in the struggle to ensure that all Americans participate fully in the electoral process."[91]

Bush v. Vera and Shaw v. Hunt

In 1996 the Supreme Court once again visited the issue of Congressional districts drawn on racial basis. This was the third time in four years the Court dealt with the controversial issue of gerrymandering. This time in two cases, *Bush v. Vera* (1996) and *Shaw v. Hunt* (1996), the Court struck down racially drawn districts in Texas and North Carolina.[92] Majority-minority districts, said the Court, cannot be drawn predominantly along racial lines. The Court said that Congressional districts may be designed for partisan politics but not for racial reasons. As in the other cases of districting, the Court's majority included Chief Justice William H. Rehnquist and Justices Sandra Day O'Connor, Anthony M. Kennedy, Antonin Scalia, and Clarence Thomas. Press comments on these decisions, and indeed a series of similar decisions since 1993, were highly conflicting as to their philosophical intent and potential impact as indicated by the following statements:

- The Voting Rights Act of 1965 has been seriously damaged, and "only the shell still stands." (Theodore Shaw of the NAACP Legal Defense and Education Fund)[93]
- The Supreme Court has replaced the law's clarity with a "you-know-it-when-you-see-it kind of standard." (Brenda Wright of the Lawyers Committee for Civil Rights Under Law)[94]

- "At night the enemies of civil rights strike in white sheets, burning churches. By day, they strike in black robes, burning opportunities." (The Reverend Jesse Jackson of the Rainbow Coalition)[95]

- We should all celebrate the Supreme Court's decision because it "closes the door on a sorry story of race-based decision making for purposes of political representation." (Abigail Thernstrom of the Institute for Justice, a nonprofit public interest law organization)[96]

- "Let's embrace the ideal of a political system as [one] that seeks out the best candidates with the best qualifications. . . . America will be far better off with color-blind political districts, not color-conscious ones." (Ken Blackwell [State Treasurer of Ohio] and Matt Fong [State Treasurer of California])[97]

Race-based Congressional districts involved in these cases were not entirely the result of pressure by the U.S. Department of Justice. They were partly the outcome of agreements between the Democratic and Republican parties. The former used them to satisfy its black and Hispanic constituencies while the latter benefited by securing the votes of whites by "insulating" the whites from minorities. Previously, in *Thornburg v. Gingles* (1986),[98] the Supreme Court had established a legal standard for creating a predominantly minority district. Under that standard, minority voters must prove that reapportionment is warranted because the challenged district minimizes or cancels out their ability to elect their preferred candidates. Thus, a bloc-voting majority is generally "able to defeat candidates supported by a politically cohesive, geographically insular minority group."[99] However, the right to vote and fair representation has never meant to guarantee proportionate electoral success.[100]

There is intense debate over whether it is desirable to increase the total number of racial minorities in the Congress even if it requires "serpentine" and "bizarre" districts as they were in the cases just described. Professor Carol M. Swain of Princeton University is of the view that instead of predominantly race-conscious districts, government should create "influence districts" in which racial minorities "constitute a significant though not a majority of the population."[101] Her data demonstrated that in 1990, before race-dominated redistricting, 40 percent of the blacks elected to the Congress were in fact elected from areas where blacks were less than 40 percent of the voting age population.[102] Quite the opposite view is expressed by the Reverend Jesse Jackson who is reported to have said that recent Supreme Court decisions on prohibiting race-based Congressional redistricting were a "kind of ethnic cleansing of blacks in Congress."[103] However, the fears of severe potential electoral losses for blacks in Congress due to redistricting proved to be unfounded in the 1996 general election. Sanford Bishop easily won reelection from Georgia's redrawn district which had 52 percent black voters in 1992 but only 35 percent in 1996. Similarly, Representative Cynthia McKinney won in a Georgia's redrawn district in which only 33 percent of the voters are black. In the nation as a whole, 14 of the 37 black Congressmen won races in districts where less than half the voters were black.[104] It is obvious that race-based gerrymandering is not only unconstitutional but unnecessary for minority political participation.

Adarand v. Pena (1995): The Supreme Court Changes Its Mind; Federal Government Now Must Live by the Same Rules as State and Local Governments

One of the most anxiously awaited decisions of the Supreme Court, *Adarand Contractors Incorporated v. Pena, Secretary of Transportation, et al.,*[105] was handed down on June 12, 1995. It involved race preference given in a federal contract under the Surface Transportation and Uniform Relocation Act of 1987. This Act provides that no less than 10 percent of contract funds must be allocated to small businesses owned and controlled by "economically and socially disadvantaged individuals," which include women, blacks, Hispanics, Native Americans, and Asian Americans. The Act's operative clause also provides that a prime contractor who awards a subcontract to an "economically and socially disadvantaged" firm, as just defined, shall be paid a bonus equivalent to 10 percent of the amount of the subcontract, not to exceed 1.5 percent of the prime contract. In this case, Mountain Gravel awarded the subcontract to build guardrails to minority-owned Gonzales Company despite the fact that its bid was higher than that of white-owned Adarand. Mountain Gravel Company's representatives testified that had it not been for the bonus money, it would have awarded the subcontract to Adarand, which had submitted a bid that was $1,700 less than that of Gonzales on a $100,000 subcontract. Adarand sued and claimed that race-based preference violates his rights guaranteed in the Fifth Amendment to the Constitution, which provides that "No person shall be . . . deprived of life, liberty, or property, without due process of law."

The U.S. District Court and the Court of Appeals held against Adarand on the grounds that the Supreme Court's previous decisions in *Fullilove*[106] (1980) and *Metro Broadcasting*[107] (1990) require only an intermediate level of scrutiny to assess the permissibility of race-conscious preferences in federal programs and actions. According to the District Court, the preference in question met this criterion; the Court of Appeals affirmed the decision. The Supreme Court by a five-to-four majority disagreed. The following is a summary of the majority opinion delivered by Justice O'Connor.

The Court gave a retrospective review of the relationship between the due process clause of the Fifth Amendment and the equal protection clause of the Fourteenth Amendment to the Constitution. Through the 1940s, the Court, in a number of cases, had held that "unlike the Fourteenth Amendment, the Fifth contains no equal protection clause, and it provides no guaranty against discriminatory legislation by Congress.[108]" However, its decisions between the mid-1950s and mid-1970s constructed a theory in which the Fifth and the Fourteenth Amendments were explicitly deemed to provide the same guaranty of equal protection.[109] In *Bakke* (1978), four Justices (Brennan, White, Marshall, and Blackmun) wanted to apply a less stringent standard of scrutiny for racial classification by a state agency "designed to further remedial purposes."[110] Then in *Fullilove* (1980), although the Supreme Court upheld the congressionally mandated 10 percent set-aside for minority-owned businesses, as in *Bakke*, it was a plurality and not a majority opinion. Similarly, in *Wygant* (1986),[111] even though the Supreme Court struck down a racial preference in public school teacher layoff policies (designed to provide "role models" for minority students), it failed to produce a majority opinion. Then in *Croson* (1989), the Supreme Court resolved the issue of race-based preferences in city contracts. By a majority opinion, it held that "the single standard of review for racial classifications should be 'strict scrutiny.'"[112] A year later, however, in *Metro Broadcasting* (1990), the Court upheld what it termed "benign" federal racial preference in the allocation of scarce broadcast licenses.[113] At that time, it rationalized its decision by stating that even if such preferences are not remedial to compensate victims of past governmental or societal discrimination, they are permissible because they serve "important governmental objectives" and because the means used were "substantially related to the achievement of those objectives."

The Supreme Court in its *Adarand* decision correctly pointed out that it is not always clear that a racial preference is in fact benign. Justice Powell had made the same point in his opinion in *Bakke*. Thus, after reviewing the decisional history of the judicial standards used to determine the constitutionality of race-based classifications by government agencies, the Supreme Court declared: "Accordingly, we hold today that all racial classifications, imposed by whatever federal, state, or local governmental actor, must be analyzed by a reviewing court under strict scrutiny. In other words, such classifications are constitutional only if they are narrowly tailored measures that further compelling governmental interests. To the extent that *Metro Broadcasting* is inconsistent with that holding, it is overruled."[114]

In *Adarand*, the U.S. Court of Appeals had upheld race-based set-asides by relying on the Supreme Court's previous decision of *Fullilove* (1980), in which a plurality had permitted a federal set-aside program by using a lenient standard of intermediate scrutiny. Thus, when the Supreme Court struck down the lenient standard of intermediate scrutiny in *Adarand*, it not only overruled *Metro Broadcasting* but also shook the foundation of *Fullilove*. Thus, any person for any reason has the right to demand equal treatment from a state agency, while unequal treatment will be subjected to strictest judicial scrutiny. The Supreme Court approvingly quoted the plurality opinion of Justice O'Connor in *Croson* (1989) that strict judicial scrutiny is applied in order to determine "what classifications are 'benign' or 'remedial' and what classifications are in fact motivated by illegitimate notions of racial inferiority or simple racial politics."[115] Neither the *Metro Broadcast-*

ing nor the *Fullilove* decision met the "intrinsically sounder" standard of strict scrutiny and, therefore, they are now not controlling.

Justices John Stevens, Ruth Bader Ginsberg, David Souter, and Stephen Breyer dissented, and together they wrote three dissenting opinions. In Justice Stevens's opinion (joined by Justice Ginsburg), the Court's majority decision has made a "sudden," "enormous," and "unjustified" departure from the reasoning in past cases, explicitly overruling *Metro Broadcasting* and undermining *Fullilove*. In a footnote in his dissenting opinion, Stevens also feared that the label "strict scrutiny" usually kills a government program based on racial classification.[116] He believed fostering diversity through racial preferences in government programs is legitimate. Justice Ginsburg (joined by Justice Breyer), in her dissenting opinion, argued that the Court should not have intervened in this case because the subject of affirmative action was currently being discussed by the political branches of the government.

The *Adarand* decision makes government-sponsored racial preference vulnerable but by no means impermissible. Now all government programs at local, state, and federal levels must meet this stringent judicial standard. These decisions since 1989 strongly suggest that the Supreme Court now has little tolerance even for "benign" racial classification in government-sponsored preference programs unless they meet its strict scrutiny test.

In the next chapter we discuss the impact of recent Supreme Court decisions on the political branches of our government and the general public.

NOTES

1. For a general discussion of the Civil Rights Act of 1991, see: Note: "The Civil Rights Act of 1991: The Business Necessity Standard," *Harvard Law Review* 106 (February 1993), 896-913; "The Civil Rights Act of 1991 and Less Discriminatory Alternatives in Disparate Impact Litigation," *Harvard Law Review* 106 (May 1993), 1621-1638; Commerce Clearing House, *Civil Rights Act of 1991: Law and Explanation* (Chicago, IL: Commerce Clearing House, 1991); David A. Cathcart and Mark Snyderman, "The Civil Rights Act of 1991," *The Labor Lawyer* 8 (Fall 1992), 849-922.

2. *Wards Cove Packing Company v. Atonio*, 490 U.S. 642 (1989).

3. Ibid., 659.

4. *Price Waterhouse v. Hopkins*, 490 U.S. 228 (1989).

5. David A. Cathcart and Mark Snyderman, "The Civil Rights Act of 1991," *The Labor Lawyer* 8 (Fall 1992), 877.

6. *Patterson v. McLean Credit Union*, 491 U.S. 164 (1989).

7. *Martin v. Wilks*, 490 U.S. 755 (1989).

8. *Lorance v. AT&T Technologies, Incorporated*, 490 U.S. 900 (1989).

9. *Equal Employment Opportunity Commission v. Arabian American Oil Company*, 111 S. Ct. 1227 (1991).

10. *Adarand v. Pena*, 115 S. Ct. 2097 (1995).

11. *Missouri, et al., v. Jenkins, et al.*, 95 *Daily Journal*, D.A.R. 7531 (June 13, 1995).

12. *Podberesky v. Kirwan*, 38 F. 3d 147 (4th Cir. 1994). Cert. Denied, 115 S. Ct. 2001 (1995); "Fourth Circuit Finds University of Maryland Minority Scholarship Program Unconstitutional," *Harvard Law Review* 108 (May 1995), 1773-1778.

13. *Podberesky v. Kirwan*, No. 93-2585 (4th Cir., October 27, 1994), 6.

14. Ibid., 20.

15. "Race-based Scholarship Ruling Will Be Appealed," *Sacramento Bee*, October 29, 1994, A11.

16. Scott Jaschik, "'No' on Black Scholarships: Supreme Court Won't Second-Guess Ruling against Race-Exclusive Awards," *Chronicle of Higher Education*, June 2, 1995, A25, A29.

17. *Chronicle of Higher Education*, January 12, 1996, A25.

18. See: Scott Jaschik, "Tough Legal Battle: Supreme Court Is Urged to Overturn Ban on Minority Scholarship"; "Organizations Backing University of Maryland's Appeal," *Chronicle of Higher Education*, May 12, 1995, A34; Scott Jaschik, "Federal Appeals Court Deals Blow to Minority Scholarships," *Chronicle of Higher Education*, November 2, 1994, A52; Carl McClendon, "Big Court Fight Looms over Scholarships for Blacks: Affirmative Action May Be Altered as Case Goes National," *San Francisco Examiner*, November 20, 1994, A4; Stephen Labaton, "Colleges Review Preferential Scholarship Plans," *San Francisco Chronicle*, October 31, 1994, A3.

19. U.S. Department of Education, Office for Civil Rights, Region X, "University of California at Berkeley School of Law," Case No. 10906001 (September 25, 1992). Letter addressed to Dr. Chang-Lin Tien, Chancellor, University of California, Berkeley.

20. Ibid., 4.

21. Ibid., 5.

22. Marcos Breton, "Berkeley Law School Is Biased, U.S. Rules: Admissions Favor Minorities, Probe Finds," *The Sacramento Bee*, September 29, 1992, A1, A14.

23. "UC's Affirmative Hyperactivity," *Sacramento Bee*, October 18, 1992, "Forum Section," 4.

24. "Cal's Law School Hit for Race 'Quotas,'" *Sacramento Union*, September 29, 1992, A3.

25. Marcos Breton, "Berkeley Law School Is Biased, U.S. Rules: Admissions Favor Minorities, Probe Finds," *Sacramento Bee*, September 29, 1992, A1, A14.

26. See, for example: Louis Freedberg, "U.S. Says UC Law School Broke Civil Rights Law: Finding Came After 2-Year Investigation," *San Francisco Chronicle*, September 29, 1992, A1; Arthur S. Hays, "Berkeley Case Troubles Law School Deans," *Wall Street Journal*, October 2, 1992, B12; "Berkeley

Law School Broke Civil Rights Law, U.S. Says," *Wall Street Journal*, September 29, 1992, B8; Scott Jaschik, "Education Department Says Affirmative-Action Policies of Berkeley's Law School Violated Federal Anti-Bias Laws," *Chronicle of Higher Education*, October 7, 1992, A21, A25.

27. Michael S. Greve, "The Newest Move in Law Schools' Quota Game," *Wall Street Journal*, October 5, 1992, A12.

28. Louis Freedberg, "Boalt Hall Admission Flap Has Nationwide Impact: Reverse Bias May Change Standards," *San Francisco Chronicle*, October 3, 1992).

29. *United States of America v. Board of Education of the Township of Piscataway*, 832 F. Supp. 836 (D.N.J. 1993).

30. Iver Peterson, "Feds Switch Sides in Civil Rights Case. Justice Department Seeks a Reversal of Discrimination Case It Won for a White Teacher in N.J.," *San Francisco Examiner*, August 14, 1994, A5; Clint Bolick, "Coronation of a Quota King at Justice," *Wall Street Journal*, August 31, 1994, 13.

31. Ibid.

32. "U.S. Agency Switches Sides in Case over Civil Rights," *Wall Street Journal*, September 7, 1994, B11.

33. *United States of America; Sharon Taxman, Plaintiff-Intervenor v. Board of Education of the Township of Piscataway*, No. 94-5090, No. 94-5112, 1996 U.S. App. Lexis 19973 (August 8, 1996), Lexis *2; also see: "Civil Rights Act of 1964—Title VII—Affirmative Action—Third Circuit Holds That Diversity Is Not, in Itself, a Sufficient Justification for Granting Preferences to Minorities—*Taxman v. Board of Education*, 91 F. 3d 1547 (3d Cir., 1996)," *Harvard Law Review* 110 (December 1996), 535-540.

34. Editorial, "A Blow to Affirmative Action in Schools, *New York Times*, August 15, 1996.

35. "High Court Seeks White House View in Race-Bias Case," *San Francisco Chronicle*, January 22, 1997, A3; "Take Side in Hiring Case, High Court Asks U.S.," *Chronicle of Higher Education*, January 31, 1997, A26.

36. David G. Savage, "Court May Review Workplace Affirmative Action," *Sacramento Bee*, June 6, 1997, A10; *Chronicle of Higher Education*, June 13, 1997, A28.

37. Linda Greenhouse, "Justices, Ending Their Term, Agree to Hear a Big Affirmative Action Case," *New York Times*, June 28, 1997, 9.

38. Douglas Lederman, "Supreme Court Agrees to Consider Affirmative-Action Case," *Chronicle of Higher Education*, July 11, 1997, A27.

39. "Justices to Decide Case about Affirmative Action," *San Francisco Chronicle*, June 28, 1997, A3.

40. "Excerpts from Affirmative Action Brief," *New York Times*, August 23,1997, 8.

41. See: Steven A. Holmes, "Rights Groups Decided to Wait for a Better Test Case," *New York Times*, November 23, 1997, 20; Stephen Labaton, "Liberals to Court: Don't Take This Case, Please," *New York Times*, November 23, 1997, WK6; Roger Clegg, "What Are Civil Rights Leaders Afraid Of?" *Wall Street*

Journal, November 24, 1997, A23; Linda Chavez, "Financial Disgrace," *Chicago Tribune,* (November 26,1997).

42. Editorial, "Settling on Affirmative Action," *New York Times*, November 24, 1997, A16.

43. Steven A. Holmes, "Major Ruling on Affirmative Action Is Likely Sooner or Later, Experts Say," *New York Times*, December 1, 1997, A11.

44. *University and Community College System of Nevada v. Yvette Farmer*, No. 25912 (January 3, 1997), 7.

45. *Wall Street Journal*, March 10,1998, B5; Douglas Lederman, "Supreme Court Turns Down Appeal of Case on Affirmative Action in College Hiring," *Chronicle of Higher Education*, March 20, 1998, A35.

46. David G. Savage, "'*Bakke II*' Case Renews Debate on Admissions," *Los Angeles Times*, July 30, 1995; Scott Jaschik, "Suit Against U. of Texas Challenges Law School's Affirmative Action Effort," *Chronicle of Higher Education*, February 9, 1994, A32-A33.

47. *Sweatt v. Painter*, 339 U.S. 629 (1950).

48. *Cheryl J. Hopwood, et al., v. State of Texas*, 861 F. Supp. 551, W.D.T. (1994). For press reports on this case see: Peter J. Riga, "Justice Isn't Color-Blind," *San Francisco Daily Journal*, September 13, 1994, 1-2; Theodore B. Olson et al., "Lily White Lies," *Docket Report* [Center for Individual Rights] (Fourth Quarter, 1995), 2; "Remedial Effort: *Hopwood, et al., v. State of Texas,*" *Docket Report* (First Quarter, 1995), 7, 9; Richard Bernstein, "Racial Discrimination or Righting Past Wrongs," *New York Times*, July 13, 1994, Education Section, B6; Scott Jaschik, "Court Backs Use of Race in Admissions," *Chronicle of Higher Education*, September 7, 1994, A40-A41, A47; "Racial Quotas on Trial in Texas," *San Francisco Chronicle*, August 1, 1994, A6; Lino A. Graglia, "In Texas a Law School Flunks the Bakke Test," *Wall Street Journal*, October 12, 1994, A17.

49. David G. Savage, "'*Bakke II*' Case Renews Debate on Admissions," *Los Angeles Times*, July 30, 1995.

50. *Cheryl J. Hopwood, et al., v. State of Texas, et al.*, No. 94-50569; No. 94-50664, 5th Cir. (1996); 1996 U.S. App. Lexis 4719; full text of the decision also in *Chronicle of Higher Education*, March 29, 1996, A28-A38. For press reports and commentaries on the Court of Appeals' decision, see: David Savage, "U.S. Court Bars Race as Admission Factor," *Los Angeles Times*, March 20, 1996, A1, A12; editorial, "A Color-Blind Constitution," *Wall Street Journal*, March 22, 1996, A12; Peter Applebome, "Ruling Threatens College Policies on Racial Entries," *New York Times*, March 21, 1996, A1, A12; Sam Howe Verhovek, "Universities Scramble to Weigh Impact of a Ruling," *New York Times*, March 21, 1996, A12; editorial, "Bad Judgment," *The Nation*, April 15, 1996; Editorial "The Death of 'Diversity'?," *Sacramento Bee*, March 21, 1996, B6; "Appeals Court Rejects Affirmative-Action Plan at Law School," *Wall Street Journal*, March 20, 1996, B9; James Richardson, "Ruling Called Tougher than UC's Affirmative Action Ban," *Sacramento Bee*, March 21, 1996, A3; "U. of Texas Halts Admissions in Wake of Ruling on Bias Suit," *New*

York Times, March 20, 1996, A12; "Court Says Colleges Can't Use Affirmative Action," *Sacramento Bee*, March 20, 1996, A1.

51. "Justice Official Blasts Affirmative Action Ruling," *Sacramento Bee*, March 22, 1996, A4.

52. "A Stunning Blow to Affirmative Action," *Chronicle of Higher Education*, March 29, 1996, A1.

53. Michael S. Greve, "Ruling Out Race: A Bold Step to Make Colleges Colorblind," *Chronicle of Higher Education*, March 29, 1996, B2.

54. Michael A. Olivas, "The Decision Is Flatly, Unequivocally Wrong," *Chronicle of Higher Education*, March 29, 1996, B3.

55. *Hopwood*, 1996 U.S. App. Lexis 4719, *35.

56. Michael J. Bowers, Attorney General, State of Georgia, Department of Law, letter addressed to Stephen R. Portch, Chancellor, Board of Regents, University System of Georgia, "Re: *Hopwood, et al., v. State of Texas, et al.*," April 8, 1996. The letter cites the Supreme Court decisions in *Adarand Constructors*, 115 S. Ct. 2097 (1995); *Shaw v. Reno*, 113 S. Ct. 2816 (1993); and *Croson*, 488 U.S. 469 (1989).

57. *Texas v. Hopwood*, No. 95-1773 (U.S. July 1, 1996); also see: Cass R. Sunstein, "Leaving Things Undecided," *Harvard Law Review* 110 (November 1996), 90-93; Douglas Lederman and Stephen Burd, "High Court Refuses to Hear Appeal of Ruling That Barred Considering Race in Admissions," *Chronicle of Higher Education*, July 12, 1996, A25, A29.

58. Douglas Lederman, "Suit Challenges Affirmative Action at U. of Wash.," *Chronicle of Higher Education*, March 14, 1997, A27.

59. Center for Individual Rights, *Docket Report*, February 1998, 11.

60. Peter Schmidt, "NIH, Texas A&M Sued over Race-Based Policy," *Chronicle of Higher Education*, March 7, 1997, A30.

61. Patrick Healy, "A Lawsuit against Georgia University System Attacks a Range of Race-Based Policies," *Chronicle of Higher Education*, March 14, 1997, A25-A26.

62. See, for example: William J. Kilberg (Editor-in-Chief), "*Hopwood v. Texas*: Further Thoughts on the Diversity Dilemma," *Employee Relations Law Journal* 22, (Autumn 1996), 1-4.

63. Center for Individual Rights, *Docket Report*, October 1997, 2-3; *Docket Report*, February 1998, 3-4; *Gratz v. Bollinger*, No. 97-75231 (E. D. Mich. filed October 14, 1997).

64. See, for example: "Adam Cohen," The Next Affirmative Action: A Lawsuit against the University of Michigan Could End Racial Preferences in College Admissions," *Time*, November 10, 1997, 52-54; Larry Reibstein, "What Color Is A? In Race-Obsessed America, Affirmative Action in College Admissions Faces Its Latest—and Sternest—Test," *Newsweek*, December 29, 1998, 76-77; Rene Sanchez, "Final Exam for Campus Affirmative Action," *Washington Post*, December 5, 1997, A1, A35, A36; Ethan Bronner, "Group Suing University of Michigan over Diversity," *New York Times*, October 14, 1997, A14;

Carol Morello, "A New Battleground for Affirmative Action: An Admission Chart May Be the 'Smoking Gun'. . . ," *USA Today*, November 28, 1997, 10A; Jonathan Chait, "TRB from Washington: Numbers Racket," *The New Republic*, December 22, 1997, 8, 41.

65. Idris M. Diaz, "Mischief Makers: The Men Behind All Those Anti-Affirmative Action Lawsuits," *Black Issues in Higher Education*, December 25, 1997, 14-19; W. John Moore, "The Influence Game: A Little Group Makes Big Law," *National Journal*, November 15, 1997, 2323.

66. See, for example: *Mainline Paving Company v. Board of Education District of Philadelphia*, 725 F. Supp. 1349 (E.D. PA, 1989); *Contractors Association of Eastern Pennsylvania v. City of Philadelphia*, 735 F. Supp. 1274 (1990); David G. Savage, "Supreme Court Rejects Minority Set-Aside Law Ruling: U.S. High Court's Decision on Public Works Spending Deals Another Blow to Affirmative Action," *Los Angeles Times*, February 19, 1997, A1, A15; *Long v. City of Saginaw*, 911 F. 2d 1192 (6th Cir. 1990); *Ohio Contractors Association v. City of Columbus, Ohio, et al.*, 733 F. Supp. 1156 (1990); *Milwaukee County Pavers Association v. Ronald Fiedler, Secretary of Wisconsin Department of Transportation*, 922 F. 2d 419 (7th Cir. 1991); *Coral Construction Company v. King County*, 941 F. 2d 910 (9th Cir.1991); *O'Donnell Construction Company v. District of Columbia*, No. 91-7056, May 5, 1992; also see: *Wall Street Journal*, May 6, 1992, B6; *Legal Times*, Week of May 25, 1992, 32; *Associated General Contractors of California v. Coalition for Economic Equity*, 950 F. 2d 1401 (1991).

67. *Howard v. McLucas*, 871 F. 2d 1000 (11th Cir.1989). Cert. denied, 493 U.S. 10002 (1989).

68. *Cone Corporation v. Hillsborough County*, 908 F. 2d 908 (11th Cir.1990). Cert. denied, 498 U.S. 983 (1990).

69. *Freeman, et al., v. Pitts, et al.*, 92 *Daily Journal*, D.A.R. 4284 (1992).

70. *Freeman*, 4291.

71. *United States v. Kirk Fordice, Governor of Mississippi, et al.*, 112 S. Ct. 2727 (1992); see: Stephen C. Halpern, "A Bedeviling and Worrisome Court Ruling on Black Colleges," *Chronicle of Higher Education*, November 4, 1992, B1-B2.

72. *United States v. Fordice*, 2736.

73. *United States v. Fordice*, 2743.

74. "Leading Cases," *Harvard Law Review* 106, (November 1992), 235.

75. *Ruth O. Shaw, et al., v. Janet Reno, Attorney General, et al.*," 93 *Daily Journal*, D.A.R. 8168, 8170 (1993); also see: "Equal Protection: Race-Based Districting and Minority Voting Rights," *Harvard Law Review* 107 (November 1993), 194-204; "Minority District 'Apartheid': Court Says Rights of White Voters May Be Violated," *The Sacramento Union*, June 29, 1993, A4; Joan Biskupic, "Court Limits Gerrymandering for Minorities: It Says Unusual Districts May Violate Rights of White Voters," *San Francisco Chronicle*, June 29, 1993, A1, A11; David G. Savage, "Justices Deal Blow to Racial Redistricting," *Sacramento Bee*, June 29, 1993, A1, A7; Elizabeth McCaughey, "Court Deals a Blow to Racial Gerrymandering," *Wall Street Journal*, June 30, 1993,

A13; editorial, "Against 'Political Apartheid,'" *Wall Street Journal*, June 30, 1993, A12; Peter Schrag, "Ethnic Gerrymander," *Sacramento Bee*, May 19, 1993, B8; editorial, "Minority Gerrymander," *Sacramento Bee*, June 30, 1993, B6; Clifford Krauss, "Muted Reaction in District That Court Opposed," *New York Times*, July 4, 1993, A20.

76. *Shaw v. Reno*, 8173.

77. *Missouri, et al., v. Jenkins, et al.*, 95 *Daily Journal*, D.A.R. 7531 (1995).

78. *Missouri v. Jenkins II*, 495 U.S. 33, 97 (1990), quoted by Chief Justice Rehnquist in *Missouri, et al., v. Jenkins, et al.*, 95 *Daily Journal*, D.A.R. 7531, 7534 (1995).

79. Ibid., 7537.

80. Ibid., 7538.

81. Ibid., 7539.

82. Ibid., 7540.

83. Ibid., 7546.

84. Ibid., 7547.

85. *Miller v. Johnson*, 95 *Daily Journal*, D.A.R. 8495 (1995); also see: "Voting Rights and Race-Based Districting," *Harvard Law Review* 109 (November 1995), 160-170; Nolan Walters, "Racial Politics at Issue in Election District Case," *Sacramento Bee*, April 20, 1995, A1, A16; Paul A. Gigot, "I Am Black and I Am a Representative," *Wall Street Journal*, June 30, 1995, A14; "Government: Georgia's Congressional Redistricting Plan Violates the Equal Rights Protection Clause," *Daily Recorder*, July 3, 1995, 7; Richard Carelli, "Redistricting Plan Vetoed by High Court," *Daily Recorder*, June 30, 1995, 1, 5; Paul M. Barrett and Gerald F. Seib, "Supreme Court Redraws Political Battleground with Broad Attack on Race-Based House [of Representatives] District," *Wall Street Journal*, June 30, 1995, A16; George F. Will, "The Voting Rights Act at 30: Racial Gerrymandering Is One Reason Newt Gingrich Is Speaker," *Newsweek*, July 10, 1995, 64; Richard Carelli, "Voting Districts Drawn by Race Ruled Unlawful," *San Francisco Chronicle*, June 30, 1995, A1, A22; "Minorities Rocked, Court Curbs Race-Based Drawing of Voter Districts," *Sacramento Bee*, June 30, 1995, A1, A20.

86. *Miller v. Johnson*, 95 *Daily Journal*, D.A.R. 8495, 8497 (1995).

87. Ibid.

88. Ibid., 8498.

89. Ibid.

90. Ibid., 8502.

91. *Wall Street Journal*, June 30, 1995, A16.

92. *Bush v. Vera*, 116 S. Ct. 1941 (1996); *Shaw v. Hunt*, 116 S. Ct. 1894 (1996); also see: "Voting Rights and Race-Based Districting," *Harvard Law Review* 110 (November 1996), 185-186; David G. Savage, "Justices Nullify Racial Districts in Texas, N.C.," *Los Angeles Times*, June 14, 1996, A1; editorial, "Achieving Fairness at Polls Demands Creative Thinking," *USA Today*, June

21, 1996, 14A; Clint Bolick, "What to Do? Nothing," *USA Today*, June 21, 1996, 14A.

93. Ellis Cose, "Voting Rights Act, R.I.P. The Supreme Court Eviscerates 'Minority' Districts," *Newsweek*, June 24, 1996, 36.

94. Ibid.

95. Ken Blackwell and Matt Fong, "Minority Candidates Don't Need Quotas," *Wall Street Journal*, July 15, 1996, A10.

96. David G. Savage, "Justices Nullify Racial Districts in Texas, N.C.," *Los Angeles Times*, June 14, 1996, A1.

97. Ken Blackwell and Matt Fong, "Minority Candidates Don't Need Quotas," *Wall Street Journal*, July 15, 1996, A10.

98. *Thornburg v. Gingles*, 478 U.S. 30 (1986).

99. Ibid., 48-49.

100. For a discussion of this issue, see: Abigail M. Thernstrom, "Vote, Right To," Kermit L. Hall (ed.), *The Oxford Companion to the Supreme Court of the United States* (New York: Oxford University Press, 1992), pp. 899-902.

101. Carol M. Swain, "The Supreme Court Rulings on Congressional Districts Could Benefit Minority Voters," *Chronicle of Higher Education*, September 27, 1996, B4.

102. Ibid.; also see Carol M. Swain, *Black Faces, Black Interests: The Representation of African Americans in Congress*, 2nd ed. (Cambridge: Harvard University Press, 1995).

103. Editorial, "Voting Integration," *Wall Street Journal*, December 2, 1996, A18.

104. Ibid. (voting data for 1996).

105. *Adarand Contractors Incorporated v. Pena, Secretary of Transportation, et al.*, 95 Daily Journal, D.A.R. 7503 (1995); also see: "Affirmative Action—Federal Minority Preference Programs," *Harvard Law Review* 109 (November 1995), 151-160.

106. *Fullilove v. Klutznick*, 448 U.S. 448 (1980).

107. *Metro Broadcasting Incorporated v. Federal Communication Commission, et al.*, 497 U.S. 547 (1990).

108. *Adarand*, 7507-8 quoting from *Detroit Bank v. United States*, 317 U.S. 329, 337 (1943).

109. *Bolling v. Sharpe*, 347 U.S. 497 (1954); *McLaughlin v. Florida*, 379 U.S. 184 (1964).

110. *Regents of University of California v. Bakke*, 438 U.S. 265, 359 (1978).

111. *Wygant v. Jackson Board of Education*, 476 U.S. 267 (1986).

112. *City of Richmond v. J. A. Croson Company*, 488 U.S. 469 (1989).

113. *Metro Broadcasting*, 564-565.

114. *Adarand*, 7512.

115. Ibid., 7512, quoting *Croson*, 488 U.S. 469, 493 (1989).

116. *Adarand*, 7524, note 1.

4

∽

Affirmative Action Diversity: A Euphemism for Preferences, Quotas, and Set-Asides

This chapter deals with the aftermath of *Adarand Contractors Incorporation v. Pena, Secretary of Transportation et al.*, (1995), particularly in government contracting, attacks on existing preferential programs, and their defense by the Clinton Administration. Details are also provided of the extent of egregious race-, ethnicity-, and gender-based preferences practiced in California's community colleges and state university systems in the employment of faculty.

EMBATTLED AFFIRMATIVE ACTION IN GOVERNMENT CONTRACTING: THE AFTERMATH OF *ADARAND*

In a significant development on October 23, 1995, the Pentagon adopted a policy that suspended (and later terminated) its $1 billion program of set-asides in contracting.[1] Known as the "Rule of Two," operating since 1987, it provided that on any Pentagon contract, if bids were submitted by two or more minority-owned companies capable of performing the contract, the Pentagon must accept one of those bids. Although in theory the set-asides were for "small disadvantaged businesses," in practice the Pentagon did not itself independently verify the social or economic "disadvantaged" status of the bidders. Turnabout on the Pentagon's policy came only after the Department of Defense faced a suit by McCrossan Construction Company of Maple Grove, Minnesota, seeking construction contracts in Las Cruces, New Mexico. The United States Justice Department believed that the Rule of Two could not meet the strict scrutiny test of *Adarand* and, therefore, decided to kill the program.

A far bigger battle has been waged against the $4.6 billion-a-year Section 8(a) program of the Small Business Administration (SBA). Under this program, the SBA serves "as an intermediary between minority-owned firms and federal agencies that want to steer work to those companies."[2] Once again, theoretically the program reserves contracts for "socially and economically disadvantaged firms," but in practice federal agencies generally consider all minorities as presumptively "disadvantaged" and allow even middle-class business owners to bid for contracts. A series of suits have been filed challenging the application of preferences in specific contracts. One of these was filed in Las Cruces, New Mexico, by McCrossan Construction Company, whose first suit had led to the demise of the Pentagon's Rule of Two. Another suit has been filed in Washington, D.C., by the San Diego–based Science Applications International Corporation, which alleges that its bid for a $500,000 contract to organize a science conference for a government department was turned down to protect a set-aside for a firm owned by an American Indian in Albuquerque, New Mexico. The Clinton Administration is defending the SBA's 8(a) program against these challenges.[3] The SBA is reported to be now more anxious to scrutinize the "disadvantaged" status of some of the bidders for Section 8(a) set-asides.[4] This program won an initial battle against the white-owned McCrossan Construction Company when on April 2, 1996, U.S. Judge Howard Bratten in Las Cruces, New Mexico, in a preliminary ruling, declined to freeze the bidding on a $15 million federal government contract at the White Sands Missile Range. The contract had been set aside for small minority-owned firms. McCrossan, relying on the *Adarand* precedent, alleged that the set-aside deprived the company of equal protection of the law and, thus, violated its constitutional rights. The District Court in its preliminary ruling said that the administration had "submitted significant evidence that the 8(a) program may survive strict scrutiny as articulated" in the Supreme Court's *Adarand* decision of 1995.[5] As may be recalled, the standard of "strict scrutiny" requires the government to demonstrate that any race-based set-aside serves a "compelling government goal" and is "narrowly tailored."

In order to cope with the mounting pressure against affirmative action preferences in government contracts, on August 14, 1997, the Clinton Administration said that it would make changes in the SBA's Section 8(a) program that would facilitate white women contractors in procuring contracts and thus broaden the political support for the bid preference program. In the fiscal year ending September 30, 1996, of the over 6,100 corporations that participated in this program, almost all were owned by minorities. The term "disadvantaged" as used by SBA covers such a wide variety of groups that in effect only white males were excluded. During the 1996 fiscal year, women received only 1.7 percent of the federal contracts. Under the proposed rules, the legal statement for proving "social disadvantage" by whites is being made less onerous—from "clear and convincing evidence" to "preponderance of evidence." Minority businesses feared that these changes, when implemented, would reduce their opportunities. Final regulations became effective in June 1998.

The Pentagon has yet another preference program under which small minority-owned businesses were awarded contracts worth $356 million in 1994. Under this program, bids submitted by minority-owned businesses are accepted even if they are up to 10 percent higher than the ones submitted by others. Kay and Associates Incorporated, an Arlington Heights, Illinois, company submitted a bid of $38.5 million to maintain naval aircrafts at China Lake, California. However, the Pentagon awarded the contract to a company owned by an African-American even though its bid was for $39.1 million. Kay and Associates challenged the constitutionality of the bid preference program as an impermissible form of affirmative action.[6] The Clinton Administration seems to plan on preserving the 10-percent bid preference program.[7] However, such programs are likely to face increased hostility by the disfavored bidders.

While the bid preference plan of the Department of Defense was under attack in the courts, in October 1994 a bipartisan statute, passed unanimously by Congress to streamline federal procurement, contained a provision that authorized other government agencies to also use the 10-percent bid preference for minority-owned firms.[8] Up until the passage of this statute in the fall of 1994, Congress's principle of race and ethnic preferences was not considered controversial even though a majority of the general public did not favor such programs.

In December 1994, then Senate Majority Leader Robert Dole requested the Congressional Research Service of the Library of Congress to compile a comprehensive list of federal statutes, regulations, programs, and executive orders that grant preferences on the basis of race, sex, national origin, or ethnicity. Preferences include goals, timetables, set-asides, and quotas. Consequently, on February 17, 1995, a 32-page list of these programs, including the titles of their enabling statutes and regulations, was submitted to Senator Dole's office.[9] Many of these programs are modeled on the affirmative action regulations drawn under Executive Orders of the early 1960s, the most prominent of which is Executive Order 11246 calling for increasing employment and contracting opportunities for minorities in federally financed construction and other contracts. Other notable statutes leading to the establishment of "goals and timetables" and requirements of demonstrating "good faith" efforts are the Equal Employment Opportunity Act of 1972 and the Civil Service Reform Act of 1978. A total of 160 such federal programs exist in public contracting, public employment, and admissions in public educational institutions.[10] Sensing that a national movement was building against preferences, in March 1995 President Clinton appointed

Christopher Edley Jr., an African-American scholar and professor of administrative law at Harvard, to review the law and practices of affirmative action.[11]

After agonizing for a few months on what position to take on affirmative action preferences. President Clinton, in a speech on July 19, 1995, at the National Archives, strongly supported the continuous use of affirmative action by declaring, "We should have a simple slogan: 'Mend it, but don't end it.'"[12] Leaders of minority groups, such as the Leadership Conference on Civil Rights and the Conference of Minority Transportation Officials, applauded the President's commitment to affirmative action, whereas a vice president of the American Business Conference said that most businesses will follow the court's decision instead and do whatever is necessary to comply with them.[13] Perhaps it was not merely coincidental that President Clinton's endorsement of affirmative action on July 19, 1995, came one day before the University of California's Board of Regents voted to repeal its affirmative action programs. This historic vote is discussed later in this chapter. The President used symbolism by making the speech in the rotunda of the National Archives, with the Declaration of Independence and the Bill of Rights resting in bronze cases in the background.

Deep division on the issue of affirmative action was apparent in the commentaries appearing in the press on the President's speech. Christopher Matthews, *San Francisco Examiner*'s Washington bureau chief, wrote, "Bill Clinton's speech on affirmative action Wednesday may have been the finest of his presidency."[14] But Joe Klein, writing in *Newsweek*, said, "In addition to its patent disingenuousness, the President's speech was a wistful, perfunctory, and intellectually flaccid affair."[15]

While strongly supporting affirmative action in general, the President ordered a review to abolish or revise those programs that are abused or poorly administered.[16] Before the President's speech in defense of affirmative action, some of the federal government agencies (notably the Commerce Department, the Agriculture Department, and the Federal Deposit Insurance Corporation) had been taking a few steps to reduce some of the preferences and to subject them to more critical review. Even these few steps were disconcerting to the Reverend Jesse Jackson of the Rainbow Coalition and to Barbara Arnwine, head of the Lawyers Committee for Civil Rights under Law.[17] By his July 1995 speech, the President sought to clarify the position of his administration and perhaps to manage the erosion of affirmative action programs regardless of the administration's position on a series of cases involving set-asides and other such preferences before various courts in the nation. Their outcomes could greatly influence the final shape and fate of these preferences.

The problem with set-asides is not simply that they result in reverse discrimination, but also that they are ideologically administered on presumptions of "underrepresentation" and "economic and social disadvantage" based simply on applicants' group identities. There are also allegations of fraud and mismanagement in these programs.[18] One of the common complaints by the opponents of such programs is that in some instances minority firms are simply used as "fronts" to receive contracts.[19]

Sixteen days after the Supreme Court handed down its landmark decision in *Adarand* (1995), Walter Dellinger, Assistant Attorney General, issued a 38-page Memorandum to General Counsels that was designed to provide preliminary guidance on the implications of that decision.[20] Following are the salient points of the memorandum, which considers both *Adarand* and *City of Richmond v. J. A. Croson Company* (1989), as interpreted by the Department of Justice.

1. From now on, the same standard of review known as strict scrutiny that was previously made applicable to state and local governments' race-based affirmative action programs shall also be applicable to federal government programs.

2. Strict scrutiny shall be applied not only to contracting, but also to health, education, hiring, and other race-based federal programs.

3. In assessing the permissibility of affirmative action programs, "Congress may be entitled to greater deference than state and local governments."[21]

4. The practice and the lingering effects of racial discrimination against minorities may in certain circumstances justify the use of race-based remedial measures.

5. The standard of strict scrutiny applied in *Croson* required that "the governmental interest underlying an affirmative action measure must be 'compelling' and the measure must be 'narrowly tailored' to serve that interest."[22]

6. Race-based affirmative action measures must not be based on generalized, historical discrimination.

7. The use of diversity as a criterion for affirmative action in settings other than educational institutions is uncertain.

8. On the basis of decisions by Courts of Appeals, in the post-*Croson* era, government must have some evidence of discrimination before instituting an affirmative action plan.

9. All Circuit courts, except the Sixth Circuit, apply an intermediate level of scrutiny to affirmative action programs for women. (The Sixth Circuit applies strict scrutiny—the same as for race-based programs.)

10. The narrow tailoring test of strict scrutiny calls for government to consider race-neutral alternatives before instituting race-conscious measures.

On February 29, 1996, Associate Attorney General John R. Schmidt issued a 19-page Memorandum to General Counsels to provide them post-*Adarand* guidance on affirmative action policy in the federal government.[23] Three key sentences in its concluding paragraphs state:

[T]he application of strict scrutiny should not require major modifications in the way federal agencies have been properly implementing affirmative action policies.

In sum, what *Adarand* requires is that in order for race or ethnicity to be used as a basis for decision making, an agency must have a demonstrable factual predicate for its actions. That predicate could be the agency's interest in remedying the effects of its discriminatory practices or the effects of employment that unintentionally have excluded minorities, or it could be based on the agency's operational needs.[24]

The memorandum also encourages government agencies to use criteria such as "confidence of the community," "community representations," "internal diversity," and "racially diverse range of views and perspectives," as justification for "nonremedial race-based actions." The memorandum relies on Justice Lewis Powell's opinion in *Bakke* concerning "diversity" as a plus factor in university admissions and encourages agencies to utilize it for giving affirmative action preferences. The document does not mention when these nonremedial preferences may be discontinued. As a policy document, it is a defense of status quo.[25] It also helpfully provides that, in hiring, government agencies may give "an applicant credit for overcoming social and economic disadvantage, which may include barriers posed by [past] discrimination based on race or ethnicity." Charles Finnie, of the *Daily Journal*, calls this "a loophole you can drive a truck through."[26] Similarly, in a press release, the Washington, D.C.–based Center for Equal Opportunity called Schmidt's memorandum an indirect contradiction with not only the spirit of the ruling of *Adarand* but also with President Clinton's public statement about "mending" affirmative action.[27]

The Justice Department's defense of affirmative action in 1996 was a surprise only because the President's call for mending the system was perceived to be a harbinger perhaps of real change in the practice of granting preferences based on race, gender, and ethnicity. However, the civil rights division of the Justice Department has been consistently and ardently supporting the affirmative action cause. As discussed previously, the Justice Department switched sides in 1994 and filed a brief in the U.S. Court of Appeals against Sharon Taxman, a white school teacher who had in 1992 won a case of reverse discrimination against the school district.[28] Similarly, in the reverse discrimination case of *Birmingham Firefighters, et al., v. City of Birmingham, et al.,* (1994), the Reagan and Bush administrations had supported the white firefighters whereas the Clinton Administration switched sides and wanted the consent decree continued.[29]

Clearly, opponents of race- and ethnicity-based government programs must resort to litigation and to Congress if they wish to bring about changes in public policies concerning set-asides and preferences in government agencies. So long as the Clinton Administration is in power, it is not likely to bring about major dismantling of these programs. "Mending" of such preferences will be minimal at best under his watch.

The opposition to affirmative action quotas, set-asides, and preferences did not emanate from Congress. In fact, Republican leadership under Senator Dole (R-Kansas) cooperated with Democrats to pass the Civil Rights Act of 1991 signed into law by President Bush on November 21, 1991. This legislation was mainly designed to restore damage done by the Supreme Court decisions handed down between 1989 and 1991 and to strengthen the rights of plaintiffs by providing monetary damages and attorneys' fees. It did prohibit race-norming, which was widely used by government agencies to evaluate the test scores for job applicants according to racial categories in which whites were compared only with whites and minorities only with the same minorities. But other than that, Congress was quiescent at least until the midterm elections in November 1994, when Republicans gained majorities in the House of Representatives and the Senate. The movement to stop preferences and set-asides in government agencies arose in California, described in Chapter 6. In any case, by spring of 1995, Congress had bestirred itself, and Senator Majority Leader Dole and Congressman Charles Canady (R-Florida) introduced companion bills to end race- and gender-based preferences and set-asides in federal employment, federal contracts, and federal government.[30] Senate Bill 1085, known as the Equal Opportunity Act of 1995, also prevents the federal government from requiring contractors to grant preferences to their subcontractors and suppliers. On September 6, 1995, Chairman of the Senate Small Business Committee, Senator Christopher Bond (R-Missouri), issued a statement calling for the evaluation of the then over $4 billion-a-year SBA program that sets aside contracts for businesses owned by minorities and presumably economically and socially disadvantaged people.[31]

On July 27, 1995, Senator Dole held a press conference at the Capitol and called for the abolition of race-, gender-, and ethnicity-based preferences and set-asides in federal contracting and employment. Speaker of the House of Representatives, Newt Gingrich, on February 27, 1996, also held a press conference and made public the Report of Minority Issues Task Force that he had established in the spring of 1995. The Report called for eliminating race- and gender-based set-asides and preferences and for substituting incentives for inner city enterprise zones, school choice vouchers, and deregulation of social services. (Alternatives to affirmative action perferences are discussed later in this chapter.)[32] Earlier, in October 1995, Gingrich threw his support behind the California Civil Rights Initiative (CCRI), which called for the elimination of discrimination or preferences in the state's public education, public contracting, and public employment.[33]

On March 7, 1996, the House Judiciary Committee's Constitution subcommittee on a straight party-line basis voted eight to five to approve the Dole/Canady Equal Opportunity Act of 1996 and sent it on for consideration of the full Committee. The bill not only prohibited outright set-asides and preferences in federal contracts and federal employment, but also banned "'numerical goals, timetables, or numerical objectives.'"[34] The bill, cosponsored by 93 House members, was fiercely opposed by Democrats. Attorney

General Janet Reno complained that the bill failed to recognize the need to correct historical vestiges of racial and gender discrimination. Contemporaneously, Clinton's Administration started to circulate a draft of new rules for federal government contracts that would "mend" the present system of preferences and set-asides to meet the stringent requirements mandated by the 1995 *Adarand* decision of the Supreme Court.

The proposed Equal Opportunity Act (S. 1085) did not prohibit or limit outreach measures that encourage the employment of and contract bidding by minorities or women so long as these measures did not involve numerical objectives or preference based on race, color, national origin, or sex. Exempted from the provisions of this proposed legislation were Indian tribes and historically black colleges and universities. Classification may legitimately be made in cases where: (1) sex is a bona fide occupational qualification; (2) it is necessary to protect the privacy of individuals; (3) national security interest is involved; and (4) armed forces are serving on active duty in a theater of combat operations. The proposed legislation was not to be retroactive and provided only injunctive or equitable relief, plus reasonable attorneys' fees and costs. The bill stalled and died in the 1996 Congress. A similar bill was reintroduced on June 17, 1997. This time it was sponsored by Senator Mitch McConnell (R-Kentucky) and Congressman Canady. It was called the Civil Rights Act of 1997. It was opposed by several civil rights organizations and consequently was killed.

It is not likely that President Clinton or another liberal president will sign a bill that would bar affirmative action preferences in federal government employment or federal contracting and alienate a core constituency of the Democratic party. However, the authors are convinced that through litigation,[35] legislation at state and federal[36] levels, and public pressure, such programs will be greatly reduced even if not completely eliminated.

PUBLIC INSTITUTIONS OF HIGHER EDUCATION: REGIMES OF QUOTAS AND PREFERENCES

In the national debate on race and ethnic preferences in higher education, California has played an important role from the very beginning of the modern civil rights era of the past three decades. Admittedly, in this period the case of *Regents of the University of California v. Bakke* (1978) was the precedent used to justify the use of race and ethnicity as a "plus" factor in college admissions. Since that decision, much has been said about the lack of clear guidance given by Justice Powell in his opinion about the exact parameters of this so-called "plus" factor. Even in 1980, Justice George Paras (concurred by Justice Robert Puglia) of the Third District Court of Appeals in California had correctly foreseen and warned that unless public universities unequivocally eliminate the use of race and ethnicity in their admissions policies, the critical question of their constitutionality will not disappear and will "inevitably return to the federal courts."[37] In *DeRonde v. The Regents of the University of California* (1980), a white man sued the University of California, Davis Law School alleging that it denied him admission while it admitted 69 of the minority applicants (Blacks, Native Americans, Filipinos, Asians, and Chicanos) who had lower academic records than his own based on a formula used by the School that combined previous academic grades and scores on the Law School Admissions Test (LSAT). The lower court held that the university had violated the Equal Protection and Due Process rights of the plaintiff guaranteed under the Federal Constitution as well as the Equal Protection and Privileges and Immunity Clauses of the California Constitution. The California Constitution provides that "[a] citizen or a class of citizens may not be granted privileges or immunities not granted on the same terms to all citizens" (Article I, Section 7[b]). The California Constitution also provides guarantees of due process and equal protection of the laws. Justice Paras noted that governmentally sanctioned favoritism in professional school admissions has a "devastating effect on the disfavored." Forecasting the trauma ahead, the justice said, that unless resolved, the constitutional issues involved will arise again.

In Paras's view, race-based preferences are not acceptable even when they are not the result of a quota system because by their very nature and logic they deny equal protection of the law to other competitors. Then criticizing Justice Powell's opinion in *Bakke*, which stated that race or ethnicity may be used as "a factor but not *the* factor," Paras said that the Supreme Court's opinion did not provide clear intellectual guidance. Paras believed that, like people of various European ethnicities who have been able to achieve equality over time, present-day minorities would be able to do the same thing through patience, pursuit of their rights, and utilization of opportunities in a free society.

However, in the opinion of the District Court of Appeals, preferential treatment was not a legally permissible means of achieving equality for numerically underrepresented minorities. This was particularly so in a university that had no past history of racial discrimination. The University of California Admissions Committee had race-normed its admissions policy under which it compared minority applicants only with one another. Justice Paras also cited *DeFunis v. Odegaard* (1974), in which liberal Justice William O. Douglas, in his dissenting opinion, had stated that any state-sponsored preference to one race over another at a professional level is invidious and violative of the constitutional guarantee of equal protection of the laws. Then in a succinct statement, Justice Paras reiterated a simple but cardinal principle: Merit rather than race, color, or ethnicity should be the sole determinant of decision making by public agencies.

For their forthright and principled opinion against preferences, Justice Paras and his concurring Justice Puglia were vilified in the press by representatives of the California Legislative Black Caucus and minority lawyers.[38]

The fact remains that the principle of merit in college admissions endorsed by Justice William O. Douglas in his dissent in *DeFunis* (1974) was avoided by the Supreme Court by declaring the case moot. Then in 1979, as discussed in Chapter 2, Justice William Rehnquist, in his dissent in *Weber*, warned that by giving race-based preference in apprenticeship training programs the Supreme Court was going against the legislative history and language of Title VII of the Civil Rights Act and had "sown the wind," thereby leaving the later courts to "face the impossible task of reaping the whirlwind." As we will describe in the following pages, for ignoring repeated warnings against race- and ethnicity-based preferences and by relying exclusively on the tenuous argument of Justice Powell's *Bakke* opinion, many public educational institutions practice blatant forms of reverse discrimination, which has resulted in a nationwide movement to abolish preferences and thus resurrect the original promise of the Civil Rights Act of 1964.

In the past two decades, institutions of higher education have undergone a profound change not only in their admissions policies but also in their philosophies, curricula, standards of performance, and employment of faculty and staff. It is outside the scope of this book to discuss in detail the particulars and magnitude of this transformation. However, we would be remiss if we did not describe at least the essence of this change and its various dimensions as viewed by a number of scholars and thoughtful commentators.

Perhaps the main argument advanced by the proponents of affirmative action in the universities is that U.S. society is rapidly becoming multicultural, and, therefore, its citizens and future leaders must be prepared to understand and appreciate the contributions and values of different ethnic groups. The census data on the racial composition of the population indicate that if the present trend of growth continues, whites who composed 73.6 percent of the population in 1995 will constitute only 52.5 percent of the population by the year 2050 (see Table 4.1).

Immigration between 1971 and 1992 shows corresponding changes. As seen in Table 4.2, the large-scale influx of immigrants from Asia, the Caribbean Islands, Central and South America, Mexico, and Africa has dwarfed the number of immigrants coming from Europe—the traditional source.

It is entirely appropriate that universities welcome qualified students of all races and ethnicities to prepare them for productive roles in our highly dynamic and competitive society. Given the population changes in this country, and the globalization of commerce and technology, it is imperative that students as well as educators and policymakers pay greater attention to the histories, institutions, belief systems, values, and norms of different cultures. This is particularly so in the case of those cultures that have hitherto received inadequate attention and recognition. The roles and contributions of women in various disciplines and their endeavors at family, community, national, and international levels must also be acknowledged and included

Table 4.1
Resident Population by Racial Origin Status

Year	Total	Hispanics[1]	White	Black	American, Indian, Eskimo, Aleut	Asian, Pacific Islander
Middle Series Projections (in thousands)						
1995	263,434	26,798	193,900	31,648	1,927	9,161
2020	325,942	51,217	208,280	42,459	2,641	21,345
2050	392,031	88,071	205,849	56,346	3,701	38,064
Percent Distribution						
1995	100.00	10.2	73.6	12.0	0.7	3.5
2020	100.00	15.7	63.9	13.0	0.8	6.5
2050	100.00	22.5	52.5	14.4	0.9	9.7

[1]Persons of Hispanic origin may be of any race

Source: U.S. Bureau of the Census, *Statistical Abstract of the United States, 1994,* 114th ed., (Washington, D.C.: Superintendent of Documents, 1994). Table 18 (extracted).

Table 4.2
Immigrants by Regions of Birth: 1971 to 1996 (in Thousands)

Countries	1971–1980	1981–1990	1991–1994	1995–1996
All countries	4,493.3	7,338.1	4,509.9	1,636.4
Europe	801.3	705.6	599.8	275.8
Asia	1,633.8	2,817.4	1,366.1	575.7
Mexico	637.2	1,653.3	1,397.9	253.7
Caribbean	759.8	892.7	441.8	213.6
Central America	132.4	458.7	266.7	76.1
South America	284.4	455.9	236.5	107.5
Africa	91.5	192.3	117.8	95.4

Source: U.S. Bureau of the Census, *Statistical Abstract of the United States, 1994 and 1998,* 114th and 118th eds. (Washington, D.C.: Superintendent of Documents, 1994 and 1998). Table 8 (extracted).

in academic curricula and must be subjects of scientific inquiries. The inclusion of these subjects or topics in college curricula and academic life, however, should not mean the suspension of critical objective judgment about the qualities and values of an ethnic community, a culture, or a society. However, understanding a culture does not, and should not, mean its uncritical glorification. Citizens should not have any hesitation in proclaiming that despite some imperfections the U.S. system of democracy does guarantee individual freedom and due process of law, to which most people of the world now aspire. It is a great achievement requiring constant vigilance and often the sacrifice of popular emotions to preserve the integrity of our principles. For over two centuries, these tenets have provided protection and refuge against religious, communal, and political persecution and have offered opportunities for a good life in the new world relatively free of class distinctions and family status. The political democracy and core culture of the United States are western, while our language and the origin of its jurisprudence of individual rights are specifically English.

There is now a cadre of American academicians who denigrate all of western civilization as oppressive and imperialistic.[39] Some feminists have joined in this chorus of discontent by alleging "male domination" and "gender inequity" in practically all social, economic, and political institutions.[40] A new category of legal writing, known as race and feminist jurisprudence, purports to prove how laws treat women and racial minorities inequitably and how law is merely an expression of white male power.[41] In educational institutions in the past several years, a virulent multicultural movement has emerged in which its leadership is not merely content to add to the curricula some subjects that may not have been hitherto adequately covered but "celebrates" a diversity that emphasizes ethnic differences as permanent and requiring special privileges. An example of this phenomenon was New York State's Social Studies Syllabus proposed in 1991 to emphasize multiculturalism. One of the dissenters from the report of the Syllabus Review Committee was Professor Arthur Schlesinger, Jr., who charged that the report, by giving an ethnic interpretation of American history and society, emphasizes *pluribus* and neglects *unum*. Then in a trenchant criticism, he made a statement that would equally apply to many public educational institutions in the country: "It is surely not the office of the public school to promote ethnic separatism and heighten ethnic tensions. The bonds of national cohesion in the republic are sufficiently fragile already. Public education should aim to strengthen not weaken them."[42]

Earlier, Schlesinger had expressed disapproval of the "cult of ethnicity" that denies the conception of America as a transforming nation.[43] There was similar controversy in 1994 when a $1.39 million federal grant was awarded to the National Center for History in the Schools at UCLA to develop national standards for United States history. The draft document of proposed standards was said to be an embodiment of political correctness that celebrated ethnicities and their origins; highlighted negative aspects of American history; and downplayed America's achievements, political freedom, and the nation's heroes.[44] In the context of this severe criticism, the U.S. Senate, by a 99-to-1 vote, censured the proposed history standards. By spring of 1996, a greatly revised report was released that was said to be appropriately balanced and that devoted due attention to the development of American democratic traditions, to individualism, and the nation's other achievements.[45] However, some critics believe that the modified history standards still unfairly attack American heritage.[46]

Much has been written about the celebration of multiculturalism and its ideology of separatism and its denial of the concept of America as a melting pot creating a distinct American identity. The allure of multiculturalism has led even Nathan Glazer, an eminent conservative academician, to conclude that African-Americans because of discrimination against them have not been fully assimilated in American society and, consequently, have become the main supporters of multiculturalist movement.[47] Glazer believes that the concept of America as a melting pot was based almost entirely on European immigrants and that blacks remain uniquely separated from them, enjoying few gains from the civil rights movement and affirmative action programs.

Multiculturalism as ideology has been manifested not only in denigrating the western culture,[48] but also of insistence by some of the accrediting agencies of institutions of higher education that inclusion of multiculturalism in curriculum and hiring be considered as a necessary standard for accreditation. Such was the initial decision of the Commission on Higher Education of the Middle States Association of Colleges and Schools (Middle States), one of the six accrediting agencies in the United States. It threatened to revoke the accreditation of Westminster Theological Seminary in Philadelphia unless it included a woman on its governing board.[49] A lack of accreditation is of great importance to the financial viability of an institution because that lack would stop all federal money, including student loans, going to it. Furthermore, it would have greatly weakened the academic status of the institution in the marketplace. The case of threatened loss of accreditation for the Westminster Theological Seminary aroused particularly strong criticism even among the liberal media because the Seminary under its religious teachings does not ordain women as ministers and elders and it requires Board members to be ordained. The Middle States also "deferred" accreditation of New York's Baruch College—one of the nation's finest business schools—for its alleged lack of "diversity" in hiring. In turn, President George Bush's incoming Secretary of Education, Lamar Alexander, delayed the renewal of the federal government's recognition of the Middle States accrediting agency pending a review of its diversity dictates.[50] Because accrediting agencies derive their authority through government recognition, the Middle States relented and made its diversity standard optional.[51] Consequently, in April 1992, the U.S. Department of Education renewed its recognition of Middle States.

ELECTION '96 AND THE NEW DEFENSE OF PREFERENCES

Despite President Bill Clinton's reelection in 1996, the Democrats were unable to take control of the U.S. Senate or the House of Representatives.

However, Mr. Clinton did especially well among working women, 57 percent of whom voted for him, as opposed to 34 percent for Robert Dole, and among union household members, who voted 60 percent for Clinton and only 29 percent for Dole.[52] However, in the Senate, Republicans gained one seat, bringing their majority to 53, compared to 47 for Democrats. In the House, Republicans' majority was cut in half—they lost 9 seats. Organized labor under the AFL-CIO's new leadership was reported to have spent about $35 million in its political campaign in the vain attempt to help Democrats win a majority in the House and the Senate.

The Republican Party, though maintaining rather significant majorities in both Houses, returned to the Capitol much chastened and vowed incessantly to cooperate with President Clinton and the Democratic Party on important public policies. It is, however, difficult to believe that leadership of the Democratic Party will willingly give significant ground on the issue of racial and gender quotas. After all, in the 1996 Democratic Party Convention, the Democratic National Committee had prescribed a precise quota by gender for "each position on each standing committee"[53] as well as race-, ethnicity-, and gender-based quotas of delegates to the Convention.[54] Given the commitment of the Democratic Party's leadership to affirmative action preferences, quotas, and the power of vested-interest lobbies, it would be unrealistic to expect that this issue could be settled simply through negotiations among leaders. Therefore, it should come as no surprise that despite the catchy slogan of "mend but not end" affirmative action, the Clinton Administration has resolved to thwart all attempts to eliminate race and gender preferences. The President vows to retain affirmative action but simultaneously professes that he does not favor quotas or reverse discrimination. His administration interprets this to mean that it should defend affirmative action programs vigorously and simply deny the empirical fact that they bestow favored treatment based on race or gender, which by definition is reverse discrimination in a highly competitive marketplace. In the 1998 midterm elections, the Republicans' majority was further reduced.

A prime example of racial favoritism in clear defiance of the law was a letter of warning issued on March 18, 1997, by Norma Cantu, the head of the U.S. Department of Education's Office for Civil Rights (and a former counsel for the Mexican-American Legal Defense Fund). Cantu asked Texas's state universities to continue to use race-based affirmative action programs, even though they had been ruled unconstitutional in March 1996 in *Cheryl J. Hopwood, et al., v. State of Texas* by the Fifth Circuit Court of Appeals and for which the Supreme Court denied certiorari. She had threatened that discontinuation of such programs might lead to the termination of federal aid to education.[55] Compliance with Ms. Cantu's wishes most likely would have made public officials of Texas personally liable for compensatory and punitive damages. The Fifth Circuit Court of Appeals had alluded to this potential personal liability in its *Hopwood* decision.

Officials in public colleges and universities in Texas were put in a no-win situation in which they would have lost as much as $2 billion in federal grants (including work study programs, student grants, and research grants) if they did not follow the U.S. Department of Education's directive that called for using a student's race in the institution's affirmative action programs. The Department of Education used the argument that such preferences were still required in Texas "to eliminate the vestiges of discrimination."[56] This is despite the fact that in *Hopwood*, the U.S. Court of Appeals had rejected this argument as lacking factual basis.

The U.S. Department of Education faced severe criticism for its obviously poor advice to the Texas authorities to ignore the law. Senator Phil Gramm (R-Texas) on March 27, 1997, in a strongly critical letter to Education Secretary Richard Riley, threatened to hold up financing for the Department of Education if Cantu's aforementioned letter was not retracted. Even Walter Dellinger, the Acting Solicitor General of the United States, strongly publicly disagreed with Cantu's position and stated that the *Hopwood* ruling was now the law in Texas. Consequently, on April 11, 1997, Cantu reversed her Department's position and stated that the *Hopwood* decision does prohibit race-based affirmative preferences to achieve diversity.[57] Not to be deterred in its zeal for preferences, in July 1997, the General Counsel of the U.S. Department of Education's Office of Civil Rights launched an investigation of the University of California's newly adopted policy of color-blind student admissions. The pretext of this investigation was that it might be a violation of nondiscrimination provisions of the federal civil rights law! The *Sacramento Bee* called it "an Orwellian misreading of the law."

Another instance of conflict between the Clinton Administration and a court decision in Texas is the case involving the Houston Metropolitan Transit Authority (HMTA) in which its affirmative action program that set aside 21 percent of the contracts to minority- and women-owned businesses was suspended in April 1996 by a federal judge, pending trials on the belief that the program was likely to be unconstitutional. Consequently, in September 1996, the HMTA replaced it with a race-neutral program. In January 1997, the Federal Transit Authority (FTA) announced that it would halt the $50 million in grants to HMTA for suspending its race- and gender-based set-aside program.

The record of Clinton's Administration, despite the President's rhetoric of "mend but not end" affirmative action, is one of unstinting support of race- and gender-based preferences, as demonstrated by the positions it took in *Birmingham Firefighters v. The City of Birmingham* (1994), *Adarand v. Pena* (1995), *Podberesky v. Kirwan* (1995), *Taxman v. Piscataway* (1996), *Hopwood v. University of Texas* (1996), and numerous similar actions by various federal government agencies. It is interesting that the Clinton Administration suffered reverses in all of those cases. In comparison, only two programs involving affirmative action preferences have been eliminated. As discussed in Chapter 2, in March 1995, affirmative action programs in the sale and purchase of broadcasting companies were repealed following the controversy in the Viacom deal. Similarly, in October 1995, the Pentagon suspended, and later terminated, its $1 billion set-aside program popularly known as the Rule of Two (discussed at the beginning of this chapter). Both of these programs were notorious for their mismanagement, lack of accountability, and exploitation by nondeserving individuals and companies. Hundreds of other affirmative action programs are operating as usual in federal, state, and local governments. Thus, it is reasonable to conclude that the opponents of unconstitutional or otherwise illegal race- or gender-based preference programs would have to persevere in a protracted struggle against the powerful vested interests of the preference lobbies and their liberal supporters in all three branches of government. The struggle will be difficult but can be done, and it will be worthwhile to resurrect the original vision of equality as contained in the Civil Rights Act of 1964.

CALIFORNIA LEGISLATURE'S ATTEMPTS TO MANDATE RACE AND GENDER PREFERENCES IN STATE'S HIGHER EDUCATION SYSTEMS

Not being content with *Bakke*'s "plus" factor for using race in university admissions, the California legislature, under the leadership of then Assembly Speaker Willie Brown, rolled out a series of bills designed to establish a regime of race- and ethnicity-based preferences in student admissions, graduation rates, and employment. These bills sought to create a system in which there was parity between the selectees and their racial or ethnic proportions in the state's population or in the student body. Following are examples of this quest for proportionality.

September 19, 1988

Governor George Deukmejian signed into law Assembly Bill 1725, sponsored by Assemblyman John Vasconcellos, which, among other things, establishes statutory duty of affirmative action in community colleges. It institutes a comprehensive plan for "addressing the goal that the system's workforce reflect proportionately the adult population of the state by the year 2005." For new faculty hires, consideration must be given to "projected California demographics, and . . . affirmative action policies and programs." Specifically, the faculty is expected "to be culturally balanced and more representative of the state's diversity."

In the hiring process for administrators and faculty, affirmative action considerations must effectively influence decisions. To achieve this end, the law requires that "[i]ndividuals, preferably minorities or women who are knowledgeable about and responsible to the community college's affirmative action goals, are included in all selection committees or similar groups."

The board of governors of the community colleges must "include adequate representation on the basis of sex and on the basis of the major racial, ethnic, and economic groups in the state." The community colleges are required to submit performance reports on affirmative action, and each college district is held accountable to meet its goals and timetables. There is also a Faculty and Staff Diversity Fund:

> The money in the fund shall be available to the board of governors upon appropriation by the Legislature for the purpose of enabling the California Community Colleges as a system to address the goal that by the year 2005 the system's workforce will reflect proportionately the adult population of the state.
>
> Also for the purpose of administering this fund, it is the intent of the Legislature that the board of governors take the steps which are necessary to reach the goal by the fiscal year 1992-93, 30 percent of all new hires in the California Community Colleges as a system will be ethnic minorities.

September 30, 1990

Governor Deukmejian vetoed Senate Bill (SB) 2843 by Senator Art Torres that in effect set up quotas and that asked the public higher education system to establish "nontraditional criteria" for faculty appointments and other employment matters. The bill would have held university administrators responsible to meet quotas for "diversity" and "historically underrepresented groups."

The governor also vetoed Assembly Bill 3993 by Assembly Speaker Willie Brown. The bill in effect called for quotas and "educational equity." Its estimated cost was $16 to $25 million.

March 8, 1991

Senate Bill 2843 was reintroduced in the State Assembly as Assembly Bill (AB) 1944 by Assembly Member Barbara Lee on March 8, 1991. It was labeled as "Postsecondary Education: Minorities."

AB 1944 called for the establishment of affirmative action programs in public higher education for women, people with disabilities, and racial and ethnic minorities who meet statewide minimum qualifications "or may become qualified through appropriate training or experience within a reasonable length of time." The bill in its generosity also provided: "The program should be designed to remedy the exclusion whatever its cause." In the course of its hearings, AB 1944 was gutted and was assigned to another completely unrelated bill that concerned the Auditor General's Office.

February 20, 1991 (amended April 17, 1991 and May 7, 1991)

Assembly Bill 617, introduced by Assembly Member Tom Hayden, called for "nontraditional criteria" including "race," "economic status," "maturity," "compassion," and "leadership potential" for admission to graduate and undergraduate programs. It was amended considerably in the Assembly.

This bill had originally been offered as AB 462 and had been vetoed by Governor George Deukmejian on September 30, 1990.

March 8, 1991

Governor George Deukmejian vetoed AB 3993 on September 30, 1990. Assembly Speaker Willie Brown reintroduced his bill (AB3993) as Assembly Bill 2150. Its goal was to achieve by the year 2000 "a diverse student body which mirrors the composition of recent high school graduates, both in first-year classes and [in] subsequent college and university graduating classes, for individuals from historically and currently underrepresented or economically disadvantaged groups." The bill stated: "It is the intent of the Legislature that educational equity be a central priority for California public educational institutions." In its egalitarian zeal, the bill required "enhanced success at all educational levels so that there are similar achievement patterns among all groups regardless of ethnic origin, race, gender, age, disability, or economic circumstances." Other requirements of this bill were: a mandatory ethnic study graduation requirement; workshops and seminars to promote sensitivity; educational equity (self-assessment); and step-by-step plans for "significant annual improvement." Performance evaluation of administrators would include achievement of "educational equity responsibility." Annual reports to this effect were to be submitted.

California Association of Scholars (CAS), an affiliate of the National Association of Scholars (NAS), was the only organization that opposed AB 2150. Testimony against the bill was given by several members of CAS. Commenting on this bill, John Leo of *U.S. News and World Report* called it "California's Racial Arithmetic,"[58] and Peter Schrag of the *Sacramento Bee* labeled it as "Higher Learning Lower Politics."[59]

April 23, 1991

The California Association of Scholars, under the leadership of the late Aaron Wildavsky of the University of California, Berkeley, held a press conference in the Governor's Press Room (arranged by State Senator Quentin Kopp) to oppose the quotas and preferences called for in Willie Brown's AB 2150, Tom Hayden's AB 617, and Barbara Lee's AB 1944. Also, written statements against these bills were issued by Professors James Q. Wilson of UCLA, Shelby Steele of San Jose State University, John Bunzel of Hoover Institution, and Stephen Barnett and John Polt of University of California, Berkeley.

On this same day, several members of CAS gave testimony against AB 617 and AB 1944. Thus, April 23, 1991, may be called the day of engagement to defend traditional academic standards and to stop the movement to further politicize the academy in California. These bills were supported by the ethnic lobbies at the State Capitol as well as by the California Faculty Association—the bargaining representative of the faculty of the California State University System.

February 5, 1992

Assembly Bill 2498, introduced by Assemblyman Richard G. Polanco, among other things required the University of California and the California State University system to "ensure that persons who determine the standards of admissions [in graduate programs] are representative of the ethnic and gender composition of California's population." It also called on these university systems to submit five-year, graduate-school affirmative action plans to the Legislature. On September 30, 1992, AB 2498 was vetoed by Governor Wilson.

Earlier, in March 1991, Assemblyman Polanco had introduced AB 2134 that required "pay for performance" for university administrators for meeting affirmative action goals and mandated that ethnic studies and women's programs be "integrated fully with the methodologies of each discipline." AB 2134 was opposed by the CAS as well as by the University of California Counsel. It was substantially amended in the form of AB 2498.

THREE EVENTS PRESAGE A MOVEMENT AGAINST PREFERENCES

At three campuses of the California State University System (CSU), uncoordinated but contemporaneous events also highlighted conflicts between the advocates of race and ethnic preferences and their opponents. The advocates of these preferences were university administrators supported by faculty organizations. The opponents were individual faculty who garnered support for their opposition to preferences. In each case, the contrarians initially faced tremendous odds, but in the end their efforts were fruitful because of their principled position of equality of opportunity. Before a discussion of these events, it needs to be emphasized that in CSU there is no evidence of a pattern of present or past effects of race or gender discrimination in faculty employment that would otherwise justify preferences as remedial measures.

Salary Supplements for "Underrepresented" Faculty

Collective bargaining agreement between the Board of Trustees of CSU and the California Faculty Association (CFA) (July 1, 1991, to June 30, 1993), which at that time covered 20 campuses, provided that minority, female, and disabled candidates in departments in which such categories of faculty were underrepresented may receive individual annual salary supplements (estimated to be between $2,000 to $5,000) for up to six years. Article 16.3 of the agreement stated that the term underrepresented "shall be determined by a comparison of the composition of departmental tenure track faculty with the composition of the CSU student body." A sum of up to $2,000,000 was to be set aside to fund this program.

This giveaway provision was incorporated into the agreement despite the fact that, in 1986, the U.S. Supreme Court in *Wygant v. Jackson Board of Education* had already ruled that absent some showing of prior discrimination by the governmental body involved, racial classification and preferences were not permissible. Furthermore, the Court said that it was unconstitutional for a school to maintain a teaching workforce in ratio to the racial composition of its student body. Earlier, in 1977, the Supreme Court in *Hazelwood School District v. United States* had held that comparison of "teacher workforce to its student population fundamentally misconceived the role of statistics." In the Court's view, the proper comparison is between the racial composition of the teaching staff and the racial composition of the qualified teacher population in the relevant employment market. The CFA-CSU collective bargaining contract also clearly violated the *Croson* (1989) principle of strict scrutiny, which requires that race and ethnic preferences in government units must be based on "compelling governmental purpose" and must not unduly trammel the interests of innocent third parties. None of the aforementioned criteria seemed to deter social engineers of the faculty union and the university system's administration from providing for the largess to remedy their ideological and extralegal notion of "underrepresentation."

The provision for salary supplement was challenged as reverse discrimination by Gary Colboth (Professor, Public Administration, CSU, Dominguez Hills) before the Equal Employment Opportunity Commission (EEOC) as well as the State of California Public Employment Relations Board. The EEOC ruled against Colboth stating that he lacked "standing" to lodge the complaint. However, after much foot-dragging and evasive legal stratagems, in October 1992, CFA and CSU, in a written agreement with Colboth, declared the controversial Article 16.3 concerning salary supplement "null and void."[60] In consideration of this stipulation, Colboth withdrew his unfair labor practice charge filed with the State of California Public Employment Relations Board. Thus, one concerned citizen-faculty saved the California taxpayers an estimated $2,000,000 that was to be spent on politically motivated preferences.

Preferences for "Diversity" at Chico

Not to be outdone by the zeal of some other campuses in CSU in the hiring of "diverse faculty" (meaning women and minorities), in 1993, the university administration at CSU, Chico, proposed a policy—the Faculty Diversity Program—that not only would give preference to "underrepresented" candidates for faculty positions but would, in effect, change the job descriptions and specifications to enable the diversity candidates to "compete" with other candidates in the pool. Positions were to be set aside for this program. Vice Provost Michael Biechler drafted and proposed a nouveau academic standard under which "unnecessary requirements for years of teaching and the longer publication lists" were not to be deemed "necessarily . . . the best match for our [Chico's] needs."[61] The standard called for the "ability to relate to an ethnically diverse student population" as a valid criterion for faculty appointment. Incensed at these measures, Professor Charles Geshekter (a specialist in African history) and a few of his colleagues led a petition drive that insisted that the university appoint "the best-qualified faculty without regard to the candidate's gender, race, religion, ethnicity, or national origin." In less than two weeks, 218 full-time faculty, constituting 40 percent of the total, signed the petition.[62] As a result, Chico State President Manuel Esteban and the Faculty Senate abandoned the Faculty Diversity Program, bringing an end to another attempt to institutionalize reverse discrimination at one university.

The Cure for Faculty "Underrepresentation" at Sacramento

The mantra of "Faculty Diversity" at CSU, Sacramento, with a student body of approximately 24,000, led to a program for "the recruitment of minority and women faculty in disciplines where minorities and/or women are underrepresented relative to the ethnic/gender composition of our student body and service area. For purposes of this program, the term *minority* includes individuals with the following ethnic backgrounds: Asian or Pacific Islander; Black or African-American; Hispanic, particularly Mexican-American; and Native American."[63]

Each year a number of faculty positions were set aside for "Opportunity Appointments." In his testimony in October 1996 before the California Assembly Budget Subcommittee on Education Finance, CSU, Sacramento, President Donald R. Gerth refused to admit that "opportunity appointments" were in fact set-asides. His explanation was: "We didn't call it that." He called them "incentive programs." For example, for the academic year 1990-1991, seven such positions were set aside. The Presidential Memorandum of February 9, 1990, gave the following helpful information for the preference program. Examples for allocating full or partial positions include when "[a] department finds two (2) underrepresented minority and/or women candidates for one advertised position; a second position could be given to provide for hiring both underrepresented minority and/or women candidates instead of one." The President's Memorandum encouraged the hiring of affirmative action faculty when "[d]uring a regular recruitment effort, a department identifies a candidate whose academic specialty does not adequately match that specified in the advertised position."[64]

On December 9, 1989, shortly before the quota program (the "opportunity appointments") was launched, Gerth "heartily endorsed" all 35 recommendations of a panel on "Racism Issues" that led to the establishment of a Multicultural Center, a program for faculty diversity, approval of a general education course in race and ethnicity as a graduation requirement, and campuswide discussion on a "celebration of diversity." The university also required each of its academic departments to elect or select an affirmative action representative for its Appointment or Selection Committee. Such a member was expected to have a politically correct view of the role. The university document "subtly" stated: "Although it is not necessary to be a member of a legally protected underrepresented class, every affirmative action representative shall be selected with a view of his or her sensitivity to the issues and commitment to the goals of affirmative action."[65]

Accordingly, in 1994, the campus had 48 affirmative action representatives plus the University Affirmative Action Officer who was required to sponsor "training" for these affirmative action representatives "to prepare them for their responsibilities." Privileged treatment to the "underrepresented" included "mini-grants," educational equity mentoring, grants from the President's discretionary "Opportunity Fund," and patronization in the form of official reception in the beginning of the academic year "Honoring New and Returning Faculty and Administrators of Color."

Concerned at the politicization of faculty employment, one of the authors (Raza) led a petition drive in the School of Business calling for hiring faculty only on the basis of their academic qualifications and merit "without discrimination as to a person's race, color, religion, sex, national origin, or disability status." Consequently, on March 13, 1992, after considerable debate, the faculty of the School by a 70 percent secret-ballot vote upheld the nondiscrimination, no-preference principle.[66] Thomas Sowell, in the *Sacramento Union*, called this vote an expression of common sense and "a revolutionary exception to current trendy thinking in academe."[67] In another action, on April 8, 1992, the Academic Council of the School of Business in a unanimous resolution asked the university to rescind the proposed race-, sex-, and ethnicity-based criteria that gave preference in the evaluation of mini-grant proposals.

From fiscal year 1990-1991 through fiscal year 1993-1994, the Sacramento campus had given out a total of $734,608 under two programs: Opportunity Appointments ($509,000) and Faculty Development Affirmative Action Grants ($225,608).[68] These affirmative action preference programs were not accompanied by any valid public study that would have established a factual predicate as to whether there was any disparity between the available academically qualified applicant pool and faculty appointments on a longitudinal basis as required by the Supreme Court's precedents on employment matters. As a matter of fact, at the very time the Sacramento campus was making affirmative action appointments and giving out race- and gender-based preferences, in its official reports, it stated that in all of its five Schools (Arts and Sciences, Business Administration, Education, Engineering and Computer Science, and Health and Human Services) as well as in Athletics and the Library, there was no underutilization of full-time minority or female faculty.[69]

Having failed to persuade the university administration to abandon its race-based preferences in faculty employment, Raza and seven of his colleagues in the School of Business through State Senator Quentin L. Kopp (I-San Francisco) requested that California Attorney General Daniel E. Lungren give an opinion on the legal status of race-, sex-, and ethnicity-based preferences in CSU, Sacramento. Extensive documentary evidence on preferences was provided to the Attorney General by the faculty group seeking the opinion. A three-attorney team from the Pacific Legal Foundation, a public interest law firm headquartered in Sacramento, also submitted extensive comments (17 pages plus attachments) to the Attorney General in support of the position that race- and gender-based preferences at the Sacramento campus were impermissible under the law. Similar supportive letters were also written by Dr. Glynn Custred of CSU, Hayward, and Dr. Thomas E. Wood, Executive Director CAS. Consequently, almost a year after the request, the Attorney General, on January 13, 1993, rendered a seven-page opinion (93-205) published in the Official Reports. The Attorney General's conclusion stated: "The California State University may voluntarily consider racial, ethnic, and gender characteristics in employing its faculty to remedy the effects of its own past discriminatory employment practices. Where evidence of such practices, which must be convincing, is based upon statistical disparity, the comparison must be between the composition of its faculty and the composition of the qualified population in the relevant labor market. The consideration must be closely related to the degree, nature, and extent of such prior discrimination."

The Vice President of University Affairs, Robert Jones, initially indicated that the university would "obey the law, whatever it is."[70] However, simultaneously, CSU spokesman Steve McCarthy, displaying affrontedness to the law, reportedly told the *Chronicle of Higher Education*: "'We're doing nothing in response to the [Attorney General's] opinion.'"[71] Senator Quentin Kopp's spokesperson, Janice Marschner, told the Bureau of National Affairs that under the Attorney General's opinion, "'academic merit triumphs over political criteria.'"[72]

The Attorney General's opinion is particularly significant in light of the fact that for faculty appointments in state university systems there were no controlling statutes or precedents for permitting affirmative action preferences. Under such circumstances, the Attorney General's opinions have been variously held to be persuasive,[73] and accorded substantial weight[74] or great weight,[75] and entitled to having a "quasi judicial character and entitled to great respect."[76]

Between 1987 and 1996, CSU granted $18 million in a Forgivable Loan Program (FLP) to minorities, women, and people with disabilities to pursue doctoral degrees in fields where these groups are "underrepresented." The system in its loan application material states: "Consideration is given to the degree of underrepresentation in the CSU faculty of the applicant's gender, ethnic group, or disability in the proposed field of study. Priority is given to applicants from historically underrepresented groups in the fields of natural sciences, computer science, mathematics, and engineering."[77]

The system did not publicly describe how it determined the "degree of underrepresentation" of each ethnic group, nor for that matter did it specify which ethnic groups were eligible for these forgivable loans. Under the program, a full-time doctoral student is eligible to receive up to $10,000 per year (not to exceed $30,000 total). If on completion of a doctorate a grantee teaches in the CSU System, then 20 percent of the loan is forgiven for every year of such full-time postdoctoral teaching.

In the nine years since the inception of the FLP, $18 million has been loaned to 875 individuals. Of these, fewer than 10 percent (85) were employed at CSU campuses, and only 3.1 percent ($560,000) of the $18 million has been repaid.[78] It is interesting to note that the CSU administration does not claim that the FLP is designed to remedy any negative effect of its past or present discriminatory policies because there's no finding to that effect. Nor does it claim that qualified "underrepresented" persons wishing to pursue doctoral programs are financially unable to do so and consequently need loans and grants. In fact, the information brochure accompanying the application generously states that: "There is no financial needs requirement for the Forgivable Loan Program. Participants may have other income or financial aid without affecting their eligibility for FLP loans."[79]

It is obvious that the FLP is designed for social engineering in which practically the only category ineligible to apply is white men. There is no pretense in this program that it meets the legal standards of permissible parameters for race-, ethnicity-, or gender-based preferences laid down by the Supreme Court. There has been no finding of prior or present discrimination so that this program can be considered remedial. Brazen disregard for the law is demonstrated by the fact that, as of February 1993, the CSU had not reviewed the Supreme Court cases to determine whether its affirmative action programs met the criteria set by the U.S. Supreme Court in its various decisions pertinent to the issue. This is despite the fact that the bureaucracy to implement affirmative action programs existed at the Chancellor's Office and on each campus.[80] (The City and County of San Francisco had also not reviewed the Supreme Court cases at the time of this survey.) Thus, as far as CSU was concerned, the Supreme Court's directive about strict scrutiny requiring a demonstration of compelling governmental interest and narrow tailoring of remedial measures was in effect irrelevant to the bureaucracy's ideological goal of curing its own version of "underrepresentation."

PATTERN AND PRACTICE OF PREFERENCES IN FACULTY EMPLOYMENT AT THE CALIFORNIA STATE UNIVERSITY SYSTEM

The events at the Dominguez Hills, Chico, and Sacramento campuses of CSU were unusual only because of the resistance and protests mounted on these campuses. Otherwise, at that time on most other campuses of the CSU system, race- and gender-based preferences in faculty recruitment and appointments were the norm rather than the exception, as the following list, taken from the Chancellor's Report,* describes. The Chancellor's Report particularly notes that successes in affirmative action goal attainment were attributed to varying strategies including: "using a majority of subject-matter experts in search committees that were sensitive to the gender and ethnic issues. . . ." (p. 15)

Bakersfield: CSU Forgivable Loan Program, 5 awards in 1991-1992: 2 Hispanics, 2 white women, 1 black woman. (p. 18)

Chico: In 1993-1994, of the 7 tenure-track hires: 5 were from "underrepresented" (3 ethnic minorities; 1 Latino, 2 Asians). (p. 20)

Dominguez Hills: CSU Forgivable Loans Program, 6 awards in 1993-1994: 3 woman, 5 minorities. (p. 22)

Fresno: "Funding for several positions has been alloted specifically for faculty diversity hires, . . ." (p. 24)

Fullerton: In 1991-1992, "Of the 21 appointments, affirmative action hires constituted 81.9 percent." (p. 26)

In 1992-1993, "Of the ten tenure-track faculty recruitments authorized for fall 1993, seven appointment offers have been made, women receiving 3 . . . and minority males receiving 2." (p. 27)

Humboldt: During 1991-1992, 77.7 percent of the tenure-track hires were affirmative action appointments.

In promotions of faculty, 90 percent of "protected-class faculty members' promotions were granted compared to 71.4 percent of white males." (p. 32)

---

*Source: California State University, Office of the Chancellor, Affirmative Action Progress Report Presented to the Board of Trustees, July 1993 (67 pp).

Long Beach: In tenure-track positions, 61.54 percent were women in 1991-1992 and 38.4 percent were minority hires.

In 1992-1993, 25 tenure-track positions undertaken. In 1993-1994, 14 appointments made effective. In 1993-1994, 9 women and 7 minorities were appointed.

Los Angeles: "For the third consecutive year, we are able to report that we have hired more females in tenure-track positions than males and over 55 percent of our total tenure-track faculty hires are ethnic minorities." (p. 37)

Sacramento: July 1, 1991, to June 30, 1992, 26 new faculty appointments completed. Of these 16 were woman, 9 minorities, and 6 white men. "Five offers to applicants of color were declined." (p. 45)

In 1992-1993, there was recruitment for 14 positions, 5 of them canceled. Appointments were made in 5 searches, of which 80 percent were diversity appointments. (p. 45)

San Bernardino: In 1993-1994, 4 were hired who had received Forgivable Loans. Also, in 1993-1994, 13 appointments were made, of which 4 were blacks, 4 Hispanics, 1 Native American; also 4 were men, and 8 were women.

"The ethnic and gender diversity indicated by those members will significantly improve the campus's prospects of reaching its affirmative action goals, i.e., a rough parity with the diversity reflected by the student body." (p. 47)

San Deigo: In 1993-1994, there were 6 searches for "special consideration positions that are vital to the department or provide an opportunity to add to the number of underrepresented faculty." (p. 50)

In 1991-1992, there were 12 new hires. Of these, 25 percent were "underrepresented" faculty. (p. 50)

San Francisco: Ethnic minorities in faculty constitute 24 percent of the total SFSU faculty.

"While the figure suggests that the university continues to move forward toward increasing the number of minority faculty, the percentages are below the populations in the Bay Area and the State of California." (p. 52)

San Jose: From June 1, 1991, to June 30, 1992, there were 79 new faculty hires. Of these, 53 percent were women and 40 percent were minority. (p. 55)

As a result of the 1990 population census, the campus has increased the goals of hiring, particularly women. (p. 55)

San Luis Obispo: In 1991-1992, 33 percent of new faculty hires were women and 7 percent ethnic minorities. (p. 57)

San Marcos: July 1, 1991, to June 30, 1992, 25 full-time faculty hired, of which 48 percent were minorities and 44 percent women. (p. 59)

"This brought the total percentage of full-time minority faculty members at CSUSM to 42 percent and female faculty members to 45 percent." (p. 59)

Sonoma: "We are pleased with the results of our 1991-1992 tenure-track hires: of the thirteen positions filled, 85 percent went to members of underrepresented groups: eight (8) to women, three (3) to ethnic minorities." (p. 62)

Stanislaus: In 1991-1992, women and ethnic minorities accounted for 62 percent of the new faculty appointments.

AVAILABLE QUALIFIED POOL FOR FACULTY APPOINTMENTS

In order to have a general idea about the extent of preferences that obviously result in reverse discrimination in faculty appointments at CSU, Tables 4.3, 4.4, and 4.5 exhibit selected data on the qualified labor pool. In most disciplines, candidates by and large must possess earned doctorates (or be working on them) to be qualified for tenure-track faculty positions. New recipients of doctorates constitute the largest portion of the qualified pool from which new faculty are drawn. Therefore, the data presented are restricted to that pool for selected years.

Table 4.3
Doctorates Awarded by Broad Field and Race 1983, 1988, and 1993

Race/Year	Science/Engineering Including Natural Sciences and Behavioral Sciences	Non-Science/Engineering Including Health, Education, Humanities, Professional, and Others
Native Americans:		
1983	28	54
1988	41	53
1993	41	78
Asians:		
1983	778	265
1988	912	323
1993	1,602	407
Blacks:		
1983	322	683
1988	346	620
1993	452	823
Hispanics:		
1983	282	326
1988	393	300
1993	536	436
White:		
1983	12,483	9,767
1988	12,326	9,131
1993	13,535	10,458

Source: National Science Foundation, *Selected Data on Science and Engineering Doctorate Awards: 1993*, NSF 94-318 (Arlington, VA: National Science Foundation, 1993). Table A, p. *x*. (extracted).

Table 4.4
Percent of Doctorates Awarded to Women 1983 and 1993

Year	Science/Engineering Including Natural Sciences and Behavioral Sciences	Non-Science/Engineering Including Health, Education, Humanities, Professional, and Others
1983	25.1	45.8
1993	29.9	52.0

Source: National Science Foundation, *Selected Data on Science and Engineering Doctorate Awards: 1993*, NSF 94-318 (Arlington, VA: National Science Foundation, 1993). Table 2, pp. 7, 12 (extracted).

Some characteristics of degree recipients are noteworthy:

- There is a significant increase in the number of women receiving doctorates over the past several years. In 1984, women earned 34.2 percent of doctorates. This number increased to 38.5 percent in 1994.[81]
- There is a marked difference in the choice of doctoral fields between men and women as well as among racial and ethnic groups, as seen in Table 4.5.

Other data for 1995 show that in all nonscience fields as a whole, women earned 52 percent of the doctorates awarded.[82] Blacks increased their share of all earned doctorates from 4.1 percent in 1994 (see Table 4.5) to 4.7 percent in 1995.

Cultural traditions and values, individual predilections, and rational calculations are largely responsible for the choices people make to pursue doctoral degrees in a particular field. Otherwise it would be difficult to explain why, for instance, more Asians relative to their population choose engineering and hard sciences than do other racial and ethnic groups. It would not be correct to say that Asians somehow have more "opportunity" to pursue engineering and hard sciences than do others. Thus, a smaller number of Ph.D.s in a particular discipline from a particular ethnic, racial, or gender group cannot be reflexively attributed simply to discrimination or to a lack of opportunity.

The American academic market for Ph.D.s is highly competitive and segmented. As a matter of fact, there are several academic markets, each having its "buyers" and "sellers" who function mostly in their specialized markets. Thus, for instance, Ivy League and research universities mostly look for different kinds of intellectual talent than do average state universities even though generally they all require their faculty candidates to have at least a Ph.D. There is fierce competition among all universities to hire ethnic and racial minorities for faculty positions. This competition is the explanation for the University of California and the California State University

Table 4.5
Characteristics of Recipients of Doctorates in 1994

Group	All Fields	Arts and Humanities	Business and Management	Education	Engineering	Life Sciences	Physical Sciences	Social Sciences	Other Professional Fields
Men	61.5%	52.3%	71.6%	39.1%	89.1%	58.4%	79.7%	50.6%	54.0%
Women	38.5	47.7	28.4	60.9	10.9	41.6	20.3	49.4	46.0
American Indian	0.5	0.6	0.8	0.6	0.2	0.4	0.2	0.5	0.8
Asian	11.5	4.6	9.4	2.8	28.5	15.5	20.6	6.0	5.6
Black	4.1	2.8	4.1	8.6	1.8	2.5	1.6	4.7	7.7
Hispanic	3.3	4.4	2.0	4.0	2.2	3.1	2.6	3.6	3.3
White	79.6	86.7	83.3	83.2	66.1	77.4	74.1	84.1	81.7
Others	1.0	0.9	0.4	0.8	1.3	1.0	0.9	1.1	0.9

Source: National Research Council, "Summary Report 1994," *Chronicle of Higher Education*, 8 December, 1995. A18 (excerpted).

systems setting aside certain slots under the designation of *opportunity positions*—a euphemism for *quota*.

The available pool of minority Ph.D.s is so small that even big-name universities that offer generous pay and fringe benefit packages and working conditions have a hard time attracting and retaining such faculty. A prime example is Duke University, which in 1988 mandated that each of its 56 departments hire at least one black faculty member by the fall of 1993. However, despite its best recruitment efforts, it was only able to increase its number of black faculty members from 31 in 1987 to 39 in fall 1993, constituting only 2.4 percent of its total full-time faculty of 1,600.[83] This is particularly telling about the paucity of available black Ph.D.s, even though some critics charge that Duke did not try hard enough to attract black professors.[84] In its defense, Duke argues that between 1988 and 1993 it actually hired 25 black faculty members, but in the same period 17 others left the university. Thus, even a prestigious university well known for its hospitable affirmative action policies was unable to meet its "goals and timetables" for "diversity" hiring. Black professors have many choices, and, consequently, they move from one university to another that offers higher salaries and perks. Some commentators call it "a game of musical chairs."[85]

NOTES

1. Ann Devroy, "President Eases Up on Contracts for Minorities: Pentagon Scraps Affirmative Action Rule for Disadvantaged," *San Francisco Examiner*, October 25, 1995, A2.

2. Paul M. Barrett, "SBA Contracts for Minorities Challenged," *Wall Street Journal*, November 22, 1995, B2.

3. Paul M. Barrett, "Foes of Affirmative Action Target SBA's 8(a) Program," *Wall Street Journal*, March 18, 1996, B2.

4. See, for example: Paul M. Barrett, "SBA Minority Set-Aside Raises Questions," *Wall Street Journal*, February 23, 1996, B2.

5. Paul M. Barrett, "Judge's Ruling Spares Set-Aside Program," *Wall Street Journal*, April 4, 1996, B5.

6. Paul M. Barrett, "Bid-Preference Plan Attacked in Legal Action," *Wall Street Journal*, November 30, 1995, A6.

7. Linda Chavez and Daniel Sutherland, "Quotamania: The Sequel," *Weekly Standard*, November 13, 1995, 11.

8. Paul M. Barrett, "Federal Preferences for Minority Firms Illustrate Affirmative Action Dispute," *Wall Street Journal*, March 14, 1995, A20.

9. Congressional Research Service, the Library of Congress, "Compilation and Overview of Federal Laws and Regulations Establishing Affirmative Action Goals or Other Preferences Based on Race, Gender, or Ethnicity" (Washington, D.C.: Library of Congress, February 17, 1995), 32 pp.

10. Tim W. Ferguson, "Race (etc.) Preferences on the Line," *Wall Street Journal*, March 14, 1995, A19. Also see: "Affirmative Action in Action," *Wall Street Journal*, February 27, 1995, A12.

11. Michael K. Frisby, "Clinton's Choice to Review Affirmative Action Underscores Delicate Nature of Undertaking," *Wall Street Journal*, March 14, 1995.

12. Louis Freedberg and Susan Yoachum, "Clinton Makes Emotional Plea for Programs," *San Francisco Chronicle*, July 20, 1995, A1, and A11.

13. Michael K. Frisby, "Clinton Expresses Strong Commitment to Continuing U.S. Affirmative Action," *Wall Street Journal*, July 20, 1995, B8.

14. Christopher Matthews, "Clinton's Stance on Affirmative Action," *San Francisco Examiner*, July 23, 1995, B11.

15. Joe Klein, "Firm on Affirmative Action: The President Pleases His Allies, But Avoids the Real Race Crisis," *Newsweek*, July 31, 1995, 31.

16. David Tell (Ed.), "Ending Affirmative Action," *Weekly Standard*, October 2, 1995, 6-9.

17. Michael K. Frisby, "Some Agencies Stage Affirmative Action Retreat While White House Still Debates Its Battle Plan," *Wall Street Journal*, March 24, 1996, A14; also see: Donna St. George, "Minority Businesses May Get Fewer U.S. Contracts," *Sacramento Bee*, March 9, 1996, A1, A17.

18. Paul M. Barrett, "SBA Minority Program Is Under Attack in GAO Report: Evidence of Cooked Books, Phony Owners May Help GOP Kill Set-Asides," *Wall Street Journal*, October 6, 1995, B2.

19. Clair Cooper, "Suit Challenges County's Affirmative Action Plan," *Sacramento Bee*, March 27, 1995.

20. Walter Dellinger, Assistant Attorney General, "Memorandum to General Counsels, re: *Adarand*" (Washington, D.C.: U.S. Department of Justice, Office of the Legal Counsel, June 28, 1995), 38 pp.

21. Ibid., 1.

22. Ibid., 2.

23. John R. Schmidt, Associate Attorney General, "Memorandum to General Counsels, re: *Adarand* Guidance on Affirmative Action in Federal Employment," (Washington, D.C.: U.S. Department of Justice, Office of the Associate Attorney General, February 29, 1996), 19 pp.

24. Ibid., 18.

25. Paul M. Barrett, "White House Memo on Federal Hiring Shows Defense of Affirmative Action," *Wall Street Journal*, March 4, 1996, B6.

26. Charles Finnie, "Set-Aside Issue Looms Large for the Presidency," *Daily Journal*, March 18, 1996, 1, 9.

27. Center for Equal Opportunity, "Justice Department Memo Defends Racial Preferences," March 6, 1996 (press release).

28. "Justice Department Drops Support of Reverse Discrimination Suit," *San Francisco Chronicle*, September 7, 1994, A3; *Sharon Taxman v. Board of Educa-*

tion, Piscataway, 832 F. Supp. 836 (1993); also see: Malcolm Gladwell, "Firing of White Teacher a Test of Limits of Affirmative Action," *San Francisco Chronicle*, September 27, 1994; "U.S. Agency Switches Sides in Case over Civil Rights," *Wall Street Journal*, September 7, 1994, B11.

29. "Court Sides with Whites in Reverse Bias Case," *San Francisco Chronicle*, May 6, 1996, A6. *Birmingham Firefighters, et al., v. City of Birmingham, et al.*, U.S. Court of Appeals for the Eleventh Circuit, No. 91-7799 (May 4, 1994). The Supreme Court declined to review the case. Linda Greenhouse, "Ruling That Bias Plan Is Unfair Stands; Justices Won't Review Ruling on Program to Promote More Blacks," *New York Times*, April 18, 1995, A12.

30. Associated General Contractors, *National Newsletter* 37 (August 11, 1995).

31. "GOP Senator Seeks to Cut Aid Program for Minority Business Firms," *Wall Street Journal*, September 7, 1995, A4.

32. Matthew Rees, "Affirmative Reaction," *Weekly Standard*, March 11, 1996, 14-15.

33. Amy Chance, "Gingrich Against Race-Based Hiring. He Backs Measure to Do Away with State's Programs," *Sacramento Bee*, October 25, 1995, A3.

34. Melissa Healy, "House Panel Backs GOP Affirmative Action Revamp. Fight Due, But Legislation Had Wide, Powerful Backing," *Sacramento Bee*, March 8, 1996, A3.

35. See, for example: Clint Bolick, "A Judge Takes on Clinton's See-No-Quota Quota Policy," *Wall Street Journal*, April 17, 1996, A21; it describes how an expansive consent order proposed by Justice Department Civil Rights Chief Deval Patrick, calling for quotas and set-asides to be imposed on the North Carolina Department of Correction, was rejected by Judge Terrence W. Boyle of a federal court in North Carolina. Boyle considered the proposed consent order as unconstitutional, denying male employees equal protection of the law.

36. Representative Jan Meyers, Chairperson of the House Committee on Small Business, is proposing to kill the so-called Section 8(a) program that awarded $5.2 billion in federal contracts to minority-owned firms in 1995. It is the biggest set-aside program for minority-owned businesses. According to the Small Business Administration, more than 90 percent of these contracts are awarded without competition. See: Stephanie N. Mehta, "SBA Program for Minorities Is Under Attack," *Wall Street Journal*, April 18, 1996, B2.

37. *DeRonde v. The Regents of University of California*, 102 Cal. App. 3d 221 (1980).

38. Steve Martini, "Minority Lawyers, Legislators Hit DeRonde Ruling as Racist," *Los Angeles Daily Journal*, January 31, 1980.

39. For information on this topic, see: Dinesh D'Souza, *Illiberal Education: The Politics of Race and Sex on Campus* (New York: Vintage Books, 1992), Chapter 3.

40. See, for example: Ibid., Chapter 7; and Richard Bernstein, *Dictatorship of Virtue: Multiculturalism and the Battle for America's Future* (New York: Alfred A. Knopf, 1994), pp. 69, 123, 144–146, 196–198, 212–214, 225.

41. Heather MacDonald, "Law School Humbug," *Wall Street Journal*, November 8, 1995, A19; "Law: The Neverending Storytelling," *Wall Street Journal*, December 8, 1995, A17 (three letters to the Editor); also see: Neil A. Lewis, "Black Scholars View Society with Prism of Race," *New York Times*, May 5, 1977, A11.

42. Arthur Schlesinger, Jr., "Toward a Divisive Diversity," *Wall Street Journal*, June 25, 1991), A18. for a detailed analysis of this issue, see his: *The Disuniting of America: Reflections on a Multicultural Society* (New York: W. W. Norton and Co., 1992).

43. Arthur Schlesinger, Jr., "When Ethnic Studies Are Un-American," *Wall Street Journal*, April 23, 1990, A14.

44. See: "Washington Update: On Campaign Trail, Senator Dole Denounces History Standards," *Chronicle of Higher Education*, September 15, 1995, A33; Lynne V. Cheney, "The End of History," *Wall Street Journal*, October 20, 1994, A26.

45. Diane Ravitch and Arthur Schlesinger, Jr., "The New Improved History Standards," *Wall Street Journal*, April 3, 1996, A22.

46. Lynne V. Cheney, "New History Standards Still Attack Our Heritage," *Wall Street Journal*, May 2, 1996, A14.

47. Nathan Glazer, *We Are All Multiculturalist Now* (Cambridge: Harvard University Press, 1997).

48. William J. Bennett, *The Devaluing of America: The Fight for Our Culture and Our Children* (New York: Summit Books, 1992).

49. "The Accreditation Wars," *Wall Street Journal*, April 23, 1991, A18. For an interview (by Carol Iannone) with Samuel T. Logan, President of Westminister Theological Seminary see: "God, Man, and Middle States," *Academic Questions* 4 (Fall 1991), 49-61.

50. U.S. Department of Education, Public Affairs, "Statement by Lamar Alexander, U.S. Secretary of Education, Before the House Government Operations Subcommittee on Human Resources and Intergovernmental Relations" (Washington, D.C.: U.S. Department of Education, June 26, 1991), 4 pp.

51. Scott Jaschik, "Group with Diversity Policy Similar to Middle States' Prepare for U.S. Review," *Chronicle of Higher Education*, April 29, 1991, A24.

52. "Election '96," *Wall Street Journal*, November 7, 1996, A14-A15.

53. "The Quota Convention," *Wall Street Journal*, August 26, 1996, A12.

54. "Quota Person," *Wall Street Journal*, February 24, 1997, A22.

55. Terrance J. Pell, "Texas Must Choose Between a Court Order and a Clinton Edict," *Wall Street Journal*, April 2, 1997, A15; Richard Starr, "Sexual Perversity in Washington: The Brave New World of Norma Cantu," *Weekly Standard*, April 7, 1997, 26.

56. A. Phillips Brooks, "Affirmative Action Laws Trap Texas in a No-Win Situation," *San Francisco Chronicle*, February 28, 1997, A6, quoting Enforcement Director of the Department of Education's Office for Civil Rights.

57. Peter Applebome, "In Shift, U.S. Tells Texas to Obey Court in Barring Bias in College Admissions," *New York Times*, April 15, 1997, A9; "A Bureaucratic Snafu Fueled a Clinton Flip-Flop on Affirmative Action," *Wall Street Journal*, April 18, 1997, A1.

58. John Leo, "California's Racial Arithmetic," *U.S. News and World Report*, June 24, 1991, 21.

59. Peter Schrag, "Higher Learning Lower Politics," *Sacramento Bee*, July 17, 1991, B6.

60. *Gary Colboth v. California Faculty Association and California State University*, Case No. LA-CE-303-H (October 14, 1992) (Stipulation and Withdrawal); also see: "Diversity Pay," *Insight*, October 7, 1991, 8.

61. Victor A. Walsh and Thomas E. Wood, *Bakke and Beyond: A Study of Racial and Gender Preferences in California Public Higher Education* (Berkeley: California Association of Scholars, 1996), p. 45.

62. Larry Mitchell, "218 Profs Oppose CSUC Diversity Plan," *Chico Enterprise Record*, February 19, 1994.

63. California State University, *Sacramento* [President's Memorandum], PM 90-05 (February 9, 1990), p. 1.

64. Ibid., 3.

65. California State University, *Sacramento*. Academic Senate, 88–102/AA, UARTP, October 13, 1988.

66. The resolution voted on was as follows:

    All recommendations concerning appointment, retention, tenure, promotion, compensation, and other terms, conditions, or privileges of employment for any faculty position must be solely based on merit without discrimination as to a person's race, color, religion, sex, national origin, or disability status. In order to fill a vacant faculty position, it shall be legitimately and widely advertised in a timely manner so that the best qualified person may be hired. Giving preference to any person on criteria other than academic merit is discriminatory and violates equal protection of the law.

67. Thomas Sowell, "Things That Make No Sense," *Sacramento Union*, July 3, 1992, A10.

68. Memorandum from Jolene Koester, Vice President for Academic Affairs, California State University, *Sacramento*, to M. Ali Raza; subject: Universitywide Faculty Diversity Programs (July 15, 1994), p. 2.

69. California State University, *Sacramento*, *Affirmative Action Plan: Statistics and Analyses* (September 1992 to October 1993), "Utilization Analysis. Utilizing 80% Rule" (Table).

70. Nora Martin, "Advisory Opinion Impacts CSU Hiring," *State Hornet*, February 11, 1994, 4.

71. Joye Mercer, "Assault on Affirmative Action: 2 Measures Sought in California Would Limit or Outlaw Policies at State Colleges," *Chronicle of Higher Education*, March 16, 1994, A25.

72. "California Colleges Told to Limit Affirmative Action to Past Practices," *Government Employee Relations Report* 32, No. 1556 (March 14, 1994), p. 364.

73. *Henderson v. Board of Education*, 78 Cal. App. 3d 875, 883 (1978).

74. *Bruce v. Gregory*, 65 Cal. 2d 666, 676 (1967).

75. *Phyle v. Duffy*, 334 U.S. 431, 441 (1948).

76. *People v. Berry*, 147 Cal. App. 2d 33, 37 (1956).

77. California State University, *1995-96 Forgivable Loan/Doctoral Program for Minorities, Women, and Persons with Disability* (n.d.) (December 1994) from information brochure and application.

78. Ali Raza and Charles Geshekter, "Race, Gender Bias Flourish in the UC [sic. CSU] System," *Orange County Register*, October 9, 1996. For a detailed account of the developments at CSU, Chico, and the general discussion of preferences in the California State University system, see: Charles L. Geshekter, "Affirmative Action in Principle, Non-Discrimination in Fact, Higher Education after Proposition 209," *Stanford Law & Policy* 10, no. 2 (Spring 1999), 205–219.

79. California State University, *1995-96 Forgivable Loan/Doctoral Program*, from information brochure and application.

80. "Survey of Affirmative Action Goal Setting Practices of Selected Public Jurisdictions," in California State Personnel Board, Memorandum to All State Agencies and Employee Organizations, Subject: Hearing on Proposed Changes to Affirmative Action Policies Affecting the Goals and Timetables Process (February 1, 1993), Attachment A, p. 17.

81. *Chronicle of Higher Education*, December 8, 1995, A18.

82. Denise K. Magner, "More Black Ph.D.s," *Chronicle of Higher Education*, June 14, 1996, A25.

83. "Bitter Debate as Duke Fails on Hiring Blacks. University Set Unrealistic Goals, Many Say—Others Assail 'Quota,'" *San Francisco Chronicle*, September 20, 1993, A7.

84. Denise K. Magner, "Duke U. Struggles to Make Good on Pledge to Hire Black Professors," *Chronicle of Higher Education*, March 24, 1993, A13.

85. Francis Mancini, "What Universities Have to Learn about Affirmative Action," *Sacramento Bee*, March 31, 1993, B7; also see: Magner, "Duke U. Struggles."

5

∽

Preferences in California's Colleges and Universities and Academic Resistance

WEST COAST ACCREDITING AGENCY DEMANDS DIVERSITY

The Western Association of Schools and Colleges (WASC) accredits over 140 four-year colleges and universities in California, Hawaii, and Guam. The list includes powerful, large universities such as the University of California (UC), California Institute of Technology (Cal Tech), and the University of Southern California (USC) as well as smaller institutions such as Thomas Aquinas College, Patten College, and Fresno Pacific College. Accreditation is important to institutions because it is a prerequisite for federal funding and student loans. In the United States, there are six accrediting associations for senior colleges and universities. Each association is recognized by the federal government for its accreditation authority within a particular region.

In 1987, WASC circulated a draft of a policy of proposed diversity standards. With some amendments, the policy was adopted in 1988. Its pertinent provision stated: "The [accredited] institution demonstrates its commitment to the increasingly significant educational role played by diversity of ethnic, social, and economic backgrounds among its members by making positive efforts to foster such diversity."[1] The policy also called for the institutions to adopt goals for undergraduate studies that include "an appreciation of cultural diversity" and to actively seek diversity in the student body and in the hiring of faculty. These affirmative action policies and procedures and their results were required to be "monitored and periodically reviewed." The policy also stated that diversity is to be sought within the "parameters defined by [an institution's] mission."

In 1987-1988 the standard did not attract the attention and scrutiny it deserved. Contemporaneously, other accrediting agencies were also adopting or enforcing diversity policies in their respective jurisdictions. For instance, in 1988, the Middle States Association of Colleges and Schools (Middle States) adopted diversity guidelines and later threatened Westminster Theological Seminary in Philadelphia and Baruch College in Manhattan with refusal to accredit unless they implemented those diversity guidelines (see Chapter 4). However, under pressure from the Bush Administration's Department of Education, Middle States modified its position by stating that institutions shall not be punished for not following the guidelines.

After putting into effect its diversity standard in July 1998, WASC increased the tempo of its public pronouncements emphasizing diversity's importance as an accreditation criterion. The administrators of WASC assumed not only that its diversity standard was unequivocally accepted by the accredited member institutions but that it was a necessary ingredient in the quality of higher education. A paper by WASC in September 1989 asserted "diversity as a fundamental element of quality" and emphasized the Association's "major new thrust" in what amounted to social engineering. An important test of the implementation of WASC's diversity standard came in the case of the renowned Rand Graduate School of Policy Studies. On November 16, 1990, Stephen S. Weiner, Executive Director of WASC's Accrediting Commission for Senior Colleges and Universities, in a letter to Charles Wolf, Jr., Dean of the Rand Graduate School of Policy Studies in Santa Monica, California, informed Wolf that although his institution fully met the standards regarding governance and academic quality, it was "missing an opportunity to take leadership and responsibility" in the areas of race and ethnicity in its policy studies. The letter further required Rand to submit a special report by May 1, 1992, on diversity. "Specifically, the Commission requests that the School more clearly delineate its goals with respect to increasing the representation of minorities and women in its faculty and student body and the inclusion of the study and analysis of issues related to diversity in its curriculum and the progress made in reaching those goals."

UCLA Professor of Management and Public Policy and eminent scholar James Q. Wilson, who served on the Academic Advisory Board of Rand, in a letter (written in a personal capacity) to Weiner strongly challenged the accrediting agency's "right, or even the competence to specify what subjects ought to be the object of research and teaching at a university." In another letter, Wilson admonished Weiner for simply demonstrating "all-too-common allegiance to a fashionable slogan: diversity," without the Commission showing why bringing race and ethnicity into greater focus in Rand's curriculum was more important than other subjects.[2] Weiner, in his response to Wilson's letter, instead of providing an explanation of the issues raised endeavored to obfuscate the matter by stating platitudes such as: it is necessary for all institutions to treat members of their respective communities with respect and "all accredited institutions, both public and private, should operate in the public interest."[3]

Weiner gave no evidence that Rand was in violation of these principles. The first major institutional effort to challenge WASC's exuberance for diversity came from Thomas Aquinas College, a small Catholic school in Santa Paula, California, with a liberal arts curriculum emphasizing the Great Books. The college president, Thomas Dillon, and his accreditation liaison officer, Richard Ferrier, valiantly fought a three-year (1991-1994) war against WASC's policy of dictating diversity in college governance, curriculum, student body, and faculty.

In January 1991, WASC sponsored a workshop on diversity. Thomas Aquinas College had been uneasy with the increasingly ideological statements about diversity by WASC generally and by the Commission's Executive Director Weiner particularly. Consequently, Thomas Aquinas College sent a large delegation to the workshop. A vigorous discussion ensued on two documents that had been produced by WASC on the issue of diversity. However, no consensus was reached on the diversity standard. There were particular misgivings about WASC's guidelines on "Do's and Don't's on Diversity" and the "outcomes" prescribed therein. Consequently, in May 1991, officials of Thomas Aquinas College wrote a thoughtful five-page letter to WASC strongly objecting to its diversity standards. The situation was greatly aggravated because of the unsubstantiated assertion of WASC that the quality of an institution is a function of, or even related to, its "diversity"—a code word for race and gender preferences. Instead of providing evidence of the presumed relationship of diversity and excellence in higher education, Weiner simply declared that "college leaders in our region agree that diversity and educational quality are intertwined."[4] This statement was simply not true.

Up to the end of 1991, opposition to the diversity standard was diffused. Two events coalesced to crystallize and strengthen the opposition to the diversity standard. First was the issuing of a report in January 1992 by the External Review Panel appointed by WASC itself that stated that many institutions had not in fact realized the importance and the extent of the diversity standard at the time of its adoption and that, therefore, unlike the other standards, it had not received appropriate peer review and hence was of questionable legitimacy. The other event was a full-scale attack on the philosophical underpinning of diversity which was perceived by some institutions as an intrusion on their autonomy. The catalyst for this opposition was Thomas Aquinas College, whose representatives had originally sounded an alarm on the reach and consequences of the diversity standard. By the middle of 1992, opposition to the standard had put WASC in a defensive position.

In retrospect, WASC's dispute with Rand Graduate School in 1990 proved to be only an opening skirmish in a four-year war between the accrediting agency and several of the colleges and universities—including the most prestigious ones. The opposition alleged that:

1. The diversity standard is vague and open to different interpretations.

2. There is no scholarly consensus that there is any relationship between diversity and excellence in education.

3. The standard politicizes the educational process.

4. It imperils the autonomy of educational institutions through increased regulatory intrusion.

5. Omission of the issue of sexual orientation in the diversity standard was unfair and consequently unacceptable.

Those expressing their dissatisfaction with the omission of sexual orientation included the President of Golden Gate University; the president of California State University, Fresno; and the Academic Senates of the California State University system, San Francisco State University, and San Jose State University. On the other hand, church-related institutions feared that the diversity standard was so vaguely written that it would require them to hire gay men and lesbians in violation of their religious tenets.[5] In order to deal with many of the criticisms, WASC prepared and distributed some explanations of its standard. But its bottomline remained the same—that an accredited institution must demonstrate its commitment to and show progress toward multicultural, multiracial diversity.

The officials of Thomas Aquinas College also protested the diversity policy through a letter in July 1991 to the U.S. Department of Education.[6] Later the California Association of Scholars, an affiliate of the National Association of Scholars, through its Executive Director, Thomas E. Wood, actively joined the opposition and published a comprehensive critique of WASC's policy on diversity.[7] The critique citing research studies concluded that there was "a lack of consensus in the academic community over policies designed to increase racial or sexual diversity through the imposition of race- and sex-based preferences."[8] The critique also pointed out that WASC had offered no empirical evidence that its conception and definition of educational quality was generally accepted by the academic community.

Martin Trow, an eminent professor of Public Policy at Berkeley (a former faculty representative to UC's Board of Regents and a former Chair of UC's Academic Senate) strongly criticized WASC for its diversity policy and said that the issue of diversity should be left up to the institutions so that they could fashion their own policies in accordance with their respective educational philosophies and missions. Instead, the drafters of diversity statements, he said, "quite clearly imagine themselves to be both wiser and more virtuous than the objects of their policy."[9] In a similar vein, Raymond A. Paredes, Associate Vice Chancellor of Academic Development at UCLA, in a letter to a member of the Accreditation Commission's Committee on Diversity stated that the university's Academic Council feels that in its diversity policy "WASC was overreaching its appropriate role."[10] Concerns were also expressed by the presidents of Pepperdine University, San Francisco Art Institute, The Master College, Biola University, Fresno Pacific College, and the Western State University College of Law.

From 1988, when WASC's Accrediting Commission for Senior Colleges and Universities adopted and implemented its diversity standard, until February 23, 1994, there was a barrage of criticism against the diversity standard. On February 3, 1994, the Faculty Senate of Stanford University in a unanimous resolution condemned WASC's policy on diversity and endorsed Stanford's President Gerhard Casper's position that WASC "is attempting to insert itself in an area in which it has no legitimate standing."[11] Steven B. Sample, president of USC, called the diversity proposal naive and hypocritical.[12] Thomas E. Everhart, president of Cal Tech, bluntly told WASC that its diversity statement was politically motivated and advised its drafters to "'stick to their knitting.'" [13] In December 1993, the Academic Council of the UC Academic Senate, without a dissenting vote passed a resolution expressing alarm over the "substantial threat to institutional autonomy" posed by the WASC report on diversity. Judith A. Merkel, representing Claremont McKenna College, in a letter to WASC wrote that "there is no clear linkage between educational quality and diversity."[14]

Before its meeting in February 1994, the Accrediting Commission endeavored to assuage its critics by declaring that WASC simply expects an institution to demonstrate its commitment to quality by "serious and thoughtful engagement with diversity," reported columnist George F. Will. This elicited a caustic comment from Will: "Do any people other than politically correct academics talk so pretentiously?"[15] The WASC standard for diversity went through a number of drafts, but as an editorial in the *Wall Street Journal* pointed out, the standard's essence remained the promotion of preferential treatment and multiculturalism.[16] Debra Saunders, a columnist for the *San Francisco Chronicle*, called WASC's diversity standard "hardball politics."[17] Peter Schrag of the *Sacramento Bee* called it "the stupid thing," because the standard "says nothing about encouragement of a diversity of ideas, outlooks, and approaches, which are among the classic fundamentals of higher education."[18] The focus of opposition was WASC's insistence that diversity is "inextricably linked" to excellence in education and that its agents can legitimately monitor an institution's commitment and progress in this matter.

Donald R. Gerth, president of CSU, Sacramento, and Chairman of the Accrediting Commission, endeavored to assure the critics "that accreditation will not be denied any college that is thoughtfully considering the matter of diversity in the context of its own institutional mission and values."[19] However, critics wanted a clear statement in the standards that diversity will not be used by the Commission "to undermine the autonomy or alter the mission of any institution."[20] This request, however, was not acceptable to WASC. Despite WASC's assurance that the diversity standard was benign, its critics were not reassured because of the zealotry of diversity proponents on the Commission and the past history of its accrediting activity. For instance, in 1990, the Commission placed on probation Westminster Theological Seminary, a small Presbyterian institution near San Diego, for, among other things, having an all-male, all-white Board of Trustees. The Seminary had to make accommodations to have its probation lifted.[21] Similar pressure for diversity was applied by WASC's visiting accreditation team on the Thomas Aquinas campus in Santa Paula when the team members wanted to have a special meeting with minority students of the campus in order to discuss "minority issues." The college refused this request on the grounds that its policy deals with students without regard to their race. Ultimately WASC relented and in March 1993 reaccredited the college. Given this background, the tenor of WASC's documents and the public statements of its officials left little doubt in the critics' minds that imposition of this standard would seriously erode the autonomy of individual institutions.

Notwithstanding these protestations, on February 23, 1994, in a meeting in San Francisco, the 15-member Commission unanimously voted to adopt the diversity standard (again).[22] It had letters of support from 92 schools— 14 schools formally opposed it. The dissenters included, among others, Stanford, USC, Cal Tech, Claremont, and Thomas Aquinas. Among the supporters was Chang-Lin Tien, chancellor of UC, Berkeley, who in a note to Professor John H. R. Polt explained his support: "My decision was based, in part, on assurances from the Accrediting Commission that accreditation will not be withheld on the grounds of diversity, thereby preserving institutional autonomy in these matters."[23]

One hopes that despite WASC's zeal for its own brand of diversity and its contradictory statements, it will allow individual institutions to develop and follow their own paths to provide quality education. In this controversy, enough public record has been generated that if WASC's diversity inspectors deny any institution accreditation on this ground it will once again become a public issue. Thus, to that extent, the principled opposition of Thomas Aquinas College to WASC's intrusion into the college's autonomy proved to be successful.

MANDATED PROPORTIONAL REPRESENTATION AT CALIFORNIA COMMUNITY COLLEGES

To our knowledge, the California Community College (CCC) system is the only statewide public entity that is required by state statute to hire its faculty and staff in proportion to its racial, ethnic, and gender representation in the state's adult population. In 1978, the Legislature passed Senate Bill 1620 requiring community colleges to develop affirmative action programs to hire underrepresented groups. In 1988, as previously stated, Assembly Bill 1725 was passed, which mandated diversity in the system's faculty and staff. For this purpose the statute set up a Faculty and Staff Diversity Fund "to address the goal that by the year 2005 the system's work force will reflect proportionately the adult population of the state" (Section 25). The statute also required the system's Board of Governors to report progress in reaching this goal. In the context of the controversy surrounding race- and gender-based preferences in public employment, public education, and public contracting generated by the California Civil Rights Initiative (CCRI), on March 30, 1995, the Board of Governors of the California Community Colleges asked the chancellor to review the system's affirmative action programs. Additionally, on June 1, 1995, Governor Pete Wilson issued an Executive Order (W-124-95) abolishing all state preferential programs based on race and gender that were directly under his executive branch. The governor asked state agencies to thoroughly review all other state affirmative action programs that were outside the scope of the executive branch and had statutory basis to ensure that they do not exceed federal law or state statutory requirements.

Responding to these developments, in September 1995, Thomas J. Nussbaum, presently Chancellor but then the General Counsel and Vice Chancellor for Legal Affairs, presented a comprehensive report on the system's affirmative action programs.[24] The report quoted the equal protection clause of the Fourteenth Amendment to the U.S. Constitution and similar guarantees provided by the California Constitution. It also cited various cases decided by the U.S. Supreme Court and the Courts of Appeals establishing the standards of "strict scrutiny" for racial and ethnic classifications, "intermediate scrutiny" for gender groupings, and "rational basis" test for other distinctions based on disability, age, or economic status.

Relying on the equal protection clause and the case law, the report concluded that the CCC's Faculty and Staff Diversity Fund was "problematic" because:

1. The "role model" theory for affirmative action was largely discredited by the Supreme Court in *Wygant* (1986).

2. "[T]he entire discussion of diversity in *Bakke* (1978) was dictum because the Court ultimately rejected the UC, Davis, admission program."

3. The California Legislature in setting up the diversity fund "did not conduct a detailed comparison between staffing rates and availability data." Hence, there's not adequate evidence that systematic discrimination had occurred.

4. There's not enough evidence to determine if the affirmative action plan was implemented only after race-neutral means had been genuinely tried.

5. The statutory goal that by the year 2005 the system's workforce will reflect proportionately the adult population of the state "is the kind of arbitrary provision which the [U.S. Supreme] Court struck down in *Croson* [1989]." It is particularly difficult to justify this goal because there has been no analysis to determine if certain groups are underrepresented.

After reviewing the impermissible aspects of the system's affirmative action program, the report concluded: "The foregoing analysis suggests that the Education Code provisions establishing the faculty and staff diversity program may be problematic from a constitutional standpoint." General Counsel Nussbaum's conclusion that the Faculty and Diversity Fund and the system's hiring goals and practices are "problematic" is obviously a deft understatement about a preference program the impermissibility of which is amply analyzed by this well researched report.

In fairness, it must be stated that the General Counsel's staff, as well as statisticians in the Chancellor's Office even earlier, had been cautioning the system's executives and managers not to use set-asides and to abandon the practice of using general population data for computation of proportionality and underrepresentation, especially for faculty recruitment.[25] However, as described by Frederick R. Lynch, the Chancellor, the affirmative action bureaucracy of the system, the president of the Board of Governors, and some of the District Chancellors and presidents of individual colleges were deeply committed to the idea that diversity and equity must be translated into proportional outcomes. Lynch described them as "militant moralists" following the political trend in the State Capitol.[26]

Following the example of a statutory requirement of proportionality in faculty and staff employment, in 1992, the Board of Governors required that the colleges should not only achieve proportional graduation rates but should also obtain equal student-transfer rates to universities.[27] Thus, the constitutional principle of equal protection of the law was transmuted into an ideology of equal outcomes mandated by the legislature and the education establishment. All of these developments occurred during a period of time when there was hardly any vocal political opposition to this policy and when affirmative action was in fact a mantra of the politically correct academicians and college administrators. Hiring data for full-time faculty for the years 1989 through 1993, cited by Victor A. Walsh and Thomas E. Wood, strongly suggested that white men were the victims of reverse discrimination, especially in social sciences and humanities.[28] This was particularly unfair to those who had served for years as part-time instructors with the hope and expectation that they would get full-time positions when available. In implementing Assembly Bill 1725, academic merit for hiring full-time faculty was often diluted by changing rank orders or by submitting unranked lists of finalists to the administration using "equivalency" degrees to satisfy minimum requirements and reinstating minorities who were initially screened out of the pool.[29] White men also suffered reverse discrimination in faculty internship programs. The impact of policies of preferences and proportionalism was somewhat mitigated due to the following: internal resistance, national-level court decisions, changed political climate, moderating influence of the Chancellor's legal and technical staff, and student demography.

1. *Internal Resistance*   On some campuses a few faculty members openly opposed the preference policy. Typically, they were tenured senior faculty who were willing to publicly speak against reverse discrimination.[30] The system's administrators recognized this resistance and often publicly remarked about it.

2. *National-level Court Decisions*   The judicial climate also played a part in dampening the zeal for preferences. Since 1989, the U.S. Supreme Court has issued a number of rulings severely restricting the permissible parameters of race and ethnic preferences. In fact, the Chancellor's General Counsel relied on these cases, particularly *Croson* (1989) and *Adarand* (1995), to warn the System that its present policies were "problematic."

3. *Changed Political Climate*   Especially in California, people now have far less tolerance for affirmative action preferences than they did in the past. Even liberal legislators and college bureaucrats recognize this seachange and have toned down their rhetoric in which essentially they used to define *equity* as "equal outcomes." Passage of the California Civil Rights Initiative in 1996 is the prime example of this political change.

4. *Moderating Influence of Chancellor's Staff*   In a staff capacity, legal experts can only advise, whereas line officials have charge of operations. The system's legal and technical staff did raise red flags against blatant preferences and advised the line officials to gather data on the qualified labor pool in the relevant labor markets for hiring purposes. There was tension between technical experts and ideological bureaucrats. This probably had a moderating influence on policies and operations.

5. *Student Demography*   Due to demographic changes, half the student population of CCC is already minorities. The system, however, seems to have given up the idea that it can achieve proportionality in transfer rates to universities. There are too many variables for the system to control in order to achieve that goal. In California's heterogeneous population, there are wide differences in cultural traditions, families' economic circumstances, and aspirations.

In 1996, the Board of Governors adopted some changes in regulations of Title V of the Education Code relating to affirmative action.[31] The goal of "proportional representation" in hiring was changed to "expected representation." But the new regulations also state that as early as 1983 there was evidence of underrepresentation of ethnic minorities, women, and people with disabilities, thereby implying that recruiters may have a justification for using these factors in their hiring decisions. Quite predictably, the Faculty Association CCC was critical of the General Counsel's Report of August 1995, which formed the basis of amendments to Title V regulations. The Association's legislative advocate said that affirmative action programs should not be dismantled based on threatened lawsuits.[32] Amendments to the regulations had a backdrop of three U.S. Supreme Court cases handed down at the end of the 1995 Court term: *Adarand v. Pena, Missouri v. Jenkins*, and *Miller v. Johnson*. In all three cases, the use of race-based preferences by the federal government was held to be unconstitutional because it failed to meet the strict scrutiny test. On July 7, 1995, Ralph Black, Assistant General Counsel of CCC, in a memorandum to the General Counsel sounded a cautionary note: "None of these cases dealt directly with an affirmative action employment program like that in place for community colleges, but . . . the Court's holdings may nevertheless have significant implications for our program."[33]

RACIALLY SEGREGATED CLASSES IN CALIFORNIA COMMUNITY COLLEGES

Over 35 of the 106 community colleges in California offered some courses, counseling, and mentoring programs exclusively for racial minorities. One such program, known as the "Puente Project," was designed exclusively for Hispanics, while the "Black Bridge Project" was for blacks only. In spring of 1994, Janice Camarena, a widowed mother of three young girls, enrolled in an English 101 course at San Bernardino Valley College. On January 19, 1994—the first day of class—the instructor asked her to leave the classroom because the class was reserved exclusively for blacks. On behalf of Camarena, the Pacific Legal Foundation, a nonprofit public interest law firm in Sacramento, sued the community college district, alleging that she suffered "humiliation, embarrassment, and extreme mental anguish when removed from class for no other reason than her race."[34]

The case could not have come at a worse time for the CCC. Its facts were stark and not contestable. A 26-year-old white mother of three young daughters (one of whom was half Hispanic) wishing to enroll in a college course to improve herself was denied admission and, consequently, deprived of her equal protection rights. This was particularly ironic in the tier of the state's higher education system that by statute is supposed to be "open" to all students who can benefit by it. Pacific Legal Foundation, long known for its vigorous efforts in support of constitutional protections, assigned the case to Robert J. Corry, a specialist in civil rights litigation. The case drew the attention of California Assemblymember Bernie Richter, Chair of the Budget Subcommittee on Education, who scheduled hearings on financial aspects of affirmative action programs. There was also a fierce political debate in California on the pros and cons of Proposition 209, which sought to outlaw discrimination as well as preferences in public employment, public education, and public contracting. The *Camarena* case was often cited by the supporters of Proposition 209 as an example of reverse discrimination that would be outlawed under the proposed law.

In June 1996, Chancellor David Mertes retired and was replaced by Thomas Nussbaum, hitherto the General Counsel, who in his August 1995 Report had warned about the "problematic" nature of the system's affirmative action programs. Given the confluence of these events and the indefensible nature of the "Black Bridge Program," in June 1996, the CCC system reached an agreement with Janice Ingraham (formerly Camarena) on the following terms:[35]

1. All academic and educational programs at the CCC (including the Black Bridge Program and the Puente Project) shall be open equally to all students regardless of race, color, national origin, or ethnicity.

2. Promotional materials on programs shall not include phrases such as "designed for African-American students" or "for Mexican-American students."

3. Colleges will not pair students with mentors or counselors based solely on their race or ethnicity of the students, mentors, or counselors.

4. The CCC system will hold workshops for informing teachers and administrators of hitherto race-exclusive programs about the terms of this agreement.

5. The CCC system shall pay $10,000 as costs and attorney's fees to the Pacific Legal Foundation.

6. The CCC system shall be prohibited from asking a student about his or her race unless required by federal and state law.

The agreement was viewed as having "broad implications" for all academic programs targeting minorities. It was also viewed as part of the nationwide controversy over affirmative action preferences.[36] Plaintiff's attorney Robert Corry called his client "a hero by any standard" who fought her case with energy and commitment and refused to be a victim.[37] Coincidentally, in the same month, Colorado's Attorney General Gale Norton said that she would probably ask public institutions of higher education to stop race-based admissions.[38] The Attorney General of Georgia had already warned his state colleges to do the same. Thus, the development in CCC was obviously a part of a national movement against affirmative action preferences.

RACE-BASED STUDENT ADMISSIONS PREFERENCES AT THE UNIVERSITY OF CALIFORNIA

Developments at UC, Berkeley

In 1989 the University of California, Berkeley, inaugurated its admissions plan under which the proportion of freshmen applicants granted admission strictly on academic criteria was increased from 40 percent to 50 percent. The increase was hailed by some observers who in the past were critical of the university's overemphasis on race and ethnicity in admissions decisions. However, as Stephen R. Barnett, Professor of Law at Berkeley, pointed out, because many of the applicants offered admission turn down the offer, under the revised system actual "yield" of applicants admitted on academic criteria would have increased from about 31 percent to 38 percent of the freshman class.[39] He also mentioned that other changes in Berkeley's admissions plan "will decrease by 22 percent, for a net loss of 10 percent, the number of students admitted primarily by academic criteria."[40] The Berkeley plan included a new category of "socioeconomic disadvantage," whose beneficiaries could not be counted against the affirmative action racial/ethnic "target groups." While the academic establishment at Berkeley was strengthening a regime of race and ethnic preferences in admissions, a coalition of minority students was demanding more diversity. On April 19, 1990, an estimated 100 students organized a protest strike in which stink bombs in many buildings led to the cancellation of dozens of classes. The protesters demanded immediate tenure for two minority professors and the hiring of at least one black professor each in English, Business Administration, Political Science, and History as "role models." The protesters also called for the immediate establishment of a bisexual, gay, and lesbian studies center; a multicultural center; and a Latino cultural center in order to remedy what the protestors alleged as "parochial" education at Berkeley.[41] In 1991, Berkeley also inaugurated an "American Cultures Breadth Requirement." At that time, this one course requirement could be met by courses offered by 30 different departments of the campus.[42] For a course to fulfill this requirement, it must take "substantial account" of at least three of the following five groups: African Americans, Native Americans, Asian Americans, Latinos, and European Americans. Three years earlier, in 1988, Stanford had also replaced its Western Culture requirement with one entitled "Culture, Ideas, and Values." These changes in the nation's two premier institutions alarmed many traditionalists who viewed them as examples of politically correct multiculturalism with its accompanying tendency to denigrate the values of western culture and its intellectual heritage. Dilution of academic criteria in admissions was criticized by some eminent Berkeley faculty members. For example, in 1990, Vincent Sarich, an anthropologist, said that the admissions policy has given Berkeley "two student populations whose academic levels barely overlap."[43] As evidence, he said that in 1987-1988, whites and Asians had a mean score of 1270 in the Scholastic Assessment Test (SAT), whereas Hispanics and blacks had a mean of about 1000. He said that minority students in more demanding courses and majors at Berkeley were not competitive with whites and Asians and, therefore, had higher dropout rates. Similar comments were also made by UC philosophy professor John Searle.

Berkeley's administration defended its admissions policy by pointing out that Berkeley, as well as other UC campuses, select their freshmen only from the top 12.5 percent of high school graduates and that by giving racial and ethnic preferences the university has not lowered its standards. Berkeley's chancellor, Ira Michael Heyman, insisted that the Supreme Court's decision in *Bakke* (1978) was the basis of these preferences and that ethnic diversity was only "one element in a range of factors" used for admission.[44] Interestingly enough, the chancellor, in quoting Justice Powell in *Bakke*, did not mention that the ethnic diversity criterion was in Justice Powell's dictum without concurrence by the other Justices.

By 1991, race and ethnic preferences in admissions and the push for "diversity" in academic programs were in full force and having some obvious and dramatic consequences. For one thing, on many campuses in California, separate graduation ceremonies were being held by different racial and ethnic groups. Some professors fretted that such separate celebrations were in fact divisive and were engendering ethnic hostility.[45] But the academic administrators supported these events as appropriate rituals to foster ethnic pride.

The success of Asians in achieving high grade point averages (GPAs) and SAT scores had a dramatic effect on their enrollment in UC, and by the fall of 1992 they outnumbered whites and became the largest ethnic group (Table 5.1). However, Asians as well as whites complained that UC's admissions policy favored other minorities with substantially lower academic records. There were news reports that campus officials defending race/ethnic preferences nevertheless feared potential "white backlash" and attributed a smaller number of white applicants to "white flight" from flagship campuses.[46] Despite preferences granted on the basis of race and ethnicity, in 1990, the freshman enrollment of blacks, Hispanics, and Native Americans in UC declined by 12.64 percent—from 4,614 to 4,031.[47] University officials attributed this decline—the first in a quarter of a century—to the fact that a greater number of those offered admission chose not to go to UC.[48] The university, defending its record, stated that from 1976 to 1990 the number of black, Hispanic, and Native American undergraduate students increased by 44 percent. This amount of progress did not satisfy the proponents of affirmative action preferences. Troy Duster, a Berkeley professor who had studied ethnic diversity on his campus, wanted the university to rely less on

Table 5.1
University of California, Berkeley, Percent of New Freshmen Registrants by Ethnicity: Selected Years

Ethnicity	1982	1984	1986	1988	1990	1992
Native American	0.3%	0.6%	0.9%	1.8%	1.4%	1.1%
Asian American	27.6	24.3	26.7	26.2	30.3	40.5
African American	5.6	7.3	8.2	10.8	6.9	6.2
Hispanic	5.7	8.8	12.4	18.6	20.9	14.0
White	57.7	55.7	45.6	37.0	34.6	30.8
Other	2.2	1.5	1.7	0.8	0.6	1.6
No Ethnic Data	0.9	1.7	4.5	4.9	5.5	5.9
Total Domestic	100.0	100.0	100.0	100.0	100.0	100.0

Source: Admissions and Enrollment, Office of Undergraduate Admissions, UC, Berkeley (figures rounded).

academic criteria such as GPA and SAT scores.[49] Pressure for greater enrollment of minority students was also being applied by several of the UC regents. Hispanic enrollment at Berkeley had dramatically increased as shown in Table 5.1.

In 1991, as discussed in Chapter 4, California Assembly Speaker Willie Brown, Jr., and Assemblymembers Tom Hayden and Barbara Lee sponsored bills that among other things called for public institutions of higher education to enroll and graduate by the year 2000 a student body proportionate to the racial and ethnic composition of the state's high school graduates. These radical legislative proposals were opposed by the California Association of Scholars—an affiliate of the National Association of Scholars—which includes many eminent scholars. Thus, within the university there arose a small but highly visible and articulate group of academicians opposed to political pressures for race- and ethnicity-based quotas for student admissions, graduation rates, and faculty recruitment.

In a newspaper opinion piece, Professor Barnett of Boalt Hall, Berkeley, pointed out that although whites represented about 52 percent of California's most recent high school graduates, their enrollment at Berkeley had fallen (from 45.6 percent in 1986) to 31 percent in 1992.[50] During the same period, enrollment of Asian Americans increased from 26.2 percent to 40.5 percent even though Asian Americans comprised only about 14 percent of California's recent high school graduates. Barnett attributed at least a part of the increase in Asian enrollment to the benefit they received from a new category of preference called "socioeconomic disadvantage status" (SES). This category went into effect at Berkeley in 1991 at the recommendation of a faculty committee chaired by Jerome B. Karbel, a professor of sociology. The committee required that 7.5 percent of the freshman class be chosen on this basis. This also helped Asian American applicants, who outnumbered whites five to one in the SES category. In 1991 and 1992, whites comprised only 10 percent and 8 percent, respectively, of this category.[51] Thus, whites were the only disfavored category in terms of affirmative action as well as SES policy.

In reviewing these data, it needs to be pointed out that just to be formally eligible for UC's nine campuses, applicants must be in the top one-eighth of their high school graduating class. In effect it means that an applicant must have a minimum GPA of 3.25. Even though the UC system has been able to accommodate all the eligible applicants, not all of them can gain admission to the campus of their choice. The demand for admission into UC's premier campuses of Berkeley and UCLA is far greater than the "seats" available. For example, in 1989, Berkeley had available only 3,500 seats for which 21,300 eligible students applied for the privilege of admission. Over 5,800 of these eligible students had straight A averages.[52] In 1991, among the applicants for Berkeley there were 8,400 straight A students. Between 50 percent and 60 percent of the admissions at freshmen level are based entirely on a combination of GPA and SAT scores. Several other supplementary categories included things such as disability, special talent, nontraditional, reentry, rural, and "special admits."[53]

Those who opposed race and ethnic preferences pointed out that the mean SAT scores of whites and Asians were about 285 points higher than those of African Americans and over 210 points higher than of Hispanics. Professor Vincent Sarich was reported to have written to the UC Board of Regents that 300 points on the SAT are worth four years of preparation and that, by admitting a large number of uncompetitive minority students, the university was subjecting them to a severe disadvantage in classroom performance.[54] While the opponents of racial preferences were providing hard data to substantiate their charge that UC was practicing a severe form of reverse discrimination against whites, the proponents of affirmative action preferences not only wanted the University to continue a race-based admission policy but, in fact, wished it to be enlarged to include other areas of education. For example, an affirmative action report for 1992-1993, submitted to the Academic Senate of the University of California, Santa Cruz, enthusiastically stated its priority: "To create class, race, ethnic, and gender equity, diversity goals need to reflect the demographic characteristics of the state. A visible commitment to equity through diversity must be made at every level of university administration, hiring, teaching, research, recruitment, retention, and staff services. We seek policies that will clearly implement this definition of diversity goals at the highest levels of the campus and systemwide administration."[55]

The report also listed sexual orientation as a demographic characteristic to be reflected in the hiring goals. The report wanted diversity goals to be broader than affirmative action goals, which it considered as "too narrow." It argued that new goals, for instance in faculty hiring, should not be related to percentage of market availability of the national doctoral pool. In the opinion of the Committee on Affirmative Action, "such a target only ratifies the race, class, and gender stratification inherent in current graduate programs and academic markets."[56] This manifesto seeking equality of results for all demographic groups by disregarding competition in the employment market as well as in student admissions was justified on the pretext of achieving "new standards of academic excellence."

UC campuses also instituted a system variously called "Appointments of Opportunity" or "Target of Opportunity Program," under which women or minorities were hired by waiving the normal search-and-appointment process for academic positions. UCLA's procedures provided that such appointments may be made "where there is substantial underrepresentation in the department, where the candidate has outstanding qualifications, and where the appointment meets a programmatic need."[57] There wasn't much public debate on the issue of this special program for minority and women faculty although privately some academicians thought that in some cases affirmative action preferences had played a role in retention, tenure, and promotion of faculty.

Open Challenge to Quotas and Preferences in UC

From 1989 to 1993, opposition to quotas in student admissions and legislative proposals for mandating college graduation rates in proportion to the demographic categories of California was fragmented and diffused. In 1993, John R. Searle, professor of philosophy at Berkeley, stated that white men were discriminated against in university admissions and faculty appointments. Then he predicted, "I believe the day will come when we will be deeply ashamed of having allowed it to occur, as we are now ashamed of previous forms of discrimination."[58] Opposition to reverse discrimination was already afoot.

Almost simultaneously in 1993, two white men, without collaboration, started a chain of events that ultimately led to the UC Regent's decision to bar race-based preferences in student admissions. Allan J. Favish, an attorney in Tarzana, California, after seeing a document of UCLA's Law School stating that race was a factor in some admissions, requested from the school data on race, GPAs, Law School Admission Test (LSAT) scores, and admissions decisions for the 1993 entering class. The school wrote him that the information requested was "unavailable."[59] However, he received the desired information after he filed a lawsuit under the California Public Records Act. The data demonstrated that in 1993 over 5,200 applicants competed for 350 slots at UCLA's Law School; among the rejected were 30 applicants who had a GPA of 3.5 or better and an LSAT score above the 92nd percentile. Of the 30 rejectees, 3 were Asians and the others were white or those who had declined to state their race (W/DS). There were other clear data that revealed favoritism toward blacks, Latinos, and Native Americans, many of whom had substantially lower academic records than those of their white counterparts. It is obvious that UCLA's Law School in 1993 was practicing egregious reverse discrimination as was Berkeley's Boalt Hall (as described early in Chapter 3).

When Jerry and Ellen Cook's son could not get admission into their hometown's UC, San Diego School of Medicine, they conducted a seven-year (1987-1993) statistical study of admissions criteria and acceptance rates of students belonging to different demographic categories. They discovered a huge difference in the academic preparation, as measured by GPA and Medical College Admission Test (MCAT) score, between minority students and nonminority students admitted to the UC San Diego School of Medicine. Figure 5.1 depicts this difference. It is true that, as in other disciplines, there are noncognitive factors in medical school admissions; however, those differences also exist in nonminorities. Thus, according to the Cooks, the probability of this distribution occurring without considerable racial prefer-

Figure 5.1
Profile of UCSD Undergraduates Admitted to the UCSD School of Medicine

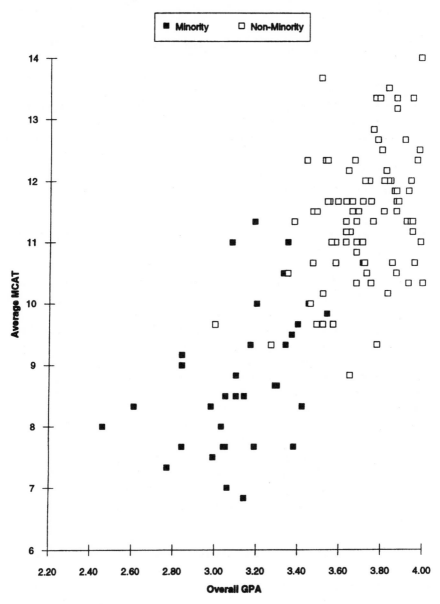

Source: Jerry and Ellen Cook.

ence is "less than one in one million, given the number of minority applicants."

The five UC medical schools at Davis, Irvine, Los Angeles, San Diego, and San Francisco received a total of 24,769 applications in the fall of 1993. Of these, about 12 percent were from minority applicants. However, of the 569 enrollees, 23 percent were minorities.[60]

Testifying before the Higher Education Committee of the California State Assembly in 1995, Ellen Cook (a statistician by profession) stated that from 1987 through 1993, students admitted under affirmative action programs in UC medical schools constituted about 32 percent of the applicants, yet they were only 13 percent of the applicant pool. "As a result of race-based admissions, the average GPA and MCAT score of accepted affirmative action students is in the lowest one percent of the other accepted students." [61] The affirmative action groups in this study included blacks, Native Americans, Mexican Americans, and people of Puerto Rican heritage but born in the United States.

It was Cook's study and complaint that aroused the initial interest and later commitment of Ward Connerly, a UC regent and a businessman in Sacramento. He persuaded the Board of Regents to ask for complete information from UC about its medical school's admissions policies. In their meeting on November 17, 1994, UC staff members still insisted "race is only one factor" in admission into the medical schools. However, they did not provide systemwide statistical analysis for medical schools. Connerly complained that UC officials had presented only one side of the story. He was quoted to have said sardonically, "Even the smallest pancake has two sides."[62] In order to justify its preference policy, UC kept repeating the eligibility gap of African Americans and Latinos. Under the Master Plan, the top 12.5 percent of California high school graduates are eligible for admission into UC. However, in 1995 only 5.1 percent of the blacks and 3.9 percent of Chicano/Latinos could meet that academic criterion, as compared to 32.3 percent of Asian Americans and 12.7 percent of whites.[63]

By spring of 1995, affirmative action policies in institutions of higher education were facing criticism in many parts of the country.[64] The University of California received the most intense scrutiny in the affirmative action program's history of over three decades. In 1994 at UCLA, in its applicant pool of 20,100 students, over 8,000 applicants had a 4.0 GPA. Among 60 percent of the freshman class admitted on academic merit, blacks made up 1.1 percent, Latinos 4.7 percent, whites 40 percent, and Asian Americans 48 percent. The second group of 40 percent was admitted through "supplementary" criteria that included race and family background as the major factors. Of all the blacks admitted, 88 percent of them got in through this route, as did 83 percent of the Latinos.[65] This category helped admit 5 percent of the white students and 17 percent of Asian Americans. Even though the admittees had a B+ average, blacks' average SAT score of 951 was 235 points below that of whites and 231 below Asians. Graduation rates in the 1990s also reflect differences in academic preparation: 80 percent of whites graduated, 77 percent of Asians, 60 percent of Latinos, and 52 percent of blacks.[66]

Throughout this controversy, UC continued to insist that race was only "one" factor in admissions and that the university must maintain racial and ethnic diversity. The university also insisted that it has only "goals" and not quotas for minority admissions. However, data issued by the UC, Berkeley, Office of Undergraduate Admissions demonstrated that even if socioeconomic status was factored in decision making, blacks would have constituted only 1.4 to 2.3 percent of Berkeley's freshman class instead of the 6.4 percent actually enrolled in 1994.[67] Similarly, Hispanics would have been only 5.6 to 10.0 percent instead of the 15.3 percent enrolled. Asian Americans and whites were the victims of reverse discrimination.

UC Regents Move to End Affirmative Action Preferences

When regent Ward Connerly announced his opposition to race-based preferences in admissions, several prominent politicians as well as a number of his colleagues on the Board of Regents severely criticized his position.[68] Anticipating a debate on this issue, UC's administration prepared a study on the potential impact on undergraduate enrollment if race and ethnicity are eliminated as admissions criteria and socioeconomic status is used in its place. On May 15, 1995, in a news release, the university claimed that such a change would result in an enrollment drop of 40 to 50 percent for blacks and 5 to 15 percent for Chicano/Latino students.[69] The enrollment of Asian Americans under the new system could rise between 15 to 25 percent, the number of white students would remain the same. The report also said that admitting students on socioeconomic status would result in a freshman class having lower academic preparation because of the correlation between socioeconomic status and academic performance. The report's main conclusions and methodology were strongly challenged by State Senator and Stanford law professor Tom Cambell, who correctly claimed that the computer simulation done by the University did "not prove what the university President claimed it did.[70] Cambell's analysis pointed out that the simulation kept race in the equation, rather than substituting socioeconomic factors for it. Furthermore, the simulation erroneously concluded that eliminating race would diminish academic qualifications of the enrollees.

The validity of UC's study was obviously dubious in view of the fact that in 1993 three-fourths of black undergraduates in UC were admitted on the basis of academic criteria and without the benefit of affirmative action.[71] Instead of admitting the fact that particularly for their leading campuses race and ethnicity were major considerations in their decisions for student admissions, the university's administration chose to misinterpret its own data. Peter Schrag, a longtime observer of the educational scene, called the report "a clumsy defense of existing race preferences. It combines strawman comparisons with statements so internally contradictory that they make your head spin."[72] It was sad to see a leading research university offer such a patently false study on a critical public policy issue of affirmative action and equal protection of the law.

While UC was insisting that it considered race and ethnicity only as plus factors in student admissions, a new study by Michael Lynch of Pacific Research Institute for Public Policy demonstrated that between 1991 and 1993 race- and ethnicity-based quotas and preferences were rampant at the UC medical schools. Minorities receiving preferences included blacks, American Indians, mainland Puerto Ricans, and Mexican Americans. This study concluded that if race and ethnicity were not major factors, the chance of so many designated minorities being admitted into the medical schools during the period under study would be "less than one in a million."[73] This was the same conclusion reached earlier by Jerry and Ellen Cook who studied the admissions rates when their son was denied admission into UC, San Diego School of Medicine.

On July 5, 1995, Ward Connerly, as a member of the University of California Board of Regents, submitted a written proposal to eliminate race-based hiring and contracting programs effective January 1, 1996, and race-based admissions practices effective January 1, 1997.[74] However, his proposal specifically stated that the university must continue those aspects of affirmative action that include advertising, outreach, and other such efforts to ensure adequate pools of qualified job applicants, students seeking admission, and contractors. (This was, of course, the original idea of affirmative action as contained in the Civil Rights Act of 1964.) He also called for increasing the percentage of students admitted effective January 1, 1997, solely on academic achievement from the existing 40 percent to 60 percent to a new rate of 50 percent to 75 percent.

In the press release, Connerly gave the following arguments for his proposal:

1. The university has been admitting some students who in fact did not meet even the minimum academic qualifications of UC.

2. Race was used not simply as a "bump" (plus factor) but as a major criterion on at least four campuses.

3. Because California has a diverse population, the university must reexamine its concept of "race problem" and discard its outmoded racial classifications.

4. Racial preferences were justified 30 years ago, but now we have reached a point of diminishing returns in race-based decision making.

5. An overwhelming majority of Americans oppose racial discrimination, and a climate of inclusion has been substantially achieved obviating the need for race-based decision making.

The reaction of Connerly's proposal was swift and intense. The Reverend Jesse Jackson decided to attend the Regents' meeting scheduled for July 20 and to speak against the repeal of affirmative action at that time.[75] Governor Pete Wilson, a supporter of Connerly's proposal, as President of the Board of Regents, also decided to attend the meeting. University of California President Jack Peltason weighed in by calling the proposed repeal a "grave mistake."[76] Four of the Regents publicly criticized Peltason for suggesting a delay in the vote to repeal preferences.[77]

The *Sacramento Bee*, in an editorial, stated that maybe a system of racial preferences in hiring and student admissions, particularly in the university's law schools and medical schools, "violates the Constitution, jeopardizes academic standards, and offends basic principles of fair play."[78] However, the paper considered the proposal premature and advised the Regents to commission an independent body to study the issue in greater depth. The *San Francisco Examiner*, anticipating a tough fight in the Board of Regents, called it "a political fight" and a "fuse burning down."[79] The *San Francisco Chronicle* advised the Board to maintain affirmative action preferences to promote racial diversity.[80] The California Association of Scholars, in a press release, stated that racial preferences in higher education lack legitimacy and cited various academic studies demonstrating "that a clear majority of students and faculty oppose race-based preferences in favor of race-blind alternative."[81]

On July 20, 1995, after a 12-hour meeting that included 6 hours of public testimony, the Board of Regents, by a vote of 15 to 10, abolished affirmative action preferences in student admissions, employment, and contracting. Those who spoke against the proposal included the Reverend Jesse Jackson and UC President Peltason. Governor Pete Wilson and Ward Connerly spoke in favor of the resolution to abolish preferences.[82] Outside and in the meeting itself, there were demonstrations, protests, and much rowdiness. Nevertheless, a historic decision of national importance had been made. The crux of the argument against affirmative action as used by the university was described by Governor Wilson in an opinion piece in a newspaper. He said that at Berkeley some minority applicants automatically qualify for admission while many Asian and white applicants with better academic records "don't even get the essays on their applications read."[83] Similarly, in 1994 at UC, Irvine, and UC, Davis, any "underrepresented" minority student meeting minimum academic eligibility requirements was automatically admitted while other ethnic minority applicants with better academic records were rejected simply "because they were not of politically correct ethnicity."

On the same page as Wilson's piece, an opposing viewpoint was given by Ralph C. Carmona, a UC regent who thought that replacing affirmative action by a "mythical meritocracy" would not serve California well because by the year 2000 about 60 percent of its high school graduates would be nonwhite.[84] These two viewpoints had, in fact, framed the issue that was finally resolved by the Board of Regents in favor of the meritocratic principle.

A week before the Regents' meeting, UC President Peltason tried to head off a negative vote by announcing a series of reviews and modifications of their affirmative action program.[85] They included ending of automatic admission of minorities at the Davis and Irvine campuses, review of the policy of admitting students who do not meet minimum academic standards of eligibility, ending of exceptions to normal search procedures for faculty hires, and ending of "special reading" of minority applications. However, the changes announced were too little, too late. After the Regents' vote, Berkeley Chancellor Chang-Lin Tien said that his campus can still achieve diversity without using race, gender, and ethnicity as criteria.[86] It is interesting to note that, to the authors' knowledge, not even the supporters of affirmative action during this whole controversy seriously argued whether the preferences practiced by the university were constitutionally permissible. As a matter of fact, the impermissibility of these practices was tacitly acknowledged by President Peltason when he introduced a series of modifications in order to avoid legal challenges. This tacit acknowledgment was duly noted by the press.[87] Another noteworthy development in the debate on this issue was widespread use of the word *preference* rather than the nebulous phrase *affirmative action*, which means different things to different people covering a variety of practices—legal and illegal.

NOTES

1. Western Association of Schools and Colleges, "Excerpts from the *Handbook of Accreditation*, July 1988" in "Statement on Diversity" (January 14, 1994), Appendix A.

2. Letters from James Q. Wilson to Stephen S. Weiner, December 18, 1990, p. 1; and February 27, 1991.

3. Letter from Stephen S. Weiner to James Q. Wilson, February 12, 1991, p. 3.

4. *Chronicle of Higher Education*, October 1991, quoted in: Linda Seebach, "Accreditation Standards Threaten Diversity of Opinion," *Los Angeles Daily News*, October 31, 1993.

5. Courtney Leatherman, "West Coast Accrediting Agency Hashes Out a Policy on Racial Diversity for Campuses," *Chronicle of Higher Education*, November 18, 1992, A15, A16.

6. Letter from Thomas Dillion, Kevin Kolbeck, and Richard Ferrier to the National Advisory Committee on Accreditation and Institutional Eligibility Accrediting Agency Evaluation Branch, Office of Postsecondary Education, United States Department of Education, Washington, D.C., July 29, 1991.

7. California Association of Scholars, *Accreditation and Diversity: A Critique of WASC's "Statement on Diversity"* (Berkeley, CA: California Association of Scholars, February 3, 1994), 59 pp.

8. Ibid., "Abstract."

9. Letter from Martin Trow to WASC Committee on Diversity, November 3, 1993, p. 2.

10. Letter from Raymond A. Paredes to Sister Magdalen Coughlin, Commission Committee on Diversity, January 25, 1993, p. 1.

11. Andy Dworkin and Colleen Krueger, "Casper, Fac Sen. Reject Statement on Accreditation," *Stanford Daily*, February 4, 1994, 1; also see: K. L. Billingsley, "Stanford Faculty Votes Unanimously Against Proposed Diversity Statement," *Washington Times*, February 5, 1994; *Chronicle of Higher Education*, February 16, 1994, A23.

12. Ralph Frammolino, "Getting Grades for Diversity?" *Los Angeles Times*, February 23, 1994, A1, West Ventura edition.

13. Ibid., A1, A15.

14. Letter from Judith A. Merkel to Dr. Steven Weiner, November 4, 1993.

15. "Accreditation Board vs. Academic Freedom in Battle over Diversity," *Sacramento Bee*, February 14, 1994, B7.

16. Editorial, "A Test of Riley," *Wall Street Journal*, February 22, 1994; also see: "WASC's More Than Academic Questions," *Washington Times*, November 11, 1993, A18.

17. Debra J. Saunders, "Thought Police, Diversity Patrol," *San Francisco Chronicle*, November 12, 1993, A22.

18. Peter Schrag, "How They Evaluate Colleges," *Sacramento Bee*, December 8, 1993, B6.

19. Donald R. Gerth, *Wall Street Journal*, January 26, 1994, A15 (Letter to the Editor).

20. Kevin D. Kolbeck (Dean of Thomas Aquinas College), *Wall Street Journal*, February 23, 1994, A21 (Letter to the Editor).

21. Editorial, "The Diversity Standard," *Wall Street Journal*, December 29, 1993, 8.

22. Debra J. Saunders, "Diversity Police Run Amok," *San Francisco Chronicle*, February 25, 1997, A22; also see: Robert D. Dávila, "Colleges to Get Diversity Rating," *Sacramento Bee*, February 25, 1997, B4.

23. Letter from Chang-Lin Tien to Professor John H. R. Polt, March 10, 1994.

24. Chancellor's Office, California Community Colleges, "Legal Analysis of Affirmative Action Programs in the California Community Colleges" (Sacramento, CA: Chancellor's Office, California Community Colleges, August 1995); also see: Kit Lively, "Cal. 2-Year Colleges, Eyeing Law, May Adjust Affirmative Action," *Chronicle of Higher Education*, October 6, 1995, A31.

25. Frederick R. Lynch, *Diversity Machine: The Drive to Change the White Male Workplace* (New York: The Free Press, 1997), pp. 241, 245, 263.

26. Ibid., p. 240

27. Ibid., p. 239.

28. Victor A. Walsh and Thomas E. Wood, Bakke *and Beyond: A Study of Racial and Gender Preferences in California Public Higher Education* (Berkeley, CA: California Association of Scholars, February 27, 1996), pp. 57-58.

29. Ibid., p. 56.

30. See, for example: Linda Seebach, "This Affirmative Action Doesn't Cut It," *Contra Costa Times*, August 25, 1996.

31. Thomas J. Nussbaum, Acting Chancellor, "Revisions to Affirmative Action and Nondiscrimination Regulations." (Amendments effective June 30, 1996, of Title V of the *California Code of Regulations*.)

32. Kit Lively, "Cal. 2-Year Colleges, Eyeing Law, May Adjust Affirmative Action," *Chronicle of Higher Education*, October 6, 1995, A31.

33. Memorandum from Ralph Black to Tom Nussbaum, "Re: Recent Supreme Court Decisions Regarding Affirmative Action." July 7, 1995, cover page (includes three and one-half pages of analysis of three cases).

34. *Janice Camarena v. San Bernardino Community College, et al.*, Case No. 95AS01512 (March 16, 1995). Filed in the Superior Court of the State of California for the County of Sacramento. The lawsuit removed to the U.S. District Court for the Eastern District of California, CIV-S-95-589 MLS GGH.

35. "Settlement Agreement and Release of All Claims," by and between Janice Ingraham (formerly Janice Camarena), Board of Governors of the California Community Colleges, and David Mertes, Chancellor, July 19, 1996.

36. Ken Chavez, "2-Year Colleges Agree to Bar Minority-Targeted Programs," *Sacramento Bee*, July 12, 1996.

37. Robert J. Corry, "Student Helps Bring Equality to Classroom," *San Bernardino Sun*, July 18, 1996.

38. Patrick Healy, "Cal. Colleges Will Stop Designing Some Classes for Specific Ethnic Groups. In Colorado, Attorney General Urges Colleges to Stop Considering Race in Admissions," *Chronicle of Higher Education*, July 26, 1996, A26.

39. Stephen R. Barnett, "Berkeley Plan: More of the Same, Only Worse," *Wall Street Journal*, October 20, 1989, A15 (Letter to the Editor).

40. Ibid.

41. Debra Levi Holtz, "Class Boycott at UC Berkeley Pushed by Minority Coalition," *San Francisco Chronicle*, April 20, 1990, A4.

42. Gregory Stephens, "UC Berkeley Launches Multicultural Requirement," *San Francisco Chronicle*, August 30, 1991, A25.

43. Vincent Sarich, "The Cost of UC's Admissions Policies," *San Francisco Chronicle*, June 16, 1990, A16. For similar comment by John Searle, see: Ben Wildavsky, "UC Berkeley Weighs Costs of Affirmative Action Policy," *San Francisco Chronicle*, May 16, 1995, A1.

44. Ira Michael Heyman, "Ethnic Diversity at UC Berkeley," *San Francisco Chronicle*, June 16, 1990, A16.

45. Diane Curtis, "Minority Students Hold Their Own Graduations," *San Francisco Chronicle*, June 1, 1991, A9.

46. Carl Irving, "New Minority Status for Whites at Cal," *San Francisco Examiner*, June 23, 1991, A1.

47. Marc Sandalow, "Minority Enrollment Drops at UC. 12.6 Percent Decline Among Blacks, Hispanics, and Native Americans Is First in 25 Years," *San Francisco Chronicle*, June 17, 1991, A15.

48. Diane Curtis, "UC Claims Rise in Minorities on Campuses. Figures Are Misleading, Some Regents Claim," *San Francisco Chronicle*, June 21, 1991, A19.

49. Sandlow, "Minority Enrollment Drops at UC."

50. Stephen R. Barnett, "Perspective on the University of California: Who Gets In? A Troubling Policy," *Los Angeles Times*, June 11, 1992.

51. University of California, Berkeley, Office of Undergraduate Admissions, "Category S.E.S. (Socioeconomic Status) Table of Ethnicity (Based on Statements of Intent to Register), Fall 1991 and Fall 1992" (Berkeley, CA: University of California, October 9, 1992).

52. Karen Paget, "Diversity at Berkeley: Demagoguery or Demography?" *American Prospect*, Spring 1992, 108.

53. University of California, Berkeley, Office of Undergraduate Admissions, "Freshman by Complemental Group" (Berkeley, CA: University of California, October 9, 1992), p. 91.

54. Linda Seebach, "UC Admission Policies Fostering Racism," *Daily News*, May 2, 1993, 3.

55. University of California, Santa Cruz, "Committee on Affirmative Action, Report for 1992-93" (Santa Cruz, CA: University of California, November 15, 1993), p. 1.

56. Ibid.

57. University of California, Los Angeles, "Academic Affirmative Action Guidelines" (Los Angeles, CA: University of California, 1994), Appendix 12, p. 156.

58. John R. Searle, "Is There a Crisis in American Higher Education," *Bulletin: The American Academy of Arts and Sciences*, January 1993, 25-26.

59. Allan J. Favish, "Preferential Admissions at UCLA Law," *Daily News*, December 11, 1994, 5.

60. Erin Allday, "Admission Criteria under Fire," *Daily Californian*, November 18, 1994, 1-2.

61. Ellen Cook, Testimony before the Higher Education Committee of the California State Assembly (April 4, 1995).

62. James Richardson, "Regents Air Views on Minority Admissions," *Sacramento Bee*, November 18, 1994, A4.

63. University of California, Testimony on Senate Constitutional Amendment 10 (March 28, 1995).

64. See: "Affirmative Action on the Line," *Chronicle of Higher Education*, April 28, 1995, A11-A33.

65. Christopher Shea, "Under UCLA's Elaborate System, Race Makes a Big Difference," *Chronicle of Higher Education*, April 28, 1995, A12.

66. Ibid., A12, A13.

67. Sarah Lubman, "Campuses Mull Admissions without Affirmative Action," *Wall Street Journal*, May 16, 1995, B1.

68. For opposing viewpoints, see: Ward Connerly, "UC Must End Affirmative Action," *San Francisco Chronicle*, May 3, 1995, A19; William K. Coblentz, "UC Affirmative Action Benefits All," *San Francisco Chronicle*, May 12, 1995, A25 (Coblentz is an attorney and former Chairman of the UC Board of Regents).

69. University of California, Office of the President, "Media Advisory," May 15, 1995; also see: James Richardson, "UC Chief Sees Big Drop in Blacks if Admission by Race Is Halted," *Sacramento Bee*, May 16, 1995, A3.

70. Tom Cambell, "UC Admission Study Prepared for Regents Meeting Challenged," document prepared by California Senator Tom Campbell and staff, July 17, 1995, p. 1.

71. James Richardson, "UC Regents Find Answers Elusive in Affirmative-Action Debate," *Sacramento Bee*, May 20, 1995, B1.

72. Peter Schrag, "Who's UC 'Eligible'?" *Sacramento Bee*, May 24, 1995, B6.

73. Michael Lynch, "Race-Based Admissions at University of California Medical Schools" (San Francisco, CA: Pacific Research Institute for Public Policy, June 1995), p. 1.

74. Ward Connerly, Press Release, July 5, 1995. For newspaper accounts, see: James Richardson, "UC Regent Submits Plans. Racial Preference Would Be Barred in Admission, Hiring," *Sacramento Bee*, July 6, 1997, A5; Pamela Burdman, "Regent's Idea to Drop UC Race Preferences," *San Francisco Chronicle*, July 6, 1995, A1.

75. James Richardson, "Wilson, Jesse Jackson to Face Off on UC Affirmative Action," *Sacramento Bee*, July 8, 1995, A7.

76. James Richardson, "Don't Scrap Affirmative Action, Regents Urged by UC President," *Sacramento Bee*, July 11, 1995, B5.

77. Edward Epstein, "Regents Hit UC President on Race," *San Francisco Chronicle*, July 15, 1995, A1.

78. Editorial, "Race Preferences at UC," *Sacramento Bee*, July 10, 1995, B4.

79. Dexter Waugh, "Tough Vote for Regents. Decision Looms on Affirmative Action," *San Francisco Examiner*, July 16, 1995, C1, C5.

80. Editorial, "Vote to Uphold UC Affirmative Action," *San Francisco Chronicle*, July 19, 1995, A18.

81. California Association of Scholars, Press Release, July 18, 1995.

82. For accounts of the regents' meeting, see: James Richardson, "UC Kills Affirmative Action," *Sacramento Bee*, July 21, 1995, A1 and A18; Susan Yoachum and Edward Epstein, "UC Regents Wrestle with Preferences," *San Francisco Chronicle*, July 21, 1995, A1, A16.

83. Pete Wilson, "Present System Isn't Fair—And Isn't Working," *San Francisco Chronicle*, July 20, 1995, A23.

84. Ralph C. Carmona, "UC Should Not Be Caught Up in Partisan Politics," *San Francisco Chronicle*, July 20, 1995, A23.

85. Scott Jaschik, "U. of California to Limit Racial Preferences in Admissions, Hiring," *Chronicle of Higher Education*, July 21, 1995, A25.

86. Kit Lively and others, "Affirmative-Action Aftermath," *Chronicle of Higher Education*, August 4, 1995, A18.

87. See, for example: Jaschik, "U. of California to Limit Racial Preferences;" Editorial, "UC: The Politics Came First," *Sacramento Bee*, July 22, 1997, B6.

6

⤳

The California Civil Rights Initiative: Proposition 209

By 1991, the enforcement apparatus of affirmative action preference had secured a tight grip on institutions in both the private and the public sectors. Politicians were acquiescent, or if they had misgivings about preferential policies, cowed into silence, as were corporate leaders who were often harassed by bureaucratic enforcers. Also the abandonment of civil rights by the elites, as defined by individual rights and equality before the law, left a vacuum in which a grievance industry thrived and in which assorted race agitators exploited both the public and the private sectors without restraint.

All the while, the majority of people, who had never had the least say in deciding the country's racial and ethnic policies over the previous 30 years, grew ever more uncomfortable with the regime that increasingly touched people's lives on all levels. Many asked the question: "If people should be treated equally regardless of their color, sex, or ethnic background, then why is it that I am passed over for employment, promotion, admission to a prestigious university, or a public contract when people less qualified, or with a higher bid on the contract than mine, are advanced over me because they are black or Hispanic or female?" For example, in 1993, 5,000 white men were told that they could not take the entrance test for the job of firefighter in Los Angeles because the department already had enough white men. Not all of those applicants would have passed that test, and among those who did, not all would have passed subsequent tests for the job. And among those hired, some would surely not have stayed through their probation period, while some would have dropped out. Yet refusing 5,000 applicants the opportunity of even taking the entrance exam solely because of their race and sex meant that 5,000 men were automatically made victims of racial and sex discrimination. Examples in other public-sector jobs and in public contracting were numerous, and the gap between what people thought was fair and what was actually happening to them grew ever more apparent.

The problem, however, was not restricted to white men. Many white women in such female-dominated jobs as teaching also felt the sting of re-jection because of race. Among such women, one heard accusations that those promoted before them because of race or ethnic identity were less qualified than those passed over. And it was not just a matter of white-Anglo against blacks and Hispanics. Asians had already complained of being pushed aside in the University of California (UC) and in San Francisco's elite Lowell High School for lower-scoring students of all other races and ethnic groups. The time, therefore, was coming for an assessment of the situation and a badly needed corrective. It was in the university that action would begin—action that would mature into the California Civil Rights Initiative, later to become Proposition 209, which would change the terms of debate and which would augment a drive toward a more equitable system within the country.

THE CORRUPTION OF THE UNIVERSITIES

Race riots of the 1960s cowed liberals, emboldened militants, and marginalized black civil rights organizations. These acts of violence contrib-uted to the eventual turning of elites away from a national consensus based on core principles and toward what has become an illiberal vision in sup-port of an antiliberal regime. An extension of the riot mentality from the street into the university was an important phase in this process. It started with protests at UC, Berkeley, San Francisco State, and New York's Colum-bia University; yet as Charles Sykes observed "it was the Ivy League that was ultimately to set the pace in the retreat of reason," a retreat that ulti-mately set the tone for colleges and universities across the country.[1]

The New Left–Black Militant Coalition

Violent black militants were joined by white radicals, who billed them-selves as the New Left, in launching this assault on the trend-setting univer-sities and, via these institutions, the entire nation. Black militants focused on heightened racial consciousness and violent attacks on white society, while the ideological formulation of the New Left was phrased, at least superfi-cially, in Marxist terms. Yet both wings of this assault on the university and on American values were more like European fascism than anything else.

Peter L. Berger observed in 1970 that unlike Marxists the New Left had no positive view of the future. And like their fascist predecessors, the New Left was simply, and violently, against the society of which it was a part and which it hated with a passion. What the New Left, like black militants, railed against were stability, capitalism, intellectualism, and rationality, claiming that liberal democracy was a fraud and rationality was a prop for an evil status quo. Like the fascists before them, the New Left–black militant coalition dehumanized its enemies and advocated violence against them.

A central feature of fascist movements was nationalism, which was indeed a defining force for black militants. Although the New Left was not nationalist in the same way, Berger pointed out that it exhibited a "vicarious nationalism," as seen in its "uncritical identification with black nationalism, not even shirking from its anti-Semitic overtone (today no longer an undertone), and vicarious solidarity with the virulent nationalisms of the Third World."[2] A defining feature of fascism, however, that was missing in both wings of the antiliberal coalition of the 1960s was authoritarianism. Berger suspected, however, that the anti-authoritarian element might have been overcome if a charismatic figure had arisen to exploit the more populist elements of New Left rhetoric.

The main target of the New Left–black militant coalition was traditional liberalism. Robert Bork, a professor at Yale University Law School in the 1960s, said that the radicals left him pretty much alone because his conservative views were well known and presumably so much in the minority that they presented no real obstacle to the radicals. In the case of his colleague constitutional scholar Alexander Bickel, however, it was quite different. Bickel, a liberal and then a law clerk for Justice Felix Frankfurter, was instrumental in achieving the liberal *Brown v. Board of Education* decision. Yet Bickel "was harassed regularly and hung in effigy in the law school courtyard during alumni weekend" for "trying to uphold standards of reason and civilized discourse and because he disapproved of the mob."[3]

The assault on the university was an assault on the liberal ideology that dominated that institution and on the very concept of a liberal democratic society, which at that time still defined the national consensus that the New Left–black militant coalition wished to destroy. What is so sad about the whole thing is that the radicals won so quickly and so easily. This was partly because some faculty members were in sympathy with the radicals and supported them. In fact, the university has always stood somewhat aloof from the society that succors it, and its faculty has for a long time been subject to intellectual fads and enthusiasms that are often at odds with the reality around them. This is infused with no little measure of snobbism. Under these conditions, some faculty support for the radical assault on the university was to be expected.

Another reason for the rapid capitulation of university faculty and administration was simple fear. Many responsible for running the university accepted the excuses given by the New Left and the black militants for their demands as a cover for buying peace at any cost. A far more pervasive reason, however, was that many in the university were unsure of liberal democracy and did not know how to defend it when the time came, especially when the assault was mounted with such violence and in the name of the very goals that liberals had so far pursued with such success. Whatever the mix of factors, the universities caved in with little resistance. Robert Bork, looking back over this sorry chapter in the history of higher education, said, "only institutions that were already soft, alienated from the surrounding society, without belief in themselves and the worth of what they did would have surrendered so easily and so completely."[4]

The violent phase of the 1960s came to an end in the universities. Yet the violence let loose by the race riots of the 1960s continued on the streets in what Fred Siegel called a "rolling riot," namely "an explosion in crime that has only now begun to subside in some cities."[5] This is just one of the ugly legacies of that unsettling period in American history. Another is that the antiliberal movement of the 1960s split into a number of single-issue groups (feminists, Hispanic grievance groups, animal rights activists, etc.). These groups spread outward, successfully subverting (sometimes with little effort) such organizations as old-line civil rights groups like the NAACP (National Association for the Advancement of Colored People), the Urban League, the ACLU (American Civil Liberties Union), and even groups unrelated to civil rights, such as the YWCA (Young Women's Christian Association), and gradually setting the cultural tone in varying degrees (depending on the social class) throughout the entire society. This was greatly facilitated by the take-over of many of the wealthiest philanthropic organizations by those on the cultural left. These foundations, unaccountable to anything except their own agendas, have lavishly funded what was once New Left and other militant groups to help create and sustain the grievance industry and to mainstream their illiberal ideas.

What these allied single-issue groups all have in common is the vision of the 1960s, which is antirational, antidemocratic, and antiliberal and which espouses a reductionist world view in which everything is narrowed to the single dimension of power. Italian Marxist Antonio Gramsci has called the infiltration of formal institutions by radical groups "the long march through the institutions to capture the culture." The theory is that a modern society can be changed by radicals once they have gained control of formal institutions (the long march) where radicals can then replace the guiding visions of the old order with a vision of society that supports and rationalizes the kind of system they intend to impose from above.

The New Left–black militant coalition has come a long way in capturing the university once the feeble resistance of the liberal elite was broken in the 1960s. By the 1970s, former radicals and those who shared their perspective to one degree or another had evolved into a loose confederation of ideas known variously as the "cultural left," "multiculturalists," and advocates of "diversity." In their most insistent and self-assertive form, they are called "postmodernists" and "deconstructionists." These are advocates of an ideology, or in some cases only a vague set of notions, based on a romantic notion of cultural relativity and radical egalitarianism, which aims at (or acquiesces in) replacing the present collective identity of a unified nation with a utopian and unworkable vision in which no one language or culture stands in a position higher than any other. The image is one of a colorful ethnic mosaic in which all celebrate their separate identities with government subsidies.

A modern nation, however, requires a common medium of discourse that all its citizens master and a common "conceptual currency" (as anthropologist Ernest Gellner calls it)—a shared language on which a consensus for public policy can be reached and maintained.[6] "Multiculturalism" throws those realities in the face of consensus by advocating what amounts to government-subsidized balkanization. This is seen today not only in separate graduation ceremonies and living facilities on university campuses, but in revisionist textbooks and curricula in public schools. However, it is evident not just in the university and public schools, but increasingly in the top echelons of business. In this regard David Rieff has noted that "the more one reads in academic multiculturalist journals and in business publications, the more one contrasts the speeches of CEOs and the speeches of noted multiculturalist academics, the more one is struck by the similarities in the way they view the world."[7] It may also be seen in the influence of "diversity consultants" originally hired by business to buy peace in the workplace, but who have become an integral part of corporate cultures everywhere.[8] Multiculturalism, therefore, is not just a harmless academic philosophy contained in the university, but a corrosive ideology in direct competition with the liberal vision that has long defined so successfully the American nation.

The National Association of Scholars

In an effort to oppose the corruption of the U.S. system of higher education, two New York academics, Steven Balch and Herbert London, formed in the 1980s an organization that they called the National Association of Scholars (NAS). Balch soon recruited an impressive cadre of scholars from the liberal tradition, many of international stature and some from the ideological left who were committed to reasoned scholarship—scholars who felt it was time to strike back and, if possible, recapture the academy. As a professor of anthropology at California State University, Hayward, Glynn Custred was asked to help organize a chapter of the NAS in California. Phillip Siegelman, professor of political science at San Francisco State University, took the lead in this effort and by the 1990s had established a branch of the NAS in California, which was called the California Association of Scholars (CAS). Its first president was University of California, Berkeley, political scientist Aaron Wildavsky. Its Board of Directors included such scholars as former Harvard University political scientist, later a faculty member at UCLA, James Q. Wilson (who is still a member of the Board of Directors) and John

Bunzel, former president of San Jose State University, former member of the U.S. Civil Rights Commission, and a senior fellow at the Hoover Institution.

The NAS (CAS) views the university as a free marketplace of ideas where rational debate is central and where teaching and research, not political indoctrination, define the mission of the institution. The NAS (CAS) is thus dedicated to promoting rational discourse in the university. It also opposes politicization of the curriculum and political correctness that stifles debate. It became clear, however, that the organization could not win back the university by fighting solely within the institution. It had to maintain a presence in the university to show that the institution was not irredeemably lost. The only way to reclaim the academy, however, was to outflank the faculty and the administration by calling on those whom the university serves to express their opinion in regard to issues of importance not only to the university, but to society as a whole.

One such issue was counting everything by race—whether in the curriculum, the faculty, or the university staff or in the police and fire departments, state and local governments, or public contracting. This issue was, in fact, so central that it would be addressed sooner or later either in the rational manner advocated by CAS or, if left to the drift of history, very likely in a manner that would draw American society closer to the Balkans, Lebanon, and Northern Ireland than anyone would want.

THE FAILURE OF REPRESENTATIVE GOVERNMENT

There was only one means available to address this issue, and that was the initiative process. This was brought home with particular force in 1991 when the Speaker of the California Assembly (now mayor of San Francisco) Willie Brown introduced a bill that would have mandated much of what was already practice in the universities. Willie Brown's bill was actually an offshoot of a much more ambitious project introduced the year before by one-time student radical and then member of the California Assembly Tom Hayden. Hayden's plan was to change the entire legal framework in which California's system of higher education operated. His bill, however, was gutted, and its various provisions were farmed out to other Democrats in the Legislature for introduction as separate bills. Willie Brown was assigned what amounted to the heart of Hayden's former legislation, which he introduced as AB 2150.

The purpose of this bill was to increase the number of minority students graduating from the state's publicly funded colleges and universities. The bill would have required that "Each segment of California public higher education [the community colleges, the California State University system, and the University of California] in conjunction with the public schools, shall strive to approximate, by the year 2000, a diverse student body which mirrors the composition of recent high school graduates, both in first-year classes and subsequent college and university graduating classes, for individuals from historically and currently underrepresented or economically disadvantaged groups."

The way to address "underrepresentation" is to ask why there is a disparity in enrollment and college performance among the races in the first place and what (if anything) can be done to change this. This is not the kind of problem solving in which the grievance industry, "multiculturalists," and Willie Brown were interested. Instead, Brown in his bill stipulated that "each of the governing boards shall hold faculty and administrators accountable for the success of the institution in achieving equity in the areas under their purview." There was no provision in that bill for funding the massive remediation that would have been necessary if such an undertaking were to be carried out in a meaningful way, nor was there any provision to help schools qualify minorities for college. Brown's bill simply mandated by law that it be done. To put some teeth in it, he went on to require that the governing boards "shall ensure that contributions toward educational equity and improvement in faculty, staff, and student diversity are incorporated, and granted significant consideration with other factors, in the performance evaluations of administrators with diversity and educational equity responsibilities," which means most, if not all, of the administration. This would have placed administrators under heavy pressure, for if they wished to protect and enhance their careers, they would have to come up with some way to show the required results. Or to put it more bluntly, as John Leo did in *U.S. News and World Report*, if administrators were to ignore the law, their jobs would be on the line.[9]

If a *quota* is a specific numerical proportion (in this case the number of minorities graduating from the state's high schools) designed to attain a specific outcome (graduation at the same rate from the state's colleges and universities) that must be reached by a given date (the year 2000) with consequences for those in authority if the goal is not reached ("significant consideration" in "performance evaluations of administrators"), then Willie Brown's bill must be considered a blatant attempt to mandate a graduation quota based on race and ethnicity.

There was no mention of the bill anywhere in the press, there was no opposition to it (except from the CAS), and there was no discussion of it on the floor. The Assembly passed the legislation on a straight party-line vote (Democrats "yes," Republicans "no") and was vetoed by Republican Governor Pete Wilson. With a Democratic governor in office (or even a different Republican governor), this outrageous bill would have quietly become law in California. The issue was by no means dead for the proponents of admissions and graduation quotas. They simply geared up for a try the following year. Their expectation, given the track record of such outrageous actions over the past 30 years, was that they would eventually win as they had so many times before. Nothing better illustrated the need for an initiative than this.

THE INITIATIVE PROCESS IN CALIFORNIA

The initiative process was introduced in California in response to a period in U.S. history when the heads of large corporations "tended not only to despise the politicians, many of whom they easily corrupted, but also to feel contempt for the government itself."[10] In fact, no other state was more subservient to the pressures of big business, in this case the Southern Pacific Railroad, than was California. As historian James Bryce observed, nowhere else were the politics and economy "so much at the mercy of one powerful corporation" than they were in California.[11]

The reform movement from 1900 to 1920, embodied in the Progressive Party and Governor Hiram Johnson, was directed toward breaking the stranglehold that this enormous business interest held on representative government. The reformers also had great faith in the efficacy of democracy, and in 1911 they instituted the initiative process so that the people could play a more direct role in their government. During the first 30 years, the initiative was used to counter the corruption that pervaded California politics. By the 1950s, however, California had developed an honest and efficient state government. From then until the 1970s, the initiative process was used only sparingly.

In the 1970s, however, use of the process once again increased as representative government failed to address issues of concern to the people. One of the most important of these issues was escalating property taxes, which the legislature consistently refused to address. In an effort to deal with this problem, Howard Jarvis and Paul Gann organized a grassroots movement, supported by homeowners' groups and funded by small donations, that qualified a measure for the 1978 election designed to bring rising property taxes under control.

That measure was known as Proposition 13, and to the very end almost all politicians resisted it, as did labor, business organizations, and the educational establishment along with such groups as the League of Women Voters, Common Cause, and even the conservative California Taxpayers Association. In short, it was the entire political elite against the people. The people came to the polls in huge numbers, nearly 70 percent of registered voters, and passed the measure by a margin of nearly two to one. This is what the initiative process was meant to do, and that indeed is what it did on the issue of property tax.

Another problem in California was the hold that professional politicians maintained on the legislature. It was reasoned that the legislature could be brought closer to the people—and, therefore, could be more responsive to their needs—if the terms of legislators could be limited. This spawned yet another popular initiative, Proposition 140, which placed severe term limits on the state Assembly and the Senate. One of the greatest effects of this measure was to end the hold of Willie Brown, who had dominated the Assembly for many years. It is still not clear, however, if the drawbacks of such a move will outweigh its benefits, yet the only chance of finding out was through the initiative process.

The California Civil Rights Initiative

Glynn Custred tried to convince members of CAS that the initiative process should be used in the struggle against balkanization in the university and elsewhere. There was no response to this suggestion at the time except from Aaron Wildavsky, who said that it was a bold idea. Others thought it simply bizarre. One day in 1991, Aaron Wildavsky received a letter from a CAS member suggesting the same action. Custred got the member's telephone number and called him. That member is Thomas Wood, a UC, Berkeley, Ph.D. in philosophy and author of three books on East Indian religion. Like many other scholars of his generation, when the supply of academic talent was outstripping demand in the universities, Wood could not find an academic job. Instead he was working in San Francisco in the research branch of the Federal Reserve Bank. Custred and Wood discussed the initiative matter over the phone and then divided up the work of researching the feasibility of an initiative. They did not actually meet for another six months, although they often spoke on the telephone.

Once they understood what it would take to put an initiative on the ballot they set to work drafting the language. This is far more difficult than it appears because a good idea discussed over the kitchen table may turn out to be a very tricky proposition when drafted as law. For example, the initiative had to be written so that it would withstand judicial scrutiny—if it were challenged in court, the initiative could be shown to be within both the language of the U.S. Constitution and the case law that interprets it. The initiative also had to be in harmony with other laws in such a way that no unintended consequences could occur. For example, the California Civil Rights Initiative (CCRI) was never meant to reverse any gains by racial minorities made over the past 30 years in civil rights law. Its only goal was to prohibit racial, ethnic, and sex preferences. Thus close attention was paid to wording so that the initiative, if enacted into law, would not infringe on or in any way make ambiguous other laws guaranteeing individual rights. It was also necessary to write the initiative so that lawyers and intellectually dishonest judges could not easily interpret it to mean what it does not say and what it was never intended to say.

To those ends, when the initiative was being drafted, a host of people around the country were consulted, especially constitutional scholars and civil rights lawyers, who freely gave their advice. Tom Wood was especially attentive to the legal side of the question, becoming expert in this domain of the law. Not only were they interested in writing sound law which would withstand judicial scrutiny, but also in an initiative which everyone could readily understand. Wood and Custred wanted people to know exactly what they were voting on, with no honest mistakes, complicated provisions, or ambiguous language to muddy the water. This meant paying close attention to brevity and clarity of language. Although hoping to keep the initiative to the 37 words of its operative clause, the drafters were unable to do this because of needed clarifications (see Appendix I). For example, clause *b* specifies that the initiative shall apply only to action taken after it is enacted and not retroactively. Clause *c* assures that the text would not interfere with such necessary or desirable distinctions by sex such as men's and women's rest rooms, boys' and girls' school athletics, the search of female criminal suspects by male authorities, and so forth. Clause *d* leaves in place those preferences mandated by consent decrees where a federal court is involved, and Clause *e* exempts programs in which federal funds may be placed in jeopardy because of conflicts between federal law or other federal mandates and the initiative. The reason for Clause *e* is to avoid problems of state and federal jurisdiction, as well as the argument that the CCRI would cost the state money if the federal government chose to withhold funds for such things as highways and schools. Avoiding conflict with the federal government was also one reason for Clause *d*; another reason was to minimize possible litigation and to accommodate a consent decree.

Clause *f* clarifies the definition of *state* to include all jurisdictions within California so that none of them, not even the local mosquito abatement district, can escape from the CCRI. Clause *g* guarantees that all people have recourse to the courts if their rights have been violated by the CCRI. Clause *h* is standard language that stipulates that if one part of the law is found in conflict with federal law, only that part and not the entire law will be struck down. Even with these necessary addenda, the CCRI consists of only nine sentences, short enough to put on a postcard and short enough to be printed on the signature petitions.

Custred and Wood tried to reassert in clear terms the color-blind principles of Title VI of the 1964 Civil Rights Act. They also paralleled the language of the Civil Rights Act as closely as possible, with only three changes. One was the insertion of the term *ethnicity*, which was more restricted in usage (although not in meaning) in the 1960s than in the 1990s. Its use enhanced and updated the language of Title VI without altering its meaning.

On advice of First Amendment experts, the initiative had no reference to religion and creed. Religious discrimination is no longer the issue it once was, and protections of religion assured under Title VI have not been undermined as have those regarding race, sex, and ethnicity. In order to retain the provision on religion, the text would have to be lengthened considerably, as the framers of Title VI had to do, in order not to interfere with religious holidays and other such considerations.

Another distinction is that the 1964 Civil Rights Act applies only to the private sector (the public sector was included in later legislation) whereas the CCRI applies only to the public sector. The authors' intention here was to ask people to vote on whether they wanted preferences to apply to the use of public money, in public policies, for the public benefit, not to mandate how companies do business. Other than these three differences, the CCRI and Title VI of the 1964 Civil Rights Act assert the same principles and prohibitions in essentially the same language.

Attention to exact language was also crucial, especially in the case of the phrase *affirmative action*. This phrase was first used in a civil rights context by President Kennedy in an executive order issued in the 1960s. Almost the same language was used later by President Johnson in an executive order that had far more effect. In both of those cases, *affirmative action* meant active measures taken to include those people who had been formerly excluded from jobs and promotions because of their race. As such, the term clearly referred to the color-blind policy that at that time was still in vogue among elites. It gradually took on new meanings as time went by and as the new regime of preferences began to assert itself. Indeed this entire period was one of semantic infiltration during which terms such as *civil rights* and even *liberalism* took on antithetical meanings as true liberalism was replaced by statism and civil rights was replaced by the atavistic regime of racial and ethnic preferences. What puzzled the CCRI's backers at first was that polling data showed that the majority approved of affirmative action when questions contained that phrase; but if questions on race policies were phrased in terms of "preference," the public overwhelmingly disapproved of them.

The most sensitive study on racial attitudes was done by Stanford University's Paul Sniderman and UC, Berkeley, researcher Tom Piazza in their 1993 *The Scar of Race*. Sniderman and Piazza, like other investigators using innovative research methods, found that the public disapproves of racial preferences by some 70 percent, a figure that corresponds with less sophisticated methodology going back to the 1970s.[12] This constancy reveals not passing fancy but deeply held values. In Sniderman's most recent book, he and his coauthor used what they call "covert measures" to try to assess what people believe.[13] They found that self-styled liberals and conservatives are equally angry about preferential policies. The attitude of many liberals, though, becomes ambiguous once the issue is subject to conditions (a fact that we discovered within the CAS among people who strongly criticized preferential policies but pulled back from the consequences of confronting it and that CAS's own polling and focus groups confirmed in a larger population).

Part of this uncertainty comes from the tension created by principles on the one hand and the need to do good and to lift up the downtrodden on the other hand. Some of it is a product of people's simple fear that if they adhere to principle the racial minorities might rise up and disturb their tranquillity. Some of the uncertainty arises when principle is trumped by partisanship, either because one's party (in this case the Democratic Party, which is firmly committed to preferences) offers some benefit that overrides principle or because fear of the opposition party (in this case the Republican Party, which is less committed to preferences) drives one to oppose whatever one's opponents might support at the time.

While drafting the initiative, however, Custred and Wood did not have access to their own polls and focus groups nor to Sniderman's latest research (although they had read *The Scar of Race*). They did, however, conduct their own experiment on language among their supporters and discovered that the term *affirmative action* should be avoided at all cost.

Puzzled by the polling data that showed approval for *affirmative action* and unequivocal hostility toward *preferences*, Custred and Wood wrote a section to the CCRI that stated, "Nothing in this section should prohibit any affirmative action policy not based on race, sex ,or ethnicity." The motive was to state that outreach policies, like those of the Kennedy and Johnson executive orders, would be allowed under the CCRI, but that preferences were prohibited. Some supporters applauded this subtle change and thought that they had captured the right nuance. Others were angry, saying that they were playing silly word games because everybody knew that affirmative action was preferences and that if they persisted in such nonsense Custred and Wood could not count on their support.

This revealed that *affirmative action* is what George Orwell called a "meaningless word"; that is, it has contradictory meanings to different people. It also revealed that it was what S. I. Hayakawa called a "snarl word" and a "purr word" at the same time, because to some it evoked the emotional overtones of "reverse discrimination," while to others it evoked some kind of warm and fuzzy benevolence. This, of course, is not the kind of language that should be used for the clear expression of one's intention and for sound law. Therefore *affirmative action* was avoided not only in the drafting of the CCRI but in the ensuing debate.

Opponents of the CCRI were furious at this wording because they knew that it was a semantic morass; and because they had no legal, practical, or moral ground on which to stand, they were forced into semantic ambiguity and confusion in order to counter the initiative. In fact, opponents sued to have the term *affirmative action* inserted in the language of the voter's handbook. The advocates resisted their case, which was argued by a cochair of the initiative and professor of law at the University of San Diego, Gale Herriot. The trial judge ordered that *affirmative action* be used at some place in the ballot description, but the appellate judge, after examining the use of that term in the law, found that it was so vague that its use in the initiative would have been deceptive.

The opposition is still angry that clear and unambiguous language was used. They preferred murky language, which was needed to deceive voters in order to protect the ethnic and racial spoils system. For example, UC, Berkeley, professor of journalism Lydia Chavez, author of an otherwise useful book on the campaign for Proposition 209, does not credit its advocates with honesty in their use of language, only with being "smart" for avoiding a device that could have been used against the CCRI.[14]

The term *preference* was also carefully chosen because its ordinary language meaning and its meaning in all branches of the law are the same. Not only did the voters understand what was meant when the CCRI said that there would be no preferences because of race, sex, or ethnicity, but there was no dispute in the law. It is interesting that the NAACP and their friends are now working to change the standard legal meaning of *preferences* in an effort to defend the ethnic and racial spoils system on which they thrive.

The Campaign

Wood and Custred started work on the CCRI in 1991. On October 15, 1993, they filed an earlier text of the initiative with the Attorney General for the November 1994 ballot. Unfortunately, they had no backing at the time, and so the initiative died. Popular initiatives find financial support from one of three quarters: economic groups, ideological (or philosophical) groups, and political interest groups. The CCRI's authors' first political contact was the Democratic Leadership Council (DLC), a group of moderates within the Democratic party, who on several occasions had stated in print the same position put forward by the CCRI. After lengthy meetings with DLC members in California and Washington, D.C., however, partisan politics won out over principle, and the DLC declined to help with the initiative.

Wood and Custred had little faith in the Republican party on this issue, yet they contacted the wealthy Lincoln Club of Orange County (California) for help. Some members were interested, but this was not an issue they cared very much about. As a result, the CCRI got no help from them until later when the California Republican Party finally came on board. And these were no ideologically or philosophically friendly groups interested in helping the CCRI financially. Most of them were involved in other issues, such as school vouchers, term limits, and so forth.

Hope for the CCRI lay with contractors, many of whom had already sued in courts across the country because of the discriminatory effects of race, sex, and ethnic preferences. Some contractor groups did help; however, the largest of these groups, the Associated General Contractors, refused help after at first showing some interest. Part of the reason, it seemed, was that some large contractors had found a way to bypass the lowest-bidder rule by co-ventures with minority contactors or by placing minorities in visible positions within their companies. Custred was told of one large San Francisco contractor who entered a co-venture with a black contractor in order to get a lucrative contract with a higher bid. When the black contractor, who had little more than a license to offer, asked what he was to do, the answer was "Keep on being black." Needless to say, the Associated General Contractors chose to stay out of the initiative-sponsoring business when it came to the CCRI.

On August 24, 1994, Wood and Custred incorporated California Against Discrimination and Preferences, a political committee that served as the organizational framework for the CCRI. And in January 1995, a campaign committee was formed with Lawrence Arnn, head of the Claremont Institute, as campaign chairman and political consultant and Arnold Steinberg as campaign strategist. Headquarters were established in Los Angeles, and a staff was hired. The formation of a campaign at that date was necessary to deal not only with problems of funding but also with the enormous press that the CCRI was getting. Early interest in the CCRI was aroused by two events with which Wood and Custred had nothing to do: the unexpected midterm victory of Republicans in Congress and the passage of Proposition 187, which was aimed at cutting off public aid to illegal aliens. The press was caught off guard with these two events, and, suspecting that CCRI would be the next big bombshell out of California, Wood and Custred found themselves inundated with reporters not only from across the nation but around the world.

In the winter of 1995, the campaign made an effort to qualify the initiative through the legislature. (If both houses approve a bill by a two-thirds vote, it automatically goes to the voters without the necessity of collecting signatures.) At that time, it was felt there was a 50/50 chance of reaching the ballot by this route because Democrats were nervous that the initiative, which was high in the polls, might cause trouble in the November election. Fearing it might have a negative effect on Democratic candidates, there was talk of putting the initiative on the March primary ballot and disposing of it in that manner. State Senator Quentin Kopp, an independent from South San Francisco, was asked by Bill Lockyear, President Pro Tem of the Senate, to sponsor the amendment in the legislature. The amendment had been previously introduced by Assemblyman Bernie Richter, but it was voted down in committee by the Democratic majority. Unfortunately Kopp's effort suffered the same fate, and once again representative government in California failed.

It was now up to the CCRI campaign to raise the money for qualification. With paid signature gatherers and volunteers, they were able to collect about half of the signatures needed to qualify. But without money for direct mail, which would have brought in millions from small donors across the country, and without some large interest group behind the CCRI, the well was fast running dry. Ward Connerly, a Sacramento businessman, a loyal Republican, and a regent on the Board of the University of California, led a successful drive to end racial and ethnic preferences at the University of California in the summer of 1995. In the fall of that year, Connerly was approached to help the CCRI. Lawrence Arnn and Tom Wood offered him the position of campaign chairman, and in November he accepted.

Once on board, Connerly used his connections in business and in the Republican party to raise the money necessary to put the initiative on the ballot. Opponents claim that Connerly was acting at the behest of Governor Pete Wilson, who wished to make this a campaign issue. From what is known, it was the other way around. Connerly is dedicated to the ideals of a color-blind America, and it is believed that it was Connerly who convinced the Republicans that this would be not only good policy but good politics. His arguments carried more weight because Connerly is black.

With the Republicans now behind the CCRI, the funds necessary to move forward and qualify were committed. On July 19, 1996, the CCRI was designated Proposition 209, and the final stage of the campaign began. Details of the story are given by Lydia Chavez in *The Color Bind*, a book that is hostile to Proposition 209 but honest and revealing in its day-to-day reporting of both sides of the campaign. One thing left out in that report, however, is the way the California Republican party played politics with the issue by trying to control the message and finally attempting, in a clumsy manner, to exploit it in the presidential campaign. This cost the CCRI votes among those Democrats and liberals who were on its side in principle, but who shied away when they suspected that the initiative was merely a Republican ploy to defeat Democrats.[15]

The initiative still won at the polls by a margin of 8 percent (54 percent to 46 percent). As discussed in the next chapter, the new law was found constitutional by the Ninth District Court of Appeals, just two days short of a year after it was passed by the voters, which vindicates the core principles of the American Creed on which Proposition 209 (now Article I Section 31 of the Constitution of the State of California) was passed. It is hoped that it will lead the way for the passage of similar laws throughout the United States. (For chronology of the developments leading to the passage of Proposition 209 and the U.S. Supreme Court's refusal to block its implementation, see Appendix II of this chapter.)

APPENDIX I   CCRI OFFICIAL TEXT

a. The state shall not discriminate against, or grant preferential treatment to, any individual or group on the basis of race, sex, color, ethnicity, or national origin in the operation of public employment, public education, or public contracting.

b. This section shall apply only to action taken after the section's effective date.

c. Nothing in this section shall be interpreted as prohibiting bona fide qualifications based on sex which are reasonably necessary to the normal operation of public employment, public education, or public contracting.

d. Nothing in this section shall be interpreted as invalidating any court order or consent decree which is in force as of the effective date of this section.

e. Nothing in this section shall be interpreted as prohibiting action which must be taken to establish or maintain eligibility for any federal program, where ineligibility would result in a loss of federal funds to the state.

f. For the purposes of this section, "state" shall include, but not necessarily be limited to, the state itself, any city, county, city and county, public university system, including the University of California, community college district, school district, special district, or any other political subdivision or governmental instrumentality of or within the state.

g. The remedies available for violations of this section shall be the same, regardless of the injured party's race, sex, color, ethnicity, or national origin, as are otherwise available for violations of then-existing California antidiscrimination law.

h. This section shall be self-executing. If any part or parts of this section are found to be in conflict with federal law or the United States Constitution, the section shall be implemented to the maximum extent that federal law and the United States Constitution permit. Any provision held invalid shall be severable from the remaining portions of this section.

APPENDIX II   CHRONOLOGY OF THE CALIFORNIA CIVIL RIGHTS INITIATIVE, PROPOSITION 209

1. Work began on the California Civil Rights Initiative by Glynn Custred (Professor of anthropology, California State University, Hayward), and Thomas Wood (Executive Director of the California Association of Scholars) in November 1991.

2. The authors completed the text of the California Civil Rights Initiative (CCRI), by the Summer of 1993.

3. Custred and Wood filed the initiative with the State Attorney General on October 15, 1993. This initiated an effort, which eventually proved to be unsuccessful, to qualify the measure for the November 1994 ballot.

4. On August 24, 1994, Californians Against Discrimination and Preferences (CADAP), a 501 (c) (4) political committee, was incorporated, which has acted as the organizational framework for the CCRI campaign. CADAP was also granted intervenor status in the suit filed in federal court challenging the constitutionality of the CCRI (Prop 209). CADAP represented the 5.4 million Californians who voted for the CCRI in the ensuing litigation.

5. In January 1995, Custred and Wood organized a political campaign for the CCRI. Lawrence Arnn, director of the Claremont Institute, was named campaign chairman, and Arnold Steinberg was named campaign consultant and strategist. Campaign headquarters were located in Los Angeles. Lawrence Arnn joined Glynn Custred and Thomas Wood on the Board of Directors of Californians Against Discrimination and Preferences.

6. In the winter of 1995, the CCRI attempted to convince the Legislature of the State of California to put the measure on the ballot by a two-thirds vote of the Legislature. State Senator Quentin Kopp introduced the bill with language slightly

modified from the 1993 version of the measure. The bill was defeated in the Democratically controlled Senate Judiciary Committee.

7. On August 7, 1995, Custred and Wood filed the same text of the initiative as that presented to the California State Senate Judiciary Committee. This was the version that was placed before the voters in the general elections of November 1996.

8. On July 20, 1995, the Board of Regents of the University of California passed two resolutions introduced by Sacramento businessman and regent Ward Connerly, which ended ethnic and racial preferences in the University of California.

9. On November 25, 1995, Ward Connerly accepted the invitation of Glynn Custred, Thomas Wood, and Larry Arnn to assume the position of Campaign Chairman of the California Civil Rights Initiative.

10. On April 15, 1996, the Secretary of State announced that the CCRI had qualified for the November 1996 statewide ballot.

11. On July 19, 1996, the CCRI was designated Proposition 209 by the Secretary of State.

12. On November 5, 1996, Proposition 209 was adopted by the voters as Article I, Section 31, of the California State Constitution by a vote of 54 percent to 46 percent.

13. Since election day, Ward Connerly had continued to work actively in the field of civil rights. His position as campaign chairman of the CCRI ended with the passage of the initiative. He then formed his own organizations to advance the issue: the American Civil Rights Institute and the American Civil Rights Coalition.

14. On November 6, 1996, the ACLU and other advocacy groups filed a complaint (*Coalition for Economic Equity v. Governor Pete Wilson, et al.*) in the U.S. District Court for the Northern District of California, alleging that Proposition 209 violated the equal protection clause of the Fourteenth Amendment of the U.S. Constitution.

15. On November 13, 1996, CADAP was granted intervenor status to defend the constitutionality of Proposition 209, representing the 5.4 million Californians who voted in favor of the initiative. Intervenor status was granted by Judge Thelton Henderson, U.S. District Court Chief Judge, who had taken control of the litigation.

16. On November 23, 1996, Judge Thelton Henderson granted the Coalition for Economic Equity, et al., a preliminary injunction against Proposition 209.

17. On January 3, 1997, CADAP appealed the preliminary injunction to the Ninth U.S. Circuit Court of Appeals. (The injunction was also appealed by State Attorney General Dan Lungren.)

18. On January 6, 1997, CADAP also filed a motion to stay the preliminary injunction before the Ninth Circuit Court of Appeals.

19. On February 10, 1997, a Ninth Circuit Court of Appeals panel consisting of Judges O'Scannlain, Leavy, and Kleinfeld heard oral arguments for a stay. At

the hearing, Attorney General Lungren joined CADAP's motion for the stay. After the hearing, the panel issued an order deferring the motion for the stay, retaining jurisdiction over the merits appeal of the preliminary injunction and expediting the briefing schedule.

20. On April 8, 1997, the panel ruled unanimously. The panel's ruling vacated the preliminary injunction. It also found that the plaintiffs had no "likelihood of success on the merits" and that "as a matter of law, Proposition 209 does not violate the United States Constitution."

21. On April 23, 1997, the Coalition for Economic Equity, et al., represented by the ACLU and others, appealed the Ninth Circuit panel's decision by filing a Petition for Rehearing and Suggestion for Rehearing before an en banc panel of the Ninth Circuit Court of Appeals.

22. On May 16, 1997, the full Ninth Circuit denied the ACLU's petition for Rehearing and Suggestion for Rehearing en banc.

23. On August 28, 1997, the federal district court's preliminary injunction against the measure was lifted and Proposition 209 became the law in California as a result of a mandate that the Ninth Circuit Court of Appeals had issued on August 26, 1997.

24. On August 29, 1997, the ACLU and a number of other organizations filed a petition Writ of Certiorari with the U.S. Supreme Court on behalf of the Coalition for Economic Equity, together with an application for Stay of the Judgment by the Ninth Circuit Court pending their petition of writ of certiorari.

25. On August 29, 1997, CADAP filed its Opposition to the Coalition for Economic Equity's Application for Recall and Stay of Mandate with the U.S. Supreme Court. (CADAP applied for recall and stay because Proposition 209 was already in effect when the ACLU's petition was filed.)

26. On September 2, 1997, the ACLU filed on behalf of the Coalition for Economic Equity, et al., a motion to strike CADAP's Opposition to Stay of the mandate of the Ninth Circuit, pending the Coalition's Petition for Writ of Certiorari. CADAP filed as respondent its opposition to the ACLU's Motion to Strike.

27. On September 4, 1997, the Supreme Court denied the ACLU's motion to block the enforcement of Proposition 209 while considering whether to review the case. (Technically, the court denied the motion for a recall and stay, pending petition for writ of certiorari.)

28. On November 3, 1997, the Coalition/ACLU's facial challenge to Proposition 209 died as the U.S. Supreme Court denied their petition for writ of certiorari.

29. In 1998, Custred and Wood founded a 501 (c) (3) organization, Americans Against Discrimination and Preferences (AADAP), designed to take to the entire nation the fight for individual rights and equality before the law for men and women of all races and ethnic backgrounds.

NOTES

1. Charles J. Sykes, *The Hollow Men: Politics and Corruption in Higher Education* (Washington, D.C.: Regnery Press, 1990), p. 145.

2. Peter L. Berger and Richard John Neuhaus, *Movement and Revolution* (Garden City, NY: Doubleday, 1970), pp. 43-47.

3. Robert H. Bork, *Slouching Towards Gomorroh* (New York: Harper Collins, 1996) p. 49.

4. Ibid., p. 50.

5. Fred Siegel, *The Future Once Happened Here: New York, D.C., L.A., and the Fate of America's Big Cities* (New York: Free Press, 1997), p. 9.

6. Ernest Gellner, *Nations and Nationalism* (Ithaca, NY: Cornell University Press, 1983), p. 34.

7. David Rieff, "Multiculturalism's Silent Partner," *Harper's*, November 1994, 65-66.

8. Frederick Lynch, *The Diversity Machine: The Drive to Change the "White Male Workplace"* (New York: Free Press, 1997), particularly Chapters 1, 2, and 4.

9. John Leo, "California's Racial Arithmetic," *U.S. News and World Report*, June 24, 1991, 21.

10. Walton Bean and James J. Rawls, *California: An Interpretive History*, 4th ed. (New York: McGraw-Hill Book Company, 1983), p. 245.

11. Cited in Walton Bean and James J. Rawls, *California*, p. 245.

12. Paul Sniderman and Tom Piazza, *The Scar of Race* (Cambridge, MA: Harvard University Press, 1993), particularly Chapters 3 and 4.

13. Paul Sniderman and Edward Carmines, *Reaching Beyond Race* (Cambridge, MA: Harvard University Press, 1998).

14. Lydia Chavez, *The Color Bind: California's Battle to End Affirmative Action* (Berkeley: University of California Press, 1998).

15. Glynn Custred, "Both Parties Lack Principles on Preferences," *Wall Street Journal*, December 2, 1996, A18.

7

⤳

The Ending of Affirmative Action Preferences in California: Testing the Constitutional Amendment

The desperate efforts to defeat Proposition 209 were exemplified by the fact that on election day, November 5, 1996, almost the entire press run of 23,000 copies of the University of California (UC), Berkeley, student newspaper (*Daily Californian*) were stolen from the racks to prevent dissemination of its editorial supporting a "yes" vote on the measure.[1] Earlier, the senior editorial board of the paper, after a vigorous debate, decided by a six-to-five vote, to recommend a "yes" vote on the Proposition and argued that affirmative action policies of the university had in fact resulted in reverse discrimination against Asians and poor whites and, therefore, urged an economic-based student admissions policy to replace the race- and gender-based policies existing at that time. This position of the *Daily Californian* was a real surprise because generally the paper takes left-of-center positions on social issues and because UC, Berkeley's Chancellor Chang-Lin Tien had opposed the UC Board of Regents' decision to eliminate the use of race and gender preferences. However, the *Daily Californian* in July 1995 had also supported the UC Board of Regents' decision to eliminate such race- and gender-based preferences. Thus, the paper's support for Proposition 209 was a logical extension of its previous position concerning the Regents' decision.

After the balloting and with all 25,348 precincts reporting, Proposition 209 was approved by a 54-to-46 ratio. Of the 58 counties in California, in only 6 counties (Alameda, Los Angeles, Marin, San Francisco, San Mateo, and Santa Cruz) did "no" votes outnumber the "yes" votes. Predictably enough, there were student demonstrations the next day at UC campuses in Berkeley and Santa Cruz against the measure approved by the voters. An attorney for the American Civil Liberties Union (ACLU) predicted, "Proposition 209 will not see the light of day." The ACLU and the Lawyers Committee for Civil Rights promptly filed a suit in the U.S. District Court in San Francisco challenging the constitutionality of Proposition 209.[2]

The Chancellor of the California State University (CSU) system said that the CSU campuses were already in full compliance with the Proposition, implying that all programs of race and gender preferences in faculty and staff employment, student education, and contracting had been stopped. The UC officials declared that they would immediately implement the new law by stopping the practice of using race as a factor in undergraduate student admissions. The UC president vowed to achieve diversity consistent with the new law. The Pacific Legal Foundation, a public interest law firm in Sacramento, commenced a lawsuit on behalf of the authors of Proposition 209 to strike down the system of race and gender preferences in employment in California Community Colleges and contracting programs in some other state entities. Governor Wilson reiterated his resolve to seek court action to have those state laws declared invalid that provide race and gender preferences.

EFFORTS TO OVERTURN THE PEOPLE'S WILL

Within less than 24 hours of the polls' closing, the opposing parties resolved to do battle in the courts. The opponents, led by the ACLU and the Lawyers Committee for Civil Rights, filed a lawsuit asking the Court to block implementation of the new measure. Separately, a group of minority female contractors also filed a suit in an effort to block the measure. The initial shots were fired almost simultaneously when, on November 6, 1996, Governor Wilson issued an Executive Order asking state officials to implement Proposition 209. Additionally, the campaign leaders asked the Court to order the implementation of the new law. It is important to note that the measure's opponents quite obviously and purposely in their public stance ignored that part of its language that stated: "The state shall not discriminate against . . . individual or group on the basis of race, sex, color, or national origin." In Washington, civil rights leaders, led by the Reverend Jesse Jackson and Patricia Ireland, President of the National Organization for Women, met with Deputy White House Chief of Staff Harold Ickes and Assistant Attorney General Deval Patrick to urge them to launch a lawsuit against Proposition 209. Additionally, they urged the Clinton Administration to withhold funds from the University of California—one of the government's biggest contractors—on the presumed grounds that the abolition of race- and gender-based preferences violates federal civil rights laws.[3] Attorney General Janet Reno was reported to have said that Proposition 209 "does not affect federal law." However, the Clinton Administration remained undecided as to any action it might take to respond to the issue.

The ACLU was successful in "forum shopping" by launching its suit in San Francisco and having a liberal judge of the U.S. District Court hear the case that was originally assigned on a random basis to the District Judge Vaughn Walker, a 1989 appointee of former Republican President George Bush. On November 13, 1996, Thelton Henderson, Chief Judge of the U.S. District Court in San Francisco, ordered the case transferred to his own court. Originally appointed to the bench in 1980 by former President Jimmy Carter, Henderson had served as a civil rights lawyer under Robert Kennedy and is the author of a string of liberal rulings. He rationalized the assignment of this case to his Court by stating that a reverse discrimination case pending before him involving a challenge by a white contractor to San Francisco's affirmative action preference program "inevitably implicates" Proposition 209. California Attorney General Dan Lungrun and Dan Kolkey, Governor Wilson's chief legal advisor, called this "judge shopping." However, such legal maneuvering is not uncommon, particularly when the stakes are so high.

While the ACLU was judge shopping, city officials of Los Angeles, San Jose, and San Francisco defiantly declared that they would either continue their preferential policies, despite the passage of the constitutional amendment, or if at all necessary make only minor changes to them. Two examples of these cosmetic changes were the renaming of San Jose's "Office of Affirmative Action" as the "Office of Equality Assurance" and the replacement of the 22-campus California State University system's African-American and Hispanic scholarship funds with a fund for disadvantaged "future scholars."[4] Thus, open resistance as well as maneuvers to finesse the newly passed law began as soon as the ballots were counted.

Some of the excuses for not immediately implementing the measure's ban against race- and gender-based preferences were disingenuous. Included in this category was a comment by a spokesperson of the California State University system who was reported to have said that the implementation of the ban would have to wait for the courts to define "what they mean by *preferences.*"[5] This is despite the fact that the word not only has a well-understood meaning in English but has been used frequently in various branches of law, including Section 703(i) of the Civil Rights Act of 1964 which states that Title VII is not applicable to any business or enterprise at or near an Indian reservation, "with respect to any publicly announced employment practice . . . under which a preferential treatment is given to any individual because he is an Indian living on or near a reservation." Throughout the campaign, sponsors and supporters of Proposition 209 continued to emphasize that it does not ban those affirmative action plans that do not result in reverse discrimination.[6] However, the Proposition's opponents refused to accept this explanation and the president of the National Organization for Women called passage of the measures the "tyranny of the majority."[7] A week before Chief Federal Judge Thelton Henderson was scheduled to hear the case, lawyers on behalf of the state of California filed a motion asking Henderson to abstain in the case. They reasoned that state courts of California should be permitted to adjudicate Proposition 209, thus avoiding the thorny issues of whether the measure violates the equal protection guarantee of the Fourteenth Amendment of the U.S. Constitution and the antidiscrimination provisions of the federal civil rights laws. The opposition charged that the state's move was merely designed to escape scrutiny of the issues by the federal court.[8]

THE SUPREME COURT REFUSES TO STOP PROPOSITION 209

Within hours after the voters of California approved Proposition 209 by a decisive 54 percent to 46 percent, the advocates of affirmative action preferences went to the U.S. District Court challenging the constitutionality of the measure and seeking an order to prevent its implementation.[9] This challenge was launched by a number of organizations including the ACLU of Northern California, the ACLU Foundation of Southern California, and the Lawyers Committee for Civil Rights. A separate suit was filed by a San Francisco private law firm on behalf of some minority- and women-owned contractors challenging the Proposition. The battle was joined by Governor Pete Wilson the day after the election when he issued an Executive Order requiring all state agencies to compile and submit to his office lists of all affirmative action programs that grant or encourage race- or sex-based preferences by them.

Because, according to the California Constitution, state statutes cannot be revoked without a ruling from the state Appellate Court, Governor Wilson moved immediately and instituted a suit to revoke a number of state laws that granted race- and gender-based preferences in public education, public employment, and public contracting. On his behalf, Pacific Legal Foundation particularly targeted such programs in California Community Colleges and contracting policies of the State Lottery Commission and the Department of General Services.

The opponents led by the ACLU and the Lawyers Committee for Civil Rights alleged that the newly passed Proposition violated the equal protection clause of the Fourteenth Amendment of the U.S. Constitution because (1) it will prevent only women and minorities from seeking preferential treatment from governmental agencies while the other groups would have no such restriction, and (2) the Initiative is in conflict with the federal civil rights legislation and regulation and in such a situation federal law must prevail.

These arguments were extensively debated in the election campaign and reported by the media. For example, in an op-ed piece in the *Los Angeles Times*, law professors Erwin Chemerinsky and Laurie Levenson charged that sex discrimination would become legal under Proposition 209.[10] It evoked a sharp rebuttal from attorney Allan J. Favish who had fought an earlier successful battle against the UCLA Law School concerning student admissions records demonstrating racial preferences.[11] The fallacious assertion that Proposition 209 discriminated particularly against women was made over and over again by the opponents in public debates and was effectively responded to by its advocates.

On a scholarly level, the issue was extensively discussed in a law review article by Vickram D. Amar, Acting Professor of Law, at UC, Davis, and Evan H. Caminker, Professor of Law at UCLA, who concluded that Proposition 209 was "racial in character" and that "under the present law of the land" it did not pass constitutional muster.[12] This article, appearing a few months before the November 1996 election, was part of a series of false allegations that included the one by the Western State University Law Review Association in its "Preliminary Findings" that Proposition 209 could endanger ethnic and women's studies university programs and ethnic holidays and celebrations.[13] Effective rebuttals of these scare tactics and illogical interpretations were offered by many academicians, as well as by practitioners of law and politics. A notable contribution in this respect was made by Eugene Volokh, Acting Professor of Law at UCLA, who in his writings and public presentations defended Proposition 209 as a constitutionally valid measure that "covers only a limited, well-defined area of government action."[14]

California's intellectuals in public debates defending the language of the Proposition included, among others, Thomas E. Wood, one of the authors of the Proposition; Richard Ferrier of Thomas Aquinas College; Charles L. Geshekter of California State University, Chico; Sacramento attorney Harvey R. Zall; Gail Heriot, professor at the University of San Diego School of Law; and attorney Robert Corry. An extensive paper in support of Proposition 209 was written by Thomas Wood. Important roles were also played by Washington, D.C.–based Dr. Michael S. Greve of the Center for Individual Rights and Linda Chavez of the Center for Equal Opportunity, both of whom supported and publicly debated the merits and the constitutionality of the Proposition. Thus, when Californians went to the polls on November 5, 1996, they were fully apprised of the plain meaning of the words and language of the Proposition and knew through their own experience how the government bureaucracy and pressure groups had perverted the ideal of nondiscrimination into preferences and quotas.

The ACLU and its coplaintiffs were successful in "judge shopping," and within a week of the institution of the suit Chief U.S. District Judge Thelton

Henderson of San Francisco ordered that the case be assigned to him. He is well known for his liberal rulings, including one that had upheld the city of San Francisco's use of race- and gender-based preferences in awarding contracts. As mentioned earlier in this chapter, the reason given by Judge Henderson for taking over the suit was that he was consolidating it with another suit pending before him involving the issue of preferences.[15] This decision of Judge Henderson's was welcomed by the opponents of Proposition 209 and denounced by its authors and advocates.[16] The California Justice Department then filed a motion asking Judge Henderson to abstain and to let the state court rule on Proposition 209.[17] This request was denied.

While political and legal maneuvering was going on in the courts, some student groups at Berkeley were doing their practiced routine of protesting and occupying a university facility. This time it was the landmark bell tower that the students occupied the day after the election. To demonstrate their commitment to preferences, some of the demonstrators chained themselves atop the tower. A statement issued by the protestors said that it symbolized Berkeley as the "Ivory Tower of elitism and exclusionsim."[18] A vast majority of the students, however, attended their classes as usual. The protest ended when police arrested the occupiers of the tower and charged them with trespassing.

At the national level, Jesse Jackson and Patricia Ireland met with officials of the Justice Department and the White House and asked that the federal government withhold funds from the University of California on the basis of the alleged violation of the civil rights laws. However, two days after the election, U.S. Attorney General Janet Reno had already said that Proposition 209 did not affect federal law.[19] Not being satisfied with the situation, Jackson emphatically stated: "'I want [the] Justice [Department] to intervene with a lawsuit.'"[20]

Defiance of the newly passed constitutional amendment was demonstrated when city officials of Los Angeles and San Francisco openly stated that they would continue to practice affirmative action preferences until all the legal challenges had been exhausted. The city officials of San Jose said that only "very minor changes" would be made in their programs,[21] despite the fact that San Jose is well known for its blatant racial and gender preferences.

The District Court issued a temporary restraining order against the implementation of Proposition 209 on November 27, 1996, and a preliminary injunction on December 23, 1996.[22] The main reasons given by Judge Henderson for his actions are:

1. Elimination of race and gender preferences would reduce opportunities in public contracting and public employment for women and minorities.
2. The enrollment of blacks, American Indians, and Hispanics would decrease, while that of Asian Americans would increase.
3. In order for women and minorities to reinstate preferences, they have to re-amend

the California Constitution, thereby imposing a substantial political burden on them.

4. Title VII of the Civil Rights Act (which bans discrimination in employment) permits public agencies to use race- and gender-based preferences in their employment policies, whereas Proposition 209 bans such preferences. Federal law preempts state law under the Supremacy Clause of the U.S. Constitution.

5. Prohibition against race and gender preferences imposes an unequal "political structure" by denying women and minorities a right to seek preferential treatment from the lowest level of government (rather than through the more arduous route of having the State Constitution amended). In support of this argument, Judge Henderson cited *Hunter v. Erickson* (1969) in which the U.S. Supreme Court struck down an amendment to the Charter of the City of Akron, Ohio. In that decision, the Akron City Council was prohibited from enacting ordinances addressing racial discrimination in housing without an approval of the Akron voters.[23] The Supreme Court had reasoned that the Charter amendment was an explicit racial classification "treating racial housing matters differently from other racial and housing matters."

6. Proposition 209 denies Equal Protection of the Law to minorities and women. In this respect, Judge Henderson cited *Washington v. Seattle School District* (1982): The Supreme Court had declared unconstitutional a State of Washington initiative in which the school boards were barred from assigning students beyond their neighborhood schools. In effect, that prevented desegregative busing.[24]

Californians Against Discrimination and Preferences (CADP), a nonprofit public interest organization founded by Proposition 209's co-authors Glynn Custred and Thomas E. Wood, granted intervenor status, asked the District Court to stay the injunction. The request was denied, and an application was made to the U.S. Court of Appeals. Among those submitting friend-of-the-court briefs in the case were the ACLU, American Jewish Congress, U.S. Department of Justice, Pacific Legal Foundation, Institute for Justice, and Independent Women's Forum. The plaintiffs included preference advocacy groups such as the National Association for the Advancement of Colored People (NAACP), AFL-CIO, and some women's and minority organizations.

The decision on April 8, 1997, was rendered by a three-judge panel consisting of Diarmuid F. O'Scannlain, Edward Leavy, and Andrew J. Kleinfeld.[25] Once again there were allegations of judge shopping. Only this time the allegation was made by the advocates of preferences. One columnist alleged that the three judges, all Republican appointees, took control of the case "under an unusual but not illegal, judicial maneuver."[26] The Court of Appeals vacated the injunction and upheld Proposition 209. In its 20-page decision, the Court rejected the argument that Proposition 209 violates the Fourteenth Amendment rights of minorities and women. On this and related issues, the Court stated, "A system which permits one judge to block with the stroke of a pen what 4,736,180 state residents voted to enact as law tests the integrity of our constitutional democracy," and it gave the following reasons for its decision to vacate Judge Henderson's injunction.

1. The district court relied on erroneous legal premise to thwart the will of the people of California.
2. It is for the people and not for the court to decide whether compelling state interests have been vindicated when and if racial classifications are used by government agencies.
3. There is a difference between what the law permits (such as racial preferences) and what it requires: "The Fourteenth Amendment, lest we lose sight of the forest for the trees, does not require what it barely permits."
4. Proposition 209 as a state law does not conflict with the federal law. Therefore, state law cannot be preempted by federal Civil Rights Act.
5. It does not stand to reason that the statewide ballot initiative was meant to deny equal protection to women and minorities that together constitute a majority of the California electorate.
6. The Fourteenth Amendment provides equal protection to individuals not to groups. "Where, as here, a state prohibits race or gender preferences at any level of government, the injury to any specific individual is utterly inscrutable."

The unanimous decision of the Court of Appeals received prominent media coverage that particularly noted the tough wording of the ruling and its implications at the national level.[27] President Clinton said that it would be a mistake not to allow disadvantaged but qualified people to participate in economic and educational life through measures that do not establish quotas. The coalition of advocacy groups that lost the ruling petitioned the full Ninth Circuit Court of Appeals to review the three-judge-panel decision.[28] On August 20, 1997, the Court of Appeals refused to review its previous decision and, six days later, declined the request to delay implementation of Proposition 209 pending its appeal to the U.S. Supreme Court.[29] Four judges of the Ninth Circuit Court of Appeals in their dissenting opinion severely criticized their three colleagues who had voted to uphold Proposition 209. They accused them of "judicial activism."[30] Some California local governments vowed to continue affirmative action preferences whereas others decided to alter them.[31]

A day after the Court of Appeals refused to delay the implementation of Proposition 209, the opponents of the Proposition requested the Supreme Court to stop its enforcement while its proponents requested the Supreme Court not to delay its implementation. On September 4, 1997, the Supreme Court refused to halt its implementation.[32] The other shoe fell on November 3, 1997, when the U.S. Supreme Court denied certiorari and let Proposition 209 stand.[33] That decision brought to success the idea two academics had of equal opportunity and who had worked tirelessly for years to achieve it through the democratic process.

CALIFORNIA ATTEMPTS TO ENFORCE EQUALITY IN POST–PROPOSITION 209 ERA

The following list illustrates the pervasive nature and extent of race- and gender-based preferences in those programs and laws that were theoretically repealed by Proposition 209 in November 1996.*

1. California Summer Science and Technology program gives emphasis to female and minority pupils of public high schools.

2. Science, Mathematics, and Technology Teacher Pipeline Program provides assistance to members of "underrepresented" groups who wish to become teachers.

3. Student preference improvement project authorizes a school district and a postsecondary education institution to apply for grants. Priority is given to schools with a concentration of students from "underrepresented" groups.

4. Existing law provides for an American Indian Early Childhood Education Program.

5. Preference given to students from "underrepresented" groups for transfer to the University of California and the California State University Systems.

6. Student Opportunity and Access Program is funded for ethnic minority students to increase their accessibility to postsecondary educational opportunity.

7. State Graduate Fellowship Program gives "priority to students who are historically disadvantaged or from groups that are underrepresented in graduate-level programs."

8. State agencies that enter into joint exercise of powers agreement "must ensure that certain minority, women, and disabled veteran business enterprise goals become part of the agreement and apply to contracts executed by the joint powers agency."

9. The Department of Transportation must comply with specified "participation goals for minority-, women-, and disabled veteran-owned firms when contracting for the services of engineers, architects, surveyors, planners, environmental specialists, and material specialists."

10. Bids for professional contract bond services must provide information regarding subcontracts to meet minority and women business enterprise "participation goals."

11. California two-year community colleges must establish and apply statewide "participation goals" for businesses owned by minorities and women.

12. Personal services contracts (under the State Civil Service Act) must include an assurance that the contractor complies with nondiscrimination affirmative action standards.

Source: California Legislature, 1997–1998 Regular Session. Assembly Bill 1700 (January 26, 1998), "Legislative Counsel's Digest," pp. 2–6 (excerpted).

13. The State Civil Service Act requires each state agency to establish an affirmative action program and "goals and timetables" designed to overcome under-utilization of minorities and women.

14. Minority Health Professions Education Foundation was established by the state to assist "underrepresented" minority groups with financial aid in the Registered Nurse Education Program and in the Geriatric Nurse Practitioner and the Clinical Nurse Specialist Scholarship Program.

15. Skilled trades and crafts apprenticeship program must ensure equal employment and affirmative action in apprenticeship of women and minorities.

16. Members of the Board of Prison Terms appointed by the governor must reflect a cross section of the racial, sexual, economic, and geographic composition of the state.

17. Every state department must award contracts to the lowest bidders who either meet "participation goals" for minority, disabled veterans, and women business enterprises or make "good faith efforts" to meet these goals.

18. Appointments to the Youthful Offender Parole Board must reflect the racial, sexual, economic, and geographic composition of the state.

Even though the described programs run counter to Proposition 209, the Constitution of California (Article III, Section 3.5) provides that the administrative agencies shall continue to enforce and administer state statutes unless an appellate court determines such statutes to be unconstitutional. That means that these laws will remain operative until either the California Legislature repeals them or the appellate courts declare them null and void. Given the fact that up to now, in both the California Assembly and the Senate, liberal Democrats are a majority, these laws are not going to be repealed. But Governor Pete Wilson, who has been a fierce opponent of such preferences at least since the spring of 1995, challenged the state lawmakers to implement Proposition 209 by repealing or modifying 35 state laws that he listed in his news conference in Los Angeles on September 9, 1997.[34] Predictably the legislature ignored his challenge.

Enter State Senator Quentin Kopp (I-San Francisco) who had been a strong supporter of Proposition 209. Senate Bill (SB) 2041, authored by Senator Kopp, was introduced in the California Senate on February 20, 1998, to eliminate provisions of many state laws that provided preferences to women and minorities. The comprehensive bill (101 pages) also provided a new outreach program for small businesses, including a "one-stop" office to provide help for small businesses seeking state contracts, and provided incentives to large prime contractors for voluntarily subcontracting with small businesses. The provisions were designed to answer the critics who constantly asked the question: What's the alternative to affirmative action in contracting? Once again, Governor Wilson appeared at a news conference at the Capitol on April 27, 1998, along with Senator Kopp and Ward Connerly, and urged the legislators to pass the bill.[35] The next day, SB 2041 was defeated in the Democrat-controlled State Governmental Organization Committee.[36]

The California Assembly, a few days earlier, defeated another bill offered by Assemblyman Bernie Richter (R-Chico), an indefatigable opponent of preference before it became a popular cause. He was a major voice in the California Assembly and in the press against race- and gender-based classifications. He introduced Assembly Bill (AB) 1700 on January 26, 1998, based on the nonpartisan Legislative Counsel's analysis that called for the elimination of a number of preferences listed earlier in this discussion. One of the authors of this book, Raza, testified in support of the bill. So did Eugene Volokh, Professor at the UCLA School of Law. The Democrats on the Judicial Committee in discussing the bill clearly wanted to lengthen the life of preferences by not repealing them and then letting the court sort out their constitutional status. Thus, the vested interests would be preserved as long as possible. It was no surprise that on April 21, 1998, the Judiciary Committee by a vote of eight to five defeated the bill—all Republicans voted "yes," and all Democrats voted "no." For over two years, liberal Democrats in the California Legislature have defeated every bill that was offered to ban preferences based on race and gender. The struggle to eliminate them will continue albeit slowly through the courts that are bound to apply Proposition 209 in eliminating them. Their demise will be hastened if the Republican party in California captures majorities in both houses of the legislature and maintains the governorship as well. That's a pretty tall order.

Not to be deterred by a series of court rulings against racial classifications, California State Senator Richard Polanco on February 18, 1998, offered a bill (SB 1735) that required that state agencies establish "outreach programs in ways that will yield diverse results in public education and public employment." In elaboration, the bill provided that the program should focus on "underrepresented" minorities and women in entry-level positions in public sector employment and educational institutions. The bill specified as to how "underrepresentation" shall be measured by a government agency:

> [U]nderrepresentation shall be determined by comparing the minority group or number of women at the governmental agency with that group's representation in the current civilian labor force in the jurisdiction of the governmental agency, or comparing the minority group or number of women at the educational institution with that group's representation in the region from which a postsecondary education, including a campus of the California State University or the University of California primarily draws its students.[37]

This bill obviously ignored the principles of strict scrutiny and rules for measuring disparity as laid down by the Supreme Court as well as by the formal Opinions of California State Attorney General Daniel E. Lungren. The Attorney General in his correspondence with Senator Polanco specifically pointed out that for measuring disparity in utilization analysis, the "comparison must be made between the composition of the relevant position at the agency and the composition of the qualified population in the relevant labor market."[38] The Attorney General cited his previous Opinion given in the case of affirmative action preferential programs for faculty hiring at California State Universities.[39] In the opinion, it was also pointed out that proper comparison must be made between the qualified available pool and its utilization, rather than with the general population.

The bill offered by Senator Polanco is an effort to circumvent Proposition 209. The Senator has been offering bills for the past several years that in one form or another call for racial and ethnic quotas in employment of faculty, graduate programs, and student admissions.[40] His previous bills were described in Chapter 4. The latest bill under the color of "outreach" was designed to lead to quotas and preferences under a sympathetic government bureaucracy.

SOME COURT CASES ON PREFERENCES: 1996-1998

Monterey Mechanical Company

An important ruling was handed down on September 3, 1997, by the U.S. Ninth Circuit Court of Appeals in *Monterey Mechanical Company v. Pete Wilson, et al.* Monterey Mechanical had competed on a construction project to connect the buildings of California Polytechnic State University, San Luis Obispo, to a central heating and air conditioning plant and to install an electrical system.[41] Despite its low bid of $21,698,000, the contract was awarded to Swinerton and Walberg, which had a bid $318,000 higher than that of Monterey Mechanical. At issue was the requirement of the California Public Contract Code, which provided that the state contracts must have subcontracting "participation goals" of at least 15 percent minority, 5 percent women, and 3 percent disabled veteran enterprises. These designated groups were exempt from this requirement. Other bidders either had to meet or make "good faith efforts to meet these goals." Not leaving anything to chance, the California statute provided that in order to prove that the requirements of good faith efforts have been met, the low bidder must prove through documentary evidence that it had: (1) contacted the contract-awarding department, other state and federal agencies, as well as local minority, women, and disabled veteran organizations to identify business enterprises owned by the designated groups; (2) advertised in trade papers and papers focusing on designated groups; (3) extended bid invitations to potential minority, women, and disabled veteran business contractors; and (4) considered available minority, women, and disabled veteran enterprises.

The California Legislature in its enthusiasm for inclusiveness identified the following "minorities" in the California Public Contract Code (Section 10115.1[d]):

[A] citizen or lawful permanent resident of the United States [who] is an ethnic person of color and who is: Black (a person having origins in any of the Black racial groups of Africa); Hispanic (a person of Mexican, Puerto Rican, Cuban, Central or South American, or other Spanish or Portuguese culture or origin, regardless of race); Native American (an American Indian, Eskimo, Aleut, or Native Hawaiian); Pacific Asian (a person whose origins are from Japan, China, Taiwan, Korea, Vietnam, Laos, Cambodia, the Philippines, Samoa, Guam, or the United States Trust Territories of the Pacific including the Northern Marianas); Asian-Indian (a person whose origins are from India, Pakistan, or Bangladesh); or any other group of natural persons identified as minorities in the respective project specifications of an awarding department or participating local agency.*

The problem arose when Monterey Mechanical, even though it had a lower bid of $21,698,000, was disqualified because it neither subcontracted out the required 23 percent of the work to minority, women, and disabled veteran business enterprises nor did it provide documentation to meet the statutory requirement of "good faith effort" to meet the "participation goals." The next lower bid by Swinerton and Walberg was accepted even though it was $318,000 higher than the one submitted by Monterey Mechanical Company. The only difference was that even though Swinerton and Walberg did not subcontract out work to the designated minority, women, and disabled veteran enterprises, it did provide documentary evidence of meeting the alternate "good faith effort" requirement of contacting and soliciting bids for subcontractors from the designated groups. Thus, California Polytech awarded the bid to Swinerton and Walberg. When Monterey Mechanical asked the university to provide it with statistics of the disparity study to justify the preference for the designated classes, it was told that there weren't any! U.S. District Court refused to grant a preliminary injunction requested by Monterey Mechanical, which then appealed to the U.S. Court of Appeals. A three-judge panel reversed the decision on the following grounds:

1. Monterey Mechanical was denied equal protection of the law in violation of its Fourteenth Amendment rights. The two companies were forced to compete on an unequal basis.

2. Because the statute allows a minority or women business enterprise to satisfy the statutory goal by allocating the percentage of work for the group itself, it gives unfair advantage in violation of the equal protection guarantee of the Fourteenth Amendment.

3. "Though worded in terms of goals and good faith, the statute imposes mandatory requirements with concreteness."[42]

4. Recent decisions of this Ninth Circuit Court of Appeals, one of the U.S. Supreme Court, and one of the Tenth Circuit Court of Appeals also state that in order to prove a violation of his constitutional rights a bidder simply needs to establish

*California Public Contract Code Section 10115.1(d).

that the state's unequal treatment imposes extra requirements, costs, and burdens on nonminority contractors.[43]

5. The appellees (that is, the trustees of California State University) had not cited any cases that contradict the logic of the decision made by the Court in the present case.

6. Even if the purpose of the statute is "attractive," it treats contractors differently and discriminatorily according to their ethnicity and sex and with respect to the "good faith" requirements.

7. Contrary to the assertion of the U.S. District Court, "there is no de minimis exception to the Equal Protection Clause [of the Constitution]. Race discrimination is never a 'trifle.'"[44]

8. General societal discrimination is not a valid justification for racial classifications and preferences. In order to justify such preferential classification, the findings must be based on prior discrimination by the public entity involved. There was no such finding in this case.

9. Even the California Legislature, in passing this statute, did not say that California State University, or the state government itself, had in the past discriminated against the preferred groups. Similarly, there is no fact finding of discrimination against the benefited groups by the U.S. District Court. Thus, preferences given by the state are neither legitimate nor remedial in character.

In conclusion, the Court said that Monterey Mechanical had suffered two harms: (1) the loss of a contract and (2) unconstitutional discrimination in the bidding process based on race and sex. Even though the legislative goal is laudable, said the Court, race, ethnic, and sex discrimination in this statute is not constitutionally justified. "We have been compelled to conclude that the statute, in so far as it classifies by ethnicity and sex, is unconstitutonal."[45]

The decision just described was given by a unanimous three-member panel consisting of Circuit Judges Kleinfeld, Leavy, and O'Scannlain. The losing parties—in the case, nominally Governor Pete Wilson, the Board of Trustees of the California State University System, and other defendants-appellees—could have requested the Circuit Court of Appeals to rehear the case en banc. They chose not to do so.[46] However, Judge Stephen Reinhardt, an active member of the same Court, sua sponte requested a vote of all the active Ninth Circuit Court of Appeals judges on whether to hear the case en banc. This request, having failed to receive a majority vote of the active judges, brought an angry response by Judge Reinhardt, joined by Judges Pregerson and Tashima. The rejection for rehearing and rebuttal of Judge Reinhardt's arguments was given by Judge Kleinfeld with whom Judges Kozinski and O'Scannlain joined, while Judge T. G. Nelson also concurred in the order rejecting the request to rehear the case en banc.

The main arguments given by Judge Reinhardt in favor of affirmative action preferences in this case and the arguments by Judge Kleinfeld against them portray not only different interpretations of the statute and its theory, but rather very differing perceptions of empirical knowledge of its implementation. Judge Reinhardt believed that the statute contained only "a benign governmental outreach program that is intended to ensure a modicum of fairness to minorities and women." He also believed that the extra steps required by the statute to prove "good faith efforts" are "innocuous" to counter the historic injustice suffered by minorities. He lamented the fact that both nationally and in California economic and political power remains "firmly and fully in the hands of [the] white majority." In a footnote he also bemoaned that in California's Ninth Circuit Court of Appeals there was no active black or Latino judge. In his view, had there been such ethnic judges, the case would not have had such "an erroneous result."

Judge Kleinfeld went to great length in answering what he called "Judge Reinhardt's ad hominem polemics against his colleagues." In his opening paragraph, Kleinfeld quoted the Declaration of Independence—"We hold these truths to be self-evident, that all men are created equal"—as well as the equal protection clause of the Fourteenth Amendment of the Constitution. He said that the Constitutional guarantees are for "any person," regardless of that person's race, ethnicity, or sex. He also said that Judge Reinhardt's characterization of the statute as "benign" does not make it so if the empirical evidence is to the contrary. His concluding paragraph commenting on the conflict between equal protection of the law and racial classification poignantly stated: "Past discrimination sometime, somewhere, is not enough. Many of us are of peoples who have suffered oppression, some recently, some long ago, some in America, some in foreign lands. There is no principle more essential to our nation than that all of our peoples have become one people, the American people."[47]

The argument between a majority of the Ninth Circuit judges and Judge Reinhardt was a classic one between conservatives and liberals in their respective view of the Constitution and of the parameters of permissible remedial compensation for discrimination versus reparation for past societal injustice. Judge Reinhardt, a graduate of Yale Law School, is well known for his exuberant liberal judicial opinions since his appointment by President Jimmy Carter in 1988. He is loved by trial lawyers for his far-fetched new theories of jurisprudence having great potential for virulent litigation and adored by radical-liberals for his support for racial preferences and ideological social and economic views. He also has the dubious distinction of being "one of the most overturned judges in history."[48] In the 1997 judicial term alone, the U.S. Supreme Court turned down unanimously seven opinions that Judge Reinhardt had written or been party to.[49] Thus, on March 9, 1998, with the Ninth Circuit Court's opinion not to hear *Monterey Mechanical* en banc, the 20-year-old provision of California Public Contract Code giving preferences to minorities and women came to an end.

The next day, Governor Pete Wilson issued an Executive Order prohibiting all state agencies, departments, boards, and commissions from enforcing the Public Contract Code's provisions concerning the "participation goals" and "good faith efforts" for designated race, sex, and ethnic minority groups. The Order maintained the existing statutory preferential treatment of disabled veteran business enterprises because they were not affected by the Ninth Circuit Court of Appeals' application of the Fourteenth Amendment in *Monterey Mechanical.*

Important Cases Outside of California

Although California continues to be the main battleground for affirmative action preferences, a few important engagements are also developing elsewhere in the nation in the form of litigation and attempts to pass legislation.

In *Metropolitan Dade County, Florida v. Engineering Contractors Association*, on March 9, 1998, the U.S. Supreme Court without comment refused to review the affirmative action preference program for black, Hispanic, and female construction contractors of Florida's Dade County.[50] The program had been struck down by the U.S. Court of Appeals in Atlanta because it did not meet the strict scrutiny test laid down in *City of Richmond v. Croson* (1989), previously discussed. The county attorney was reported to have said that the strict standard "'should be somehow meetable.'" The minority contractors in this case believed that although discrimination continues to exist, it is very difficult to prove.

Another set-aside program suffered demise at the hands of U.S. District Court Judge Lynn N. Hughes who ruled on November 13, 1997, that Houston's Metropolitan (Metro) Transit Authority's affirmative action preferences were unconstitutional. Houston's program called for 21 percent of the Metro's construction contracts to be subcontracted to women- or minority-owned enterprises. The Court rejected Metro's contention that 21 percent was a "goal" and not a quota. Judge Hughes said that white male contractors unfairly lost business due to discrimination against them. "The Constitution disallows collective guilt. . . . We do not accept the concept that a person is responsible for what others of her race, town, profession, or politics may have done."[51]

There was an extraordinary twist to this case. In April 1996, Judge Hughes had issued a preliminary injunction against Metro's affirmative action program. However, the Federal Transit Administration (FTA) then decided to withhold several million dollars in grants from Metro contending that Metro was obligated under federal law to have an affirmative action program. The *Houston Chronicle* subsequently reported that, in response to pressure from Republicans in Congress, the FTA released over $100 million to Metro.

In an attempt to bolster its justification for race- and sex-based preferences, the City of Houston had prepared a disparity study that the Judge called "bureaucratic stuff," lacking "intellectual depth," and not meeting the "standard of even weak sociological science."[52] Predictably enough, the proponents of affirmative action preferences attacked Judge Hughes's opinion on race- and gender-based preferences as counter to civil rights legislation!

Earlier (at the end of Chapter 2), the *Lamprecht*[53] (1992) decision was described: The Washington, D.C., Circuit Court invalidated the Federal Communication Commission's (FCC) "program diversity" standard as arbitrary. In that case, the FCC had declined a license to a radio broadcasting applicant for not meeting that standard. The Center for Individual Rights was responsible for achieving that precedent-setting victory on behalf of its client.

In 1998, a three-judge panel of U.S. Court of Appeals for the Washington, D.C., Circuit once again dealt a blow to affirmative action preferences in a case involving the Lutheran Church and the FCC.[54] This was the first case in which a U.S. Court of Appeals applied the strict scrutiny test to an affirmative action program for employment of minorities. (As may be recalled, the *strict scrutiny* standard requires that for legitimate race classification, a public agency must prove that: (1) compelling governmental interest justifies the exception; (2) the program is narrowly tailored and does not unnecessarily trammel the rights of innocent third parties; (3) race-neutral means have been found to be inadequate; (4) present discrimination or the present effects of past discrimination are due to the government agency's actions themselves. This last criterion is deemed to be a legitimate basis to establish compelling government interest in that matter.)

The case arose out of a petition filed by the NAACP against a radio station owned by the Lutheran Church and operated from the campus of Concordia Seminary charging that the station did not employ an adequate number of minorities and, therefore, its broadcasting license should be rescinded. The FCC had an affirmative action program that encouraged broadcasting companies to employ minorities (blacks, Asian Pacific Islanders, Hispanics, and American Indians). Its justification was to diversify radio and television programming. The FCC did not define what it meant by "diversity in programming." Faced with the problem of how to measure adequate "representation of minorities," the FCC compared the percentage of minority employees at the ratio station with the percentage of qualified minority employees in the community served by the radio station. Although the FCC renewed the license, it fined the station $25,000 and issued detailed instructions on increasing the proportion of minority employees and submitting biennial reports to the FCC. The church group had argued that its employees require a knowledge of Lutheran doctrine and classical music and that few blacks are qualified to meet these criteria. Nevertheless, these arguments were dismissed by the FCC as not meeting the "good faith effort" criterion of the agency for hiring minorities.

The U.S. Court of Appeals rejected the agency's contention that its affirmative action program was simply designed to create "diversity." In the Court's view, the diversity criterion has been used "'as a permanent justification for policies seeking racial proportionality in all walks of life.'"[55] The Court was also dismissive of the Justice Department's argument that the federal agency's recruitment plan was merely outreach effort to expand the qualified labor pool and not a hiring quota. The Court said that it was immaterial whether that affirmative action program "imposes hard quotas, soft quotas, or goals";[56] each one induces a numerical target that, in effect, will result in race-based preferences.

The proponents of affirmative action pointed out that this decision wiped out an affirmative action program that had been in effect for 30 years. In 1971 minorities accounted for only 9.1 percent of employees in radio and television. That number increased to 19.9 percent at the time of this decision in 1998. This decision did not affect the affirmative action program for women, but proponents of such programs feared that the approach of strict scrutiny used by the Court for minorities may be used as a precedent for attacking such goals for women.

California Constitutional Amendment Proves Fatal to Two Racial Preferences

As described earlier, the operative clause of Proposition 209 (Cal. Const. Art. I, Sec. 31(a)) prohibits discrimination or preferential treatment on the basis of race, sex, color, ethnicity, or national origin in public employment, public education, or public contracting.

The City of San Jose, California, ostensibly to comply with Proposition 209, adopted a resolution modifying its affirmative action program in city contracting. Under the new system, each general contractor bidding on a city project had to demonstrate that it did not discriminate on the basis of race or sex by either (1) an evidentiary presentation of subcontracting with an appropriate number of business enterprises owned by minorities and women, or (2) certification of its good faith outreach efforts to increase minority participation (bids). Contractors were not required to provide any information to nonminority business enterprises.

The program was challenged by Hi-Voltage Wire Works, and others, as a violation of Proposition 209 approved by California voters. The City argued that its "evidentiary presumption" and "outreach" were merely "screening" or detection devices to ensure nondiscrimination and were not meant to bestow preferences on minorities or women. The Superior Court of California, County of Santa Clara, in its opinion discussed the U.S. Ninth Circuit Court of Appeals's *Monterey Mechanical Company* decision in which similar outreach goals were declared unconstitutional.[57] The Superior Court also noted California's newly enacted Constitutional provision against discrimination and preferences and ruled that the City of San Jose's screening device "is simply another name for participation goals that are prohibited by Proposition 209."[58] It ruled the City's outreach program "flawed" and a violation of the California Constitution's Article I, Section 31(a). It granted plaintiff's motion for summary judgment.

Proposition 209 was also the basis of a ruling on March 20, 1998, by Presiding Justice Robert Puglia of California's Third District Court of Appeals. It was the first such case of the application of Proposition 209 at the District Court of Appeals level. Pacific Legal Foundation, a public interest law firm based in Sacramento, brought the case on behalf of Edward Swiden, a white, and William Kidd, a Native American, who were passed over by the State's Department of Fish and Game, which had given jobs to lower-scoring minorities and women. The Department of Fish and Game did this under a state law passed in 1977 that required government agencies to increase the representation of women and minorities. In a three-to-zero ruling, Presiding Justice Puglia said that the Court is not convinced "that in this state 'merit' is defined by one's sex or by the color of one's skin."[59] This observation was influenced by the Department of Fish and Game's policy instituted in 1981 under which 60 percent of the new hires were to be women and minorities even if their test scores were lower than those of whites and men. At the time this policy was instituted, the State Personnel Board found that there was an underrepresentation of minorities and women in the Department of Fish and Game.[60] Justice Puglia was of the opinion that such hiring preferences were unconstitutional even before Proposition 209 was passed in November 1996. Governor Pete Wilson, an ardent opponent of these preferences, hailed the court decision. For the Pacific Legal Foundation, it was another victory in its decades' old war against racial preferences in public agencies.

LEGISLATIVE ATTEMPTS TO BAN PREFERENCES AND CHANGES IN SECTION 8(A) PROGRAM

In 1996, attempts by some Republican legislators failed to ban affirmative action preferences. Once again, in 1997, a bill offered by Congressman Charles T. Canady (R-Florida) would have, among other things, prohibited the use of race in any student financial aid program. A similar measure was introduced in the Senate by two Republican Senators, Mitch McConnell of Kentucky and Orin Hatch of Utah. The Senate bill would have barred federal agencies from using race classifications in making grants and awarding contracts.[61] A House of Representatives panel approved the Canady bill in July 1997, but it made no further progress.

On November 6, 1997, another opportunity to ban preferences was lost when the House of Representatives' Judiciary Committee, by a vote of 17 to 9, tabled a bill offered by Canady.[62] The bill would have barred the use of race in student aid programs. However, the bill did not prohibit colleges and universities from using race as a plus factor in student admissions. It also exempted the historically black colleges and American Indian tribal colleges from the prohibition concerning student aid. In the House Judiciary Committee, all 13 Democrats and 4 Republicans voted to table the bill. The successful motion to table the bill made by Republican Congressman George Gekas was greeted with cheers by the Committee Democrats and members of the audience, which included the Reverend Jesse Jackson. The explanation for the motion by Gekas was that affirmative action programs were already crumbling and that there was disagreement among Republicans themselves on the course to take on this sensitive issue. Commenting on his hesitancy, Linda Chavez, President of the Center for Equal Opportunity and an opponent of preferences, said that the Republicans must take a principled and courageous stand against race and sex-based affirmative action preferences.[63] She was particularly referring to the reauthorization of a major highway and transportation bill that included a 10 percent national goal for minority contractors. The lack of nerve among Republicans to ban preferences was also the topic of a column by George Will.[64] However, despite the failure of these bills, the movement to prohibit preferences in government programs still showed some sign of life. As a matter of fact, even in the fall of 1997, some reports indicated that assault on preferences remained a priority for the GOP, which kept alive a bill "that would jettison race-and-gender-based preferences in 160 programs."[65] These are the programs that the White House is trying to save through its new regulations announced on June 24, 1998.

In March 1998, Representative Frank Riggs (R-California) introduced a bill that would have banned the use of race, sex, national origin, or ethnicity in student admissions in public colleges and universities receiving federal funds.[66] The language used was in some respects similar to that of California's Proposition 209 passed by the voters in November 1996. The bill was offered as an amendment to the Higher Education Act. The National Association of Scholars (NAS) strongly supported the Riggs Amendment, quoting survey data indicating "overwhelming opposition among American higher education faculty to the use of ethnicity and race in college admissions decisions."[67] The NAS thought that the proposed amendment should have covered not just public institutions but also private ones. The NAS dismissed the American Council of Education, which opposed the Riggs Amendment, as "an organized advocate for racially discriminatory preferences in higher education." On May 6, 1998, the House of Representatives, by a vote of 249 to 171, rejected the Riggs Amendment.[68] Those opposing the Riggs Amendment included 193 Democrats, 55 Republicans, and one Independent. The Republicans feared a veto by President Clinton if the amendment had been part of the Higher Education Act. Representative Riggs, in an effort to garner support for his amendment, had modified his bill twice before it was voted down. Originally, his bill barred preferences in both public and private institutions.[69] But the threat of a veto to a bill that among other benefits cut interest rates for students loans from 7.6 percent to 6.8 percent, provided large increases in Pell Grants from $3,000 to $4,500 in 1999 and in stages to $5,300, and provided block grants to states for teacher training was simply too powerful politically for the Republicans to try to override. Opposition by the higher education's bureaucracy organized under the banner of the American Council on Education was perhaps also a factor in the Republicans' unwillingness to fight a veto. Writing in the *New York Times*, Anthony Lewis thought that the defeat of the Riggs Amendment was perhaps a "turn of the tide" in the affirmative action controversy.[70] An amendment authored by Senator Mitch McConnell (R-Kentucky) and Representative Marge Roukema (R-New Jersey) similar to that of Riggs was offered in the Senate by McConnell. It also failed, by a vote of 37 for to 58 against.[71]

The demise of bills concerning affirmative action in higher education was similar to that of the attempts to attach anti-set-aside language to the transportation bills offered a few weeks earlier. On March 6, 1998, the Senate voted 58 to 37 to defeat a proposal that would have ended the current requirement of giving 10 percent of all federally funded contracts to companies owned by women and minorities. (In 1996 these two groups received 15 percent, that is, $2 billion, of all federally financed highway contracts.)[72] Once again, 15 Republicans voted with the Democrats to defeat the proposal, while only one Democrat voted in favor. The failed proposal was offered as an amendment to the $173 billion highway bill that contained construction projects for every state. Legislators from both parties wanted to have a bill that brought money and jobs to their respective states. Once again, President Clinton had threatened to veto the bill if it eliminated the set-asides. The author of the amendment, Senator Mitch McConnell, was reported to have remarked that the Senate's effort was the last best chance to roll back preference programs in 1998.[73] Given the summer recess and the midterm elections, Senator McConnell's assessment was very realistic. Majority Leader Trent Lott of Mississippi was disappointed at the senators' failure to eliminate set-asides and remarked that the American people want these programs eliminated. Then he said: "Maybe it will take an election to get them in tune with America."[74] That election was in November 1998 when the Republican majority was in fact reduced. However, observers are not very confident that Congressional Republicans are willing to make preferences a pivotal election issue, despite the fact that a large majority of voters disapprove of favored treatment based on race, sex, and ethnicity, particularly when given by government agencies.

Since the Supreme Court's 1995 decision, and particularly since the passage of California's Proposition 209, the Clinton Administration has been trying to find ways to preserve affirmative action preferences as much as possible by thwarting attempts to dismantle the regime of quotas and set-asides that often are euphemistically called "goals," "good faith efforts for participation," "diversity," and "multicultural outreach" programs for "disadvantaged" and "underrepresented" groups. As described previously in Chapter 3, the Supreme Court in *Adarand* (1995) ruled that the 10 percent bid advantage given to "disadvantaged business enterprise" did not meet the strict scrutiny standard and hence violated the equal protection rights of the dispreferred Adarand Constructors. On remand, the U.S. District Court in June 1997 called the extra compensation paid to the prime contractor a "gratuity" or "bonus" that "'encourages, entrenches, subsidizes, or results in racial discrimination.'"[75] The judge also said that it is a flawed presumption that all those in the designated minority groups are "disadvantaged."

The Clinton Administration, on August 14, 1997, announced plans to modify its Small Business Administration's (SBA) Section 8(a) program that gives bid preferences to minority-owned businesses. In fiscal year 1995-1996, under this program, a total of 6,115 companies owned by minorities received federal contracts amounting to $6.4 billion.[76] Until this proposed change, only 27 of these companies received contracts under SBA's Section 8(a) program. Of the total $197.5 billion in federal contracts during fiscal year 1995-1996, women-owned businesses received only 1.7 percent of the dollar amount. It was only 1.3 percent in fiscal year 1991-1992.[77] The planned changes did contemplate that whites could also be eligible for consideration if they could provide "preponderance of evidence" of their disadvantaged status. Government contracts as a whole are an important part of the nation's economy. Of the total federal procurement contracts (of which Section 8(a)'s program accounts for only 3.2 percent), "small disadvantaged businesses" in fiscal year 1995-1996 received 20 percent."[78] The problem is that under the Section 8(a) program, an owner of a company would be considered "disadvantaged" if he or she had a personal net worth of less than $250,000. As Steven A. Holmes pointed out, it is "a criterion that more than 90 percent of the Americans could meet."[79] Under that proposed rule, blacks, Hispanics, Asians, and many other racial minorities are presumed to be disadvantaged, while whites have to prove that they are socially disadvantaged to be eligible. It was generally believed that white men would be the only other disfavored class under the proposed rules.

After studying the issue of preferences in government contracts for over two years, on June 24, 1998, the federal government announced another new affirmative action policy in response to the *Adarand* (1995) decision of the Supreme Court. Under this newest policy, affirmative action preferences would still be given in awarding contracts amounting to "about three-quarters of the money Government spends on procurement contracts with small businesses."[80] The policy still gives a break of as much as 10 percent on a bid to "disadvantaged" businesses. The White House claims that the policy is based on its study of 70 industries and that affirmative action will now be allowed only in those industries where there are disparities between the availability of qualified entrepreneurs and their underutilization by contractors and government agencies. In those industries where there is no underutilization, the lowest bidders will receive contracts without the use of 10 percent price breaks. Under this approach, for instance, affirmative action will be used in textile mills but not in food manufacturing, forestry, or fishing. Although detailed analyses of the newest policy await, Abigail Thernstrom, an expert on the economic aspects of race relations and a senior fellow at the Manhattan Institute, called the latest policy "'old wine in new bottles.'"[81] The government claimed to have studied 73 sectors of the economy for determining if minority firms were being discriminated against. Much will depend on the validity of the statistical data, measurement, and methodology used to determine if it meets the strict scrutiny test. Regardless of all that, it is still a policy that does not treat business entrepreneurs individually but rather classifies them according to race and ethnicity. To that extent, it divides rather than unites our nation. It is what *Business Week* calls "back door affirmative action."[82]

IMPACT OF MERIT-BASED POLICIES ON UC ADMISSIONS

Despite all the provocative and deceptive rhetoric of the defenders of affirmative action preferences that implementation of color-blind admissions policies will "resegregate" higher education, for the academic year 1998-1999, a much larger number of California blacks and other minorities applied for freshman admission to the University of California than in the previous year. Applications from blacks, American Indians, Mexican Americans, and Filipino Americans rose by 3.1 percent, 9.3 percent, 10.1 percent, and 0.5 percent, respectively. There was a drop of 1.8 percent in applications from Asian Americans.[83] The *New York Times* called the relatively small drop "A Surprise after End of Affirmative Action."[84] Minority applications, excluding Asian Americans, totaled 9,979 out of a total of 49,648 California applicants. There was a drop of 10.0 percent in freshman applicants from California whites and other groups. However, there was a sharp drop in non-Asian minority enrollment in the University of California's law and business schools for the academic year 1998-1999.[85] These schools had relied heavily on standardized test scores and on grade point averages (GPAs). Asian Americans, who excel in these two criteria, markedly achieved increased enrollment in law schools by 32 percent and business schools by 9 percent. There was a sharp drop in 1998 compared to 1997 in the number of minority enrollment in UC's law schools: blacks from 43 students to 16, Mexican Americans/Latinos from 89 to 59, and American Indians from 10 to 4. The number of white students in these law schools increased from 464 to 589. The drop in non-Asian minority enrollment in UC's business schools was also significant: blacks from 27 to 20 and Mexican American/Latinos from 54 to 25. Enrollment of Asian Americans and whites, on the other hand, increased by 9 percent and 5 percent, respectively. In UC's graduate programs, with a total of 7,040 new students enrolled in the 1998 academic year, black students increased from 213 to 218, and there was little change in the overall demographic composition of the student body. This was also true of UC's five medical schools.

The Clinton Administration continued its support of affirmative action preference programs. In its view, even though blacks receive preference in admissions in elite schools, it does not greatly harm the opportunities of whites or Asian Americans. For the first time, the President's Council of Economic Advisers included a chapter on racial inequality in its 1998 annual report. It called for continued use of preferences in university admissions because, in its view, students given preferences based on race or ethnicity ultimately succeed in their university work.[86] The 1600-point Scholastic Assessment Test (SAT) designed to measure verbal and math reasoning has become a target of those who think that it prevents non-Asian minorities from getting a fair opportunity for admission into elite universities. Included in this group is Eugene Garcia, Dean of the Graduate School of Education at UC, Berkeley, who believes that the universities should simply eliminate the SAT. Others, however, argue that the SAT is a nationally uniform standard, and in the words of David Murray, Director of Research at the Statistical Assessment Service, getting rid of this standard is akin to shooting the messenger of bad news.[87] Despite this controversy, UC continues to rely heavily on SAT scores in its admission decisions. The university has concluded that in view of different school districts using different academic standards and grading policies, the SAT provides a good uniform measure. Furthermore, the university's analysis indicates that eliminating the SAT in admissions decisions is likely to result in an overall decrease of minority enrollment.[88]

There are some efforts in California to adopt the new Texas system—after the *Hopwood* case of reverse discrimination, a state law has been passed that provides the top 10 percent of high school graduates the assurance of admission into the university of Texas system. A plan in California has been debated that would automatically make eligible for admission into UC the top 4 percent of the seniors in each high school. (At present, UC eligibility is to the top 12.5 percent of all California high school graduates.) Although this proposal has the support of UC officials, others fear that its adoption will lower academic standards.[89]

Interest in rethinking admissions standards is understandable especially in view of the very sharp decline in minority enrollment at the elite law schools of UCLA and UC, Berkeley, in the immediate wake of Proposition 209. At UCLA, black applicants accepted for admission dropped from 104 in 1996 to 28 in 1997. Of these, only eight enrolled plus two others who were accepted in 1996 but had deferred enrollment until 1997. At UC, Berkeley's law school, blacks accepted for admission dropped from 74 in

1996 to 15 in 1997. More dramatically indeed, none of those blacks admitted chose to enroll. Instead, only one black who had deferred enrollment from the previous year chose to enroll in 1997.[90] This is not to imply that those who chose not to enroll, or those who were not offered admission to the Boalt Hall School of Law at UC, Berkeley, or to the UCLA School of Law suffered serious career damage. In fact, many of those admitted, as well as those declined admission, usually have many other similar, or even better, offers from other prestigious law schools. (The average GPA of an admittee at Boalt Hall is 3.74 and an average Law School Admission Test (LSAT) score in the 97th percentile.)

Slowly (some say too fast), the University of California system is making the necessary adjustments to comply with the law barring racial discrimination or preference in public education. For instance, the University of California, Davis, has added overcoming adversity as a factor in its admissions criteria.[91] However, despite this effort, minority admissions dropped in 1998 by 23.5 percent as compared to the pre-Proposition 209 figures of 1997, whereas Asian Americans achieved increased enrollment of 8.3 percent. Even white admissions dropped by 9.8 percent.[92]

Earlier optimism of the potential for maintaining demographic diversity at UC based on the flood of applications from all racial and ethnic groups in January and February of 1998 turned into disappointment when in the spring UC officials looked at the data on admissions. In three UC campuses, declines were particularly significant as shown in Table 7.1.

Precise decline in the admission of ethnic and racial groups could not be measured because of an interesting development: Twice as many applicants as before declined to identify their ethnicity. At Irvine, the number of applicants declining to identify their ethnicity rose from 442 in 1997 to 1,423 in 1998.[93] The UC campuses at Riverside and Santa Cruz, being relatively less selective, showed increases in black and Hispanic admittees.

Table 7.1
University of California Admissions at San Diego, Davis, and Irvine

	San Diego		Davis		Irvine	
	1997	1998	1997	1998	1997	1998
Blacks	373	203	518	332	303	246
Hispanics	1,427	979	1,626	1,302	1,412	1,291
American Indians	105	66	122	100	66	57
Whites	5,309	4,790	5,615	5,064	3,770	3,375
Asian Americans	4,548	4,400	3,813	4,130	5,389	5,309

Source: Data extracted from Associated Press story, "Minority Admissions Decline with New California Policy," *New York Times* (March 18, 1998), A19.

The declines in minority enrollment at UC, Berkeley, and UCLA, the premier campuses of the system and the most selective public institutions of higher education in the United States, were particularly dramatic. At Berkeley, Hispanics and American Indians together dropped from 23.1 percent of the freshman admission pool in 1997 to 10.4 percent in 1998. At UCLA this group's admissions dropped from 19.8 percent to 12.7 percent.[94] It is generally agreed that blacks admitted to UC belong to the middle class and are second- or third-generation collegians. Relatively speaking, Asian students come from economically less well-off families. In fact, many of the Asian American students come from poor families. [95] The law of averages would indicate that a majority of the poor in this country are whites.

Berkeley, as the most selective public university in the nation, accepted only 27 percent of the 29,821 students who applied. UCLA accepted only a third of its applicants. It is reported that of the "underrepresented" minority applicants at Berkeley, 800 had high school GPAs of 4.0 and SAT scores of 1200 out of a possible 1600.[96] The University and public policy makers continue to be surprised at the number of applicants who did not check off the ethnic identity box on their admission applications. As compared to 1997 when 5,355 such applicants left the ethnicity box blank, in 1998 their number in the UC system as a whole rose to 13,575.[97]

If one looks at the eight-undergraduate-campus system of UC as a whole, the drop in minority enrollment is less dramatic than was feared initially. In the UC system in 1998, 18 percent fewer blacks and 7 percent fewer Latinos were admitted than in the pre-Proposition 209 year of 1997. Of the 60,912 applicants to UC in 1998, a total of 44,393 (that is, 72.88 percent) received admission to at least one campus of the system.[98] The statistics are a far cry from the dire prediction of "resegregation" made by the advocates of racial preferences. Nor is the *New York Times* editorial heading—"Proposition 209 Shuts the Door"—justified.[99]

The problem of admission at selective Berkeley is that it cannot admit all the qualified applicants. In fact, for the fall of 1998, it declined admission to about 6,000 students who had 4.00 GPAs. This included 800 "underrepresented" minority students. In an effort to counteract Proposition 209, California Senator Teresa Hughes (D-Inglewood) has offered a constitutional amendment (SCA 7) that would require UC to admit the top 12.5 percent of graduates from each high school in California. The existing law requires UC to accept the top 12.5 percent of high school graduates statewide.[100] A longtime observer of education, Peter Schrag of the *Sacramento Bee*, believes that this proposal is not realistic because it could bring into a rigorous academic setting students whose chances of success would be rather small.[101] There are other bills in the California Legislature designed to boost the pool of minorities for admission into UC.[102]

The fiercely competitive admissions standards are demonstrated by the fact that not everyone who is admitted to UC elects to enroll. For example, in 1996, UC offered admission to 40,400 students for its freshman class. However, only 23,200 of them elected to enroll. Similarly, in 1998, out of the 33,000 admitted, only about 22,000 in fact enrolled. Thus, it would not be true to say that minority students are being denied opportunity to receive good education. In this regard, Peter Schrag says: "[W]ell qualified minority students are sought and fought over by admissions officers from one end of the country to the other. The only difference is that Harvard and Princeton can consider race, while UC can't."[103]

The drop in enrollment of "underrepresented" minorities at UC has, however, generated controversy in which the old advocates of preferences call for restoring affirmative action while others call for implementing the letter and spirit of Proposition 209 and taking steps to improve the quality of education in grades K through 12.[104] Supporters of affirmative action particularly cite the significant drop in admission of black and Hispanic applicants at UC's flagship campus of Berkeley as well as at UCLA.[105] This has led Nathan Glazer, the noted Harvard sociologist who until recently was an articulate foe of affirmative action preferences, to change his position and ask for rethinking of this issue.[106] There has been a similar reaction from Glen C. Loury, Professor of Economics at Boston University and a former aide in the Reagan Administration. Loury, who was previously opposed to preferences in public employment and public contracting, has also asked for rethinking of the issue of college admissions. He argues that because there is a great economic disparity between blacks and whites, affirmative action still has an important role to play.[107] However, data on the economic status of racial groups in California demonstrates that Asian Americans with greatly lower family incomes academically outperform blacks with much higher family incomes. Asian Americans are only one-ninth of California's population, but they constitute one-third of those admitted into the Fall 1998 class at the University of California.

Up to now there has been a great disparity among racial and ethnic groups in the dropout rates and correlated graduation rates. The figures cited by Stephen and Abigail Thernstrom of those who were admitted into Berkeley's freshman classes between 1987 and 1990 and who were able to complete the degree within six years are as follows: blacks 58 percent; Hispanics 67 percent, and whites 84 percent.[108] In their view, the students admitted under the new color-blind policies and on an equal basis are likely to have the same graduation rates. It will be several years before this prediction can be judged.

The bureaucracy of higher education continues to push for affirmative action preferences albeit under the slogan of "diversity" in student bodies, faculties, and staff. A statement entitled "On the Importance of Diversity in Higher Education" and endorsed by 57 associations supposedly representing 3,000 American colleges and universities piously states: "Achieving diversity on college campuses does not require quotas. Nor does diversity warrant admission of unqualified applicants."[109] The statement lists a series of benefits of diversity, such as enriched educational experience, personal growth, and economic competitiveness. Although the statement laments "precipitous declines in the enrollment of African American and Hispanic students," it still does not recognize that the main reason for that is the elimination of racial and ethnic preferences by force of law in some jurisdictions. Also, the notion that diversity based on racial preferences, even though a violation of the equal protection clause, is somehow desirable must be rejected. The universities have grossly misused the diversity rationale in student admissions since the *Bakke* case over 20 years ago. That rationale is no longer acceptable to deny Fourteenth Amendment rights to individuals. Those who emphasize "diversity" in education typically are talking about racial and ethnic makeup of the student body, faculty, and staff and are recommending preferences on that basis. Yet as Professor James Q. Wilson aptly points out: "Real diversity is the diversity of ideas and beliefs that produce challenging discussions, new theories, and revised explanations."[110]

Data of student admissions at UC issued on May 20, 1998, indicate that although the enrollment of "underrepresented" minorities (defined officially as blacks, Hispanics, and American Indians) dropped substantially for the Fall 1998 freshman class at Berkeley and UCLA, it has led to increases on UC's other six campuses. This redistribution has led to an overall decrease of non-Asian minorities to 10.5 percent from 1997 to 1998.[111] University officials worked very hard to encourage students to enroll after their applications were accepted. Universitywide underrepresented minorities made up 15.2 percent of the Fall 1998 freshman class compared with 17.6 percent in 1997. Berkeley's Chancellor Robert M. Berdah felt relieved and is reported to have said that their worst fears had not been realized.[112] Minority students offered admissions to Berkeley or UCLA have many options of enrolling at other excellent universities if they so wish.[113]

PUBLIC POLICY AND PREFERENCES

On March 11, 1998, the Institute for Justice, a public interest organization in Washington, D.C., launched a nationwide campaign to ask state attorneys general "to examine all race-conscious statutes, policies, and practices" under their jurisdiction and to comply with U.S. Supreme Court decisions "that limit the use of racial classifications in all but the most extreme and exceptional circumstances."[114] The sponsors of the project include former Attorney General Edwin Meese, the American Civil Rights Institute, and the Center for Equal Opportunity (CEO). Under this project, attorneys general of all 50 states have been contacted, and Roger Clegg of the CEO will monitor compliance efforts by the states to determine whether racial preferences are being modified or eliminated in accordance with Supreme Court precedents.

The nation expects its President and Congress to provide leadership and reasonable solutions to its problems. On his part, President Bill Clinton had adopted three approaches simultaneously to deal with our racial problems.

1. He believes we should "mend but not end," affirmative action programs—his mantra since 1996. His Justice Department has defended every affirmative action program challenged in the courts. Examples are the *Hopwood* and *Taxman* cases discussed earlier.

2. He has made appointments, or nominated people, who are ardent defenders of race-based preferences. Examples are the 1993 nomination of Lani Guinier to be Assistant Attorney General for Civil Rights—a post which, after Guinier's withdrawal, went to Deval Patrick, and after his resignation in 1997 to Bill Lann Lee (all advocates for preferences). One should add to this list of affirmative action advocates Norma Cantu, the U.S. Education Department's Assistant Secretary for Civil Rights.

3. In San Diego on June 14, 1997, he announced an initiative on race relations.

We believe that the president has every right to nominate to federal positions people who are in tune with him and his political party's expectations. However, on matters of race relations, the president's actions and philosophy of affirmative action preferences run counter to the sentiments of the general public. Public opinion polls consistently favor equal opportunity but oppose preferences based on race.[115] The very week President Clinton announced his race initiative in June 1997, a Gallup Poll showed that whereas 60 percent of blacks thought that government should do more to help them, the same percentage of whites thought that blacks should do more to help themselves.[116] Given this divided opinion, it is quite appropriate that measures should be adopted that create a common understanding of the problem. This is particularly important for California, which now has a demographic composition of 52 percent white, 30 percent Latino, 10 percent Asian, 7 percent black, and 1 percent American Indian.[117] The authors do not believe that the answer to the nation's racial divide lies in adopting the Reverend Jesse Jackson's suggestion of continued aggressive enforcement of affirmative action to close, what he terms, the "opportunity gap" and more government spending to close the "investment gap."[118] Nor does the answer lie in establishing a national commission that is diverse only in ethnic and racial makeup but homogeneous in philosophy. As viewed by Derrick Bell, "Mr. Clinton's new board will be as inadequate as it is unoriginal."[119] The Commission (Advisory Board) headed by eminent historian John Hope Franklin, was part of President Clinton's much touted initiative involving the nation in "a great and unprecedented conversation about race."[120] The president tried to frame the issue as if the movement against affirmative action preferences was aimed at "resegregation."[121] This was, of course, not true and was, in fact, a desperate effort to show "leadership" on this important and sensitive issue. It was countered by Newt Gingrich, Speaker of the House of

Representatives, and Ward Connerly, Chairman of the American Civil Rights Institute, who in an op-ed commentary urged the president to "abandon the misguided belief that our society should ever use discrimination to end discrimination."[122] They also pointed out the failure of President Lyndon B. Johnson's Great Society programs, which cost the nation $5.4 trillion dollars as analogous to the failed policy of racial preferences.

The initial uncertainty over the president's approach to a race initiative was shared by liberals and conservatives alike. The *New York Times* in its editorial commenting on the president's speech proposing a year-long initiative on race called it "a sermon with little sanctimonious preaching."[123] While the president was talking about a race initiative, he called the voter-approved Proposition 209 "devastating" [124] and harmful to education.

In a speech on June 14, 1997, at the University of California at San Diego,[125] President Clinton inaugurated the race initiative. The following were the main developments in race relations from then until the end of June 1998:

- A resolution was offered by Representative Tony Hall (D-Ohio) and six Democrats and six Republicans proposing an apology for slavery. It did not receive enthusiastic welcome in the Congress. Many feared that the next step would be proposals and demands for reparations.[126] President Clinton decided not to apologize at the time but will consider it in the future.

- A group of House Republicans introduced a bill, titled Civil Rights Act of 1997, calling for ending race- and gender-based preferences in a variety of government programs.[127]

- The panel on race held a number of public meetings but was criticized for its lack of focus.[128] It also decided not to consider the views of foes of affirmative action preferences because, in the opinion of the panel's Chairman, John Hope Franklin, such opponents were not likely to contribute to this discussion.[129]

- In order to enliven the race initiative and in response to criticism, President Clinton invited nine prominent opponents of preferences to a meeting with him in the White House.[130] The critics charged that the race panel was one-sided.

- President Clinton, visiting Uganda, expressed regret on slavery in America.[131]

- A group of prominent conservatives, headed by Ward Connerly, have established a group on race issues claiming that the panel established by President Clinton was one-sided and hostile to opposing viewpoints.[132] American Indians have also complained that the president's Advisory Board did not have a representative of their own on it, while Asian Americans claimed that the panel was too preoccupied with African American issues.[133] President Clinton, himself, was short tempered in a town hall meeting on December 3, 1997, with Abigail Thernstrom, a critic of his affirmative action policies.[134]

Originally, the Advisory Board for the president's Initiative on Race was expected to submit its report within a year, that is, by June 14, 1998. However, that deadline was extended. The Board was beset with organizational problems, with a lack of focus, and with a lack of interest in the country as a whole to have a "dialogue" with a panel that was obviously one-sided. After holding a series of meetings in the fall of 1998, the Board submitted its report entitled "One America in the 21st Century." Based on its 15-month-long study, it recommended that a permanent race commission be established not only to continue the dialogue but also to make recommendations on economic policies to the president. The report was strikingly pessimistic and unimpressed with the progress made so far in race relations in the past 40 years. It made a number of recommendations, including greater racial and ethnic tolerance, special training for teachers to work in poor neighborhood schools, better portrayals of minorities in the media, and increasing the minimum wage. Both the findings and the recommendations were stereotypical liberals' solutions to the complex problems of our nation's race relations and economic disparities. As of early 1999, President Clinton had not acted upon the Board's main recommendations.

The authors do not believe that a creative new public policy will emerge on the affirmative action issue during the tenure of President Clinton's Administration. By continuing to support affirmative action programs that go beyond the letter and spirit of the Civil Rights Act, the Clinton Administration preserves its liberal constituency but without popular support on this issue. The advocates of preference programs refuse to admit that American culture has greatly changed in the past 40 years. Economic, social, and political progress has been made by African Americans because discrimination based on race (and gender) is no longer acceptable in the nation as a whole.[135] The nation has come a long way and progress continues to be made. It is time now to discard the notion that race-, ethnicity-, or gender-based preferences that deny others equal protection of the law are either desirable or viable in a democratic society that has built-in corrective mechanisms. Americans should reaffirm the moral and legal commitment that there shall be no discrimination and no preference on account of one's race, ethnicity, and sex in both the public and private sectors. Let the principle of merit prevail. The authors agree with Representative Charles T. Canady, who on February 25, 1998, in his opening statement in Oversight Hearing on the Civil Rights Division of the U.S. Department of Justice, said: "Eventually, discriminatory preferences will end. When we look back, we will wonder why the United States Department of Justice [in President Clinton's administration] supported the differential treatment of human beings on the basis of their immutable characteristics, and stood on the wrong side of history."[136]

NOTES

1. Elaine Herscher, "*Daily Cal* Stolen Off Racks—Editor Cites Prop. 209," San Francisco Chronicle, November 6, 1996, B4; "Cal Newspapers Stolen Off Racks," *Sacramento Bee*, November 6, 1996, A15.

2. Ken Chavez and Clair Cooper, "New Arena for Prop. 209: Battle Over Affir-

mative Action Adjourns to Courts," *Sacramento Bee*, November 7, 1996, A1, A9.

3. Associated Press, "Rights Leaders Urge White House to Take Prop. 209 to Court," *San Francisco Chronicle*, November 9, 1996, A2.

4. G. Pascal Zachary, "Some Major Cities Thumb Their Noses at California Ban on Affirmative Action," *Wall Street Journal*, November 15, 1996, A18.

5. Peter Schmidt, "Vote in California to Ban Racial Preferences Sparks Lawsuits and Student Protests," *Chronicle of Higher Education*, November 15, 1996, A35.

6. Ibid.

7. Peter Schmidt, "Political and Legal Maneuvering Follows California Vote to Ban Racial Preferences," *Chronicle of Higher Education*, November 22, 1996, A28.

8. Claire Cooper, "State Wants Its Courts to Rule on Prop. 209. Asks Federal Judge to Abstain in Case," *Sacramento Bee*, November 20, 1996, A3.

9. Edward W. Lempinen and Reynolds Holding, "Newly Passed Prop. 209 Already Mired in Lawsuits. Wilson Orders Immediate Enactment—Foes Sue," *San Francisco Chronicle*, Novemer 7, 1996, A1, A15; Ken Chavez and Claire Cooper, "New Arena for Prop. 209. Battle Over Affirmative Action Adjourns to Courts," *Sacramento Bee*, November 7, 1996, A1, A9.

10. Erwin Chemerinsky and Laurie Levenson, "Sex Discrimination Made Legal," *Los Angeles Times*, January 10, 1996, B9.

11. Allan J. Favish, "Response to *L. A. Times* News Article," *Los Angeles Daily Journal*, March 12, 1996, 6.

12. Vikram D. Amar and Evan H. Caminker, "Equal Protection, Unequal Political Burden, and the CCRI," *Hastings Constitutional Law Quarterly* 23 (Summer 1996), 1019-1056.

13. Western State University Law Review Association, "Preliminary Findings: Legislative Impact of Proposition 209" (1996), cited by Eugene Volokh in, "The California Civil Rights Initiative: An Interpretive Guide," *UCLA Law Review* 44 (June 1997), p. 1337, Note 3; also see: "Proposition 209: Not as Radical as Advertised," *The Recorder*, November 15, 1996, 1.

14. Volokh, 1336.

15. Harriet Chiang, "Prop. 209 Opponents Win a Round. Liberal Judge Decides to Review 2 Lawsuits," *San Francisco Chronicle*, November 15, 1996, A21.

16. Claire Cooper, "Judge Switch Upsets Prop. 209 Supporters," *Sacramento Bee*, November 14, 1996; also see: Clint Bolick, "The ACLU Takes Aim at the California Civil Rights Initiative," *Wall Street Journal*, November 13, 1996, A23.

17. Claire Cooper, "State Wants Its Courts to Rule on Prop. 209. Asks Federal Judge to Abstain in Case," *Sacramento Bee*, November 20, 1996, A3.

18. Peter Schmidt, "Vote in California to Ban Racial Preferences Sparks Lawsuits and Student Protests," *Chronicle of Higher Education*, November 15, 1996, A35.

19. "Rights Leaders Urge White House to Take Prop. 209 to Court. California Affirmative Action Ban," *San Francisco Chronicle*, November 9, 1996, A2.

20. "White House Considers Joining Legal Assault on Prop. 209," *Sacramento Bee*, November 9, 1996, A3.

21. G. Pascal Zachary, "Some Major Cities Thumb Their Noses at California Ban on Affirmative Action," *Wall Street Journal*, November 15, 1996, A18.

22. *The Coalition for Economic Equity v. Wilson*, 946 F. Supp. 1480, 1520-21 (N.D. Cal., 1996).

23. *Hunter v. Erikson*, 393 U.S. 385 (1969).

24. *Washington v. Seattle School District*, 458 U.S. 457 (1982).

25. *The Coalition for Economic Equity, et al.; Plaintiff/Appelles v. Pete Wilson, Governor, et al., Defendants/Appellants*, Nos. 97-15030, 97-15031 (U.S. Court of Appeals, 9th Cir., 1997).

26. Dan Walters, "Judge Shopping Pays Off Again," *Sacramento Bee*, April 9, 1997, A3.

27. See for example: Harriet Chiang, "Court Upholds Prop. 209," *San Francisco Chronicle*, April 9, 1997, A1, A11; G. Pascal Zachary, "Initiative to Ban Race Preference in California Gets Court's Support," *Wall Street Journal*, April 9, 1997, B8; Editorial, "Affirming The Voters," *Wall Street Journal*, April 9, 1997, A14; Tim Golden, "Federal Appeals Court Upholds California's Ban on Preferences," *New York Times*, April 9, 1997, A1, A18; Claire Cooper, "Prop. 209 Ruled Constitutional," *Sacramento Bee*, April 9, 1997, A1, A12; Editorial, "The Proposition 209 Challenge," *Sacramento Bee*, April 10, 1997, B6; Peter Schmidt, "A Federal Appeals Court Upholds California Measure Barring Racial Preferences," *Chronicle of Higher Education*, April 18, 1997, A28; Harry Jaffa, "Why CCRI Is Constitutional," *The Weekly Standard*, April 21, 1997, 24-27; Center for Individual Rights, *Docket Report* (Special Issue) (April 1997), 1-4.

28. Claire Cooper, "Review of Prop. 209 Ruling Asked," *Sacramento Bee*, April 23, 1997, A4.

29. Associated Press, "California Poised to Enforce Anti-Preference Law," *New York Times*, August 27, 1997, A12; Dan Smith, Dorsey Griffith, and Emily Bazar, "Prop. 209 Takes Effect Today as Battle Goes On," *Sacramento Bee*, August 28, 1998, A1; Pascal Zachary, "California Proposal 209 Takes Effect. Some Cities to Ignore Ban on Preferences Until Law Is Clarified," *Wall Street Journal*, August 29, 1997, A12; Peter Schmidt and Douglas Lederman, "Legal Barriers Removed to California's Ban on Racial Preferences," *Chronicle of Higher Education*, September 5, 1997, A47.

30. Claire Cooper, "Judges Chide Peers for Prop. 209 Support," *Sacramento Bee*, August 29, 1997, A4.

31. Tim Golden, "California Adapts as 1996 Initiative Ends Preferences," *New York Times*, August 29, 1997, A1.

32. Linda Greenhouse, "Justices Allow Anti-Bias Law to Go into Effect," *New York Times*, September 5, 1997, A16; Peter Schmidt, "Supreme Court Refuses

to Stay Proposition 209," *Chronicle of Higher Education*, September 12, 1997, A42.

33. Louis Freedberg, "U.S. Top Court Lets 209 Stand," *San Francisco Chronicle*, November 4, 1997, A1, A13; Douglas Lederman, "Supreme Court Refuses Appeal on California Measure Barring Affirmative Action," *Chronicle of Higher Education*, November 14, 1997, A34.

34. Dan Smith, "Wilson Takes Aim at 35 Laws. Act Under Prop. 209, He Urges Legislature," *Sacramento Bee*, September 10, 1997, A1.

35. Jon Matthews, "Wilson Wants All State Preferences Deleted. He Pushes for Passage of Bill That His Critics Claim Is Rash," *Sacramento Bee*, April 28, 1998, 2.

36. Capitol Bureau, "Affirmative Action Measure Rejected," *Sacramento Bee*, April 29, 1998, A15.

37. State of California, SB 1735 (February 18, 1998, as amended in Senate, April 20, 1998).

38. Letters from Attorney General Daniel E. Lungren to Senator Richard Polanco re: SB 1735 (April 20, 1998, and May 21, 1998).

39. 77 Ops. Cal. Atty. Gen. 1 (1994).

40. See, for instance, AB 2134 (March 8, 1991); AB 2498 (March 11, 1992) vetoed by Governor Pete Wilson (September 30, 1992).

41. *Monterey Mechanical Company v. Pete Wilson, et al.*, 125 F. 3d 702 (9th Cir. 1997).

42. Ibid., 711.

43. The court referred to: *Northeastern Florida Contractors v. Jacksonville*, 508 U.S. 656 (1993); *Bras v. California Public Utilities Commission*, 59 F. 3d (9th Cir. 1995); *Coral Construction Company v. King County*, 941 F. 2d 910 (9th Cir. 1991); and *Concrete Works of Colorado, Inc. v. City and County of Denver*, 36 F. 3d 1513 (10th Cir. 1994). (10th Circuit covers Colorado, Kansas, New Mexico, Oklahoma, Utah, and Wyoming.)

44. *Monterey Mechanical*, p. 712.

45. *Monterey Mechanical*, p. 175.

46. *Monterey Mechanical Company v. Pete Wilson, et al.*, 98 Daily Journal D.A.R. 2317 (March 10, 1998).

47. Ibid., 2319.

48. Matthew Rees, "The Judge the Supreme Court Loves to Overturn," *Weekly Standard*, May 5, 1997, 27.

49. Ibid., 27.

50. *Metropolitan Dade County v. Engineering Contractors Association; Allied Minority Contractors v. Engineering Contractors Association*, *Wall Street Journal*, March 10, 1998, B5; "High Court Declines Bias Case. Florida Plan Backed Aid to Minority Firms," *Sacramento Bee*, March 10, 1998, E5.

51. Dan Feldstein, "Metro's Policy on Race, Sex Loses in Court," *Houston Chronicle*, November 13, 1997.

52. Deborah Tedford, "Judge Criticizes Study on Affirmative Action," *Houston Chronicle*, November 14, 1997.

53. *Lamprecht v. Federal Communications Commission*, 958 F. 2d 382 (D.C. Cir., 1992).

54. *Lutheran Church v. Federal Communications Commission*. See: Steven A. Holmes, "F.C.C. Requirement on Minority Hiring Is Voided by Court," *New York Times*, April 15, 1998, A1, A20; Scott Ritter, "Court Overturns Radio, TV Rules on Minority Hiring," *Wall Street Journal*, April 15, 1998, B16; editorial, "Defining Affirmative Action," *Wall Street Journal*, April 20, 1998, A18. For a critical review of this decision, see: "Constitutional Law—Equal Protection—D.C. Circuit Finds FCC's Equal Employment Opportunity Regulations Unconstitutional. *Lutheran Church—Missouri Synod v. FCC*, 141 F. 3d 344 (D.C. Cir.), rehearing en banc denied, 154 F. 3d 487 (D.C. Cir. 1998)," *Harvard Law Review* 112 (February 1999), 988-993.

55. Holmes, A20.

56. Ritter, B16.

57. *Hi-Voltage Wire Works, Inc., et al., v. City of San Jose, et al.*, Case No. CV768694 (February 9, 1998).

58. Ibid., 4.

59. Associated Press, "Appeals Court Rules Hiring Quota Violates Prop. 209, Merit Policy," *Sacramento Bee*, March 21, 1998.

60. Dan Morain, "Appeals Court Ends Hiring Preferences for State Jobs," *Los Angeles Times*, March 21, 1998.

61. Karla Haworth, "Bill Would Bar U.S. Use of Affirmative Action," *Chronicle of Higher Education*, August 15, 1997, A27.

62. Bryan Mealer, "House Panel Tables Bill to Bar Affirmative Action," *Chronicle of Higher Education*, November 14, 1997, 40; "Bill to End Affirmative Action Postponed," *San Francisco Chronicle*, November 7, 1997, A3.

63. Linda Chavez, "Party of Lincoln or of Quotas? GOP Must Decide," *Wall Street Journal*, October 7, 1997, A22.

64. George Will, "Republicans' Cowering Crouch on Preferences," *San Francisco Chronicle*, November 17, 1997.

65. Susan B. Garland and Amy Borrus, "The GOP Assault on Affirmative Action Is Getting Serious," *Business Week*, November 17, 1997, 55.

66. *Chronicle of Higher Education* (March 20, 1998), A33; "End Preferences, Riggs Proposes," *Sacramento Bee*, March 5, 1998, A12; *Chronicle of Higher Education*, May 1, 1998, A40.

67. National Association of Scholars, "NAS Applauds Policy of Riggs Amendment Banning Racial and Sexual Discrimination in College Admissions" (press release), April 30, 1998, 2.

68. Stephen Burd, "House Votes Down Proposal to Bar Racial Preferences in Admissions," *Chronicle of Higher Education*, May 15, 1998, A35-A37; Robert Green (Associated Press), "House Passes Higher Education Bill. Legislators

Reject Efforts to End Affirmative Action at Colleges, Universities," *Sacramento Bee*, May 7, 1998, A14.

69. Douglas Lederman, "Jockeying Intensifies over Proposal to Bar Racial Preferences in Admissions," *Chronicle of Higher Education*, May 8, 1998, A36.

70. Anthony Lewis, "Turn of the Tide?" *New York Times*, May 18, 1998, A23.

71. Equal Opportunity Foundation, "Memo from Linda Chavaz," June 12, 1998.

72. James Dao, "Senate Stops Bid to End Road-Work Set-Asides," *New York Times*, March 7, 1998, A9.

73. Ibid.

74. Lawrence M. O'Rourke, "Senate Backs Affirmative Action Program," *Sacramento Bee*, March 7, 1998, A18.

75. Terry Eastland, "Federal Set-Asides: Just Another Name for Discrimination," *Wall Street Journal*, July 9, 1997, A15.

76. Steven A. Holmes, "U.S. Acts to Open Minority Program to White Bidders. Women Would Be Most Likely to Benefit from Changes for Federal Contracts," *New York Times*, August 15, 1997, A1.

77. "SBA Set-Aside Will Aid Women-Owned Businesses," *Wall Street Journal*, August 14, 1997, B2.

78. Ibid.

79. Steven A. Holmes, "Defining Disadvantage Up to Preserve Preferences," *New York Times*, August 24, 1997, E3.

80. David E. Rosenbaum, "White House Revises Policy on Contracts for Minorities," *New York Times*, June 25, 1998, A1; also see: Jonathan Peterson, "U.S. Rewrites Rules on Favoring Minority Contractors," *Sacramento Bee*, June 24, 1998, A8; for details, see: The White House, Office of the Press Secretary, "Statement by the President," and its attachment "Procurement Reforms: SDB Certification and the Price Evaluation and Adjustment Program"(Washington, D.C.: The White House, Office of the Press Secretary (June 24, 1998); and *Federal Register* 63 (June 30, 1998), 35714-35780, "Federal Acquisition Regulation for Small Disadvantaged Businesses: Notice and Rules."

81. Rosenbaum, *New York Times*, June 25, 1998, A1.

82. "Back Door Affirmative Action," *Business Week*, July 6, 1998, 40.

83. Data from University of California in: Brad Hayward, "Applications Climb for 1998 UC Admission," *Sacramento Bee*, January 29, 1998, A3.

84. William H. Honan, "Minority Applicants Rise at California, Easing Fears. A Surprise after End of Affirmative Action," *New York Times*, January 29, 1998, A14; Pamela Burdman, "UC Sees Record Number of Applicants," *San Francisco Chronicle*, January 29, 1998, A1.

85. Julianne Basinger, "U. of Cal. Reports on Minority Enrollment," *Chronicle of Higher Education*, January 30, 1998, A28.

86. Jodi Enda, "Report Lauds Affirmative Action Impact," *Sacramento Bee*, February 10, 1998, A1, A12.

87. June Kronholz, "As States End Racial Preferences, Pressure Rises to Drop SAT

to Maintain Minority Enrollment," *Wall Street Journal*, February 12, 1998, A24.

88. Brad Hayward, "SAT Test Still UC's Standard of Choice. Talk of Dropping Disputed Exam Fades," *Sacramento Bee*, February 17, 1998, A1, A16; also see: Adrian Wooldridge, "A True Test," *New Republic*, June 15, 1998, 18-21 (Wooldridge believes that without SAT minorities would do even worse).

89. Brad Hayward, "Admission Proposal Praised by UC Officials," *Sacramento Bee*, February 20, 1998, A3; Patrick Healy, "U. of Cal. Weighs Admitting Top 4% of Students," *Chronicle of Higher Education*, March 6, 1998, A37.

90. Jeffrey Rosen, "Damage Control," *New Yorker*, February 23 and March 2, 1998, 61. For detailed discussion of law school admissions issues, see pp. 61-64.

91. Brad Hayward, "Diverse UCD is Goal of Strategy," *Sacramento Bee*, February 23, 1998, A1, A12.

92. Brad Hayward, "Minority Numbers Drop at UC Davis," *Sacramento Bee*, March 17, 1998, A1, A10.

93. Karla Haworth, "Minority Admissions Fall on 3 Cal. Campuses," *Chronicle of Higher Education*, March 27, 1998, A41.

94. Ethan Bronner, "U. of California Reports Big Drop in Black Admission. Effect of a Referendum," *New York Times*, April 1, 1998, A1, A23.

95. Ibid., A23.

96. Steve Stecklow, "Minorities Fall at Universities in California," *Wall Street Journal*, April 1, 1998, A1, A3, A8.

97. "Fewer U. of California Applicants Reveal Race," *New York Times*, April 2, 1998, A12.

98. Brad Hayward, "Drop in Blacks, Latinos Admitted to All of UC Less Than at Cal, UCLA," *Sacramento Bee*, April 3, 1998, A4.

99. Editorial, "Proposition 209 Shuts the Door," *New York Times*, April 4, 1998, A22.

100. Phil Garcia, "Officials Weigh the Cost of UC Diversity," *Sacramento Bee*, April 5, 1998, A1, A25.

101. Peter Schrag, "UC Admissions: Is Podunk High School World Class?" *Sacramento Bee*, February 18, 1998, B7.

102. Notable bills are: Tom Hayden's SB 1697 and Carole Migden's AB 1292.

103. Peter Schrag, "UC Admissions Criteria: The Virtues of a Little Fudging," *Sacramento Bee*, April 8, 1998, B7.

104. See for example: "Time to Restore Affirmative Action?" *New York Times*, April 7, 1998, A26 (Letters to the Editor).

105. Jame Ramage, "Berkeley and UCLA See Sharp Drops in Admission of Black and Hispanic Students," *Chronicle of Higher Education*, April 10, 1998, A43.

106. Steven A. Holmes, "Re-Rethinking Affirmative Action," *New York Times*, April 5, 1998, WK5; Nathan Glazer, "In Defense of Preference," *New Republic*,

April 6, 1998, 18-21, 24-25; also see: "Gazing Glazer," *New Republic*, May 11, 1998, 4-5 (Letters to the Editor).

107. Glenn C. Loury, "The Hard Questions: Unequalized," *New Republic*, April 6, 1998, 10-11; also see: "Arguing Inequality," *New Republic*, May 18, 1998, 4-5 (Letters to the Editor).

108. Stephen Thernstrom and Abigail Thernstrom, "The Consequences of Colorblindness," *Wall Street Journal*, April 7, 1998, A18.

109. American Council on Education, "On the Importance of Diversity in Higher Education" (updated March 11, 1998), 2 pp.

110. James Q. Wilson, "Education. The Meaning of Fewer Minorities at UC, UCLA," *Los Angeles Times*, April 5, 1998.

111. Dob Kollars, "Many Losses, a Few Gains in UC Fall Minority Enrollment," *Sacramento Bee*, May 21, 1998, A1, A19.

112. Ethan Bronner, "Minority Enrollment at U. of California Will Dip in Fall," *New York Times*, May 21, 1998, A20.

113. Frank Bruni, "Black Students May Prefer to Say No to Berkeley. Prospective Freshmen Pursued in Effort to Preserve Diversity," *New York Times*, May 2, 1998, A1, A7.

114. "New Front on Race Preferences," *Liberty and Law* 7, 2 (May 1998), 6.

115. For a scholarly analysis of this issue, see: Paul M. Sniderman and Thomas Piazza, *The Scar of Race* (Cambridge: Harvard University Press, 1993).

116. Louis Freedberg, "President Clinton's Ultimate Challenge," *San Francisco Chronicle*, June 15, 1997, A9.

117. Editorial, "The President Takes on Nation's Toughest Issue," *San Francisco Chronicle*, June 13, 1997, A26.

118. Louis Freedberg, "Clinton Race Initiative Drawing Skepticism," *San Francisco Chronicle*, June 11, 1997, A1, A6.

119. Derrick Bell, "A Commission on Race? Wow," *New York Times*, June 14, 1997, 19; also see Carol Ness, "Cheers, Boos for Clinton on Race," *San Francisco Examiner*, June 15, 1998, A17, A26.

120. Peter Baker, "President Tilts at Great Divide," *San Francisco Examiner*, June 15, 1997, A1, A15.

121. Alison Mitchell, "Defending Affirmative Action, Clinton Urges Debate on Race. Calls Diversity Essential and Issues Warning on Resegregation," *New York Times*, June 15, 1998, 1, 14, 15.

122. Newt Gingrich and Ward Connerly, "Face the Failure of Racial Preferences," *New York Times*, June 15, 1997, 15 (Section 4).

123. Editorial, "Opening a Conversation on Race," *New York Times*, June 16, 1997, A14.

124. Ronald Brownstein, "Clinton Calls Prop. 209 'Devastating,'" *San Francisco Chronicle*, June 16, 1997, A1, A6.

125. "Excerpts from President Clinton's Speech on America's Racial Divide," *New York Times*, June 15, 1998, Y15; Kim Strosnider, "Clinton Defends the Use of

Affirmative Action in Education," *Chronicle of Higher Education*, June 27, 1997, A31.

126. "Apology for Slavery Gets Tepid Reception. Congress Concerned about Reparations," *San Francisco Chronicle*, June 17, 1997, A3; Christopher Matthews, "A Peculiar Apology for Slavery," *San Francisco Examiner*, June 22, 1997, D7.

127. Louis Freedberg, "GOP Seeks Federal Ban on Affirmative Action. Response to Clinton's Crusade on Race," *San Francisco Chronicle*, June 18, 1998, A1, A11.

128. Steven A. Holmes, "Critics Say Panel on Race Is Going Nowhere Slowly," *New York Times*, October 12, 1998, 14.

129. Steven A. Holmes, "Race Panel Keeps Out Opponents of Its Views," *New York Times*, November 20, 1997, A1, A16; editorial, "Stifling the Race Debate," *New York Times*, November 21, 1998, A26.

130. James Bennet, "Clinton Debates 9 Conservatives on Racial Issues," *New York Times*, December 20, 1998, A1, A8; "Excerpts from Round Table with Opponents of Racial Preferences," *New York Times*, December 22, 1997, A16.

131. James Bennet, "In Uganda, Clinton Expresses Regret on Slavery in US," *New York Times*, March 25, 1998, A1, A11.

132. Steven Holmes, "Conservative Scholars Plan Rival Group on Race Issues," *New York Times*, April 30, 1998, A18; "Clinton's Initiative on Race Is Challenged," *Sacramento Bee*, April 30, 1998, A5.

133. Steven A. Holmes, "Indians Are Latest to Disrupt Race Panel," *New York Times*, March 25, 1998, A14.

134. Editorial, "Yes or No, Mr. President," *Wall Street Journal*, December 5, 1997, A18; editorial, "Talking about Race in Akron," *New York Times*, December 5, 1997, A22; James Bennet, "Clinton at Meeting on Race Struggles to Sharpen Debate," *New York Times*, December 4, 1997, A1, A18.

135. For a scholarly and comprehensive analysis on the progress made by African Americans, see: Stephen Thernstrom and Abigail Thernstrom, *America in Black and White. One Nation Indivisible* (New York: Simon and Schuster, 1997).

136. February 25, 1998, Committee on the Judiciary—Canady Statement, http://www.house.gov/judiciary/222321.htm).

Index

~

About the Authors

M. ALI RAZA teaches at the College of Business Administration at California State University, Sacramento. He served as a visiting Fulbright Professor at Vidyodaya University in Sri Lanka and as a senior adviser to the Government of Sri Lanka's United Nations' Development Program.

A. JANELL ANDERSON teaches Business Law and Organizational Behavior at the College of Business Administration at California State University, Sacramento. She and M. Ali Raza co-authored *Labor Relations and the Law* (1996). She has published other works on government regulation of business.

HARRY GLYNN CUSTRED, JR. is Professor of Anthropology at California State University, Hayward. His field is cultural and linguistic anthropology. He is co-author and principal of California's Proposition 209 which ended racial, ethnic, and sex preferences in the public sector.

ISBN 0-275-96713-1

HARDCOVER BAR CODE